W9-BKC-941

COOKING
Hints & Tips

COOKING
Hints & Tips
Christine France

A DK PUBLISHING BOOK

Project Editors Judy Garlick, Jo Richardson
Project Art Editor Sarah Hall
Editor Colette Connolly
US Editor Laaren Brown
Designer Helen Benfield
Series Art Editor Jayne Carter
Managing Editor Stephanie Jackson
Managing Art Editor Nigel Duffield
Senior Managing Editor Krystyna Mayer
Senior Managing Art Editor Lynne Brown
Production Controller Sarah Coltman
DTP Designer Jason Little

First American Edition, 1997
2 4 6 8 10 9 7 5 3
Published in the United States by
DK Publishing, Inc., 95 Madison Avenue,
New York, New York 10016

Visit us on the World Wide Web at
http://www.dk.com

Copyright © 1997
Dorling Kindersley Limited, London

Library of Congress
Cataloging-in-Publication Data

France, Christine
    Cooking hints and tips / by Christine France
        – 1st American ed.
        p.   cm.
    Includes index.
    ISBN 0-7894-1447-3
    1. Cookery.   I. Title.
TX651.F37 1996
641.5--dc20   96–33575
                                          CIP

Reproduced by Chroma Graphics, Singapore
Printed and bound in Italy by Lego

CONTENTS

INTRODUCTION 6

KITCHEN EQUIPMENT 10

PREPARED INGREDIENTS 30

FRESH INGREDIENTS 44

PREPARING INGREDIENTS 58

COOKING METHODS 74

ENTERTAINING 118

INTRODUCTION

HERE IS NO SECRET RECIPE FOR GOOD COOKING, but by learning some of the helpful tips and tricks in this book you will be able to prepare and cook food successfully in a well-organized kitchen. Shortcuts and alternative methods of doing ordinary and out-of-the-ordinary kitchen tasks are described, too.

USING THIS BOOK

EQUIPPING YOUR KITCHEN

Organizing your kitchen well is the first step towards successful cooking. *Kitchen Equipment* describes how best to plan a kitchen and choose and maintain appliances and cooking utensils for maximum performance. *Prepared Ingredients* tells you how to set up and maintain a useful pantry – an essential in any kitchen – and describes the best ways to store dried foods. It lists healthy basics as well as convenience foods, and suggests a range of clever ways to combine the two. This chapter also gives advice on keeping a ready supply of ingredients with which to rustle up a quick, healthy meal at only a moment's notice.

Enriching dried fruits
To learn how to transform a selection of dried fruits into a richly flavored and luxurious compote, turn to page 36.

Chilling fish
To find out how to select the best fresh fish, chill it quickly, and store it safely, see page 54.

CHOOSING AND PREPARING FRESH FOODS

Good cooking starts with sensible shopping to buy the finest, freshest ingredients, which then need safe storage and careful preparation so that you can extract the very best from them during cooking. *Fresh Ingredients* tells you everything you need to know about choosing, buying, and storing all kinds of fresh foods safely. *Preparing Ingredients* takes you clearly and concisely through all the basic methods of food preparation, and includes numerous simple but effective ideas for adding flavour and variety to enhance a wide range of familiar foods.

COOKING FOR FAMILY AND FRIENDS

Making the very best of good food and enjoying it to the fullest requires a little basic knowledge of a few simple cooking techniques. *Cooking Methods* describes how to improve the many different methods of cooking, from achieving the best results with grilled or barbecued foods, to preventing the problems associated with baking and preserving. Once you feel confident about using the basic techniques, you can enjoy cooking for friends as well as family. *Entertaining* takes you from the planning and preparation of a wide variety of special occasions – formal and informal – to the cooking and presentation of food.

Garnishing effectively
To discover how to add the finishing touches to dinner-party food by making effective garnishes, turn to page 131.

To discover how to add the finishing touches to dinner-party food by making effective garnishes, turn to page 131.

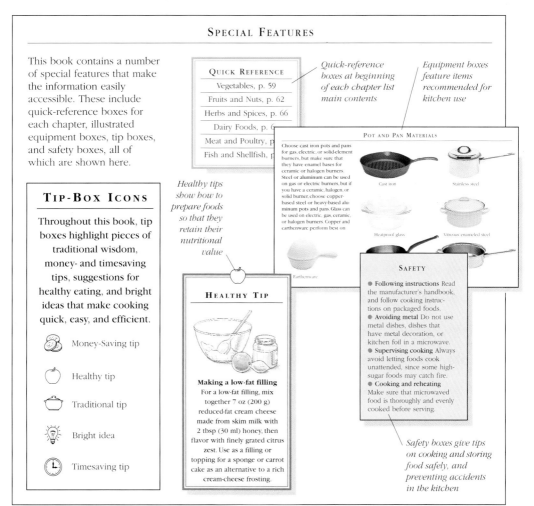

SPECIAL FEATURES

This book contains a number of special features that make the information easily accessible. These include quick-reference boxes for each chapter, illustrated equipment boxes, tip boxes, and safety boxes, all of which are shown here.

Quick-reference boxes at beginning of each chapter list main contents

Equipment boxes feature items recommended for kitchen use

QUICK REFERENCE

Vegetables, p. 59
Fruits and Nuts, p. 62
Herbs and Spices, p. 66
Dairy Foods, p. 6
Meat and Poultry, p
Fish and Shellfish, p

Healthy tips show how to prepare foods so that they retain their nutritional value

POT AND PAN MATERIALS

Choose cast iron pots and pans for gas, electric, or solid-element burners, but make sure that they have enamel bases for ceramic or halogen burners. Steel or aluminum can be used on gas or electric burners, but if you have a ceramic, halogen, or solid burner, choose copper-based steel or heavy-based aluminum pots and pans. Glass can be used on electric, gas, ceramic, or halogen burners. Copper and earthenware perform best on

Cast iron
Stainless steel
Heatproof glass
Vitreous enameled steel
Earthenware

TIP-BOX ICONS

Throughout this book, tip boxes highlight pieces of traditional wisdom, money- and timesaving tips, suggestions for healthy eating, and bright ideas that make cooking quick, easy, and efficient.

Money-Saving tip

Healthy tip

Traditional tip

Bright idea

Timesaving tip

HEALTHY TIP

Making a low-fat filling
For a low-fat filling, mix together 7 oz (200 g) reduced-fat cream cheese made from skim milk with 2 tbsp (30 ml) honey, then flavor with finely grated citrus zest. Use as a filling or topping for a sponge or carrot cake as an alternative to a rich cream-cheese frosting.

SAFETY

● **Following instructions** Read the manufacturer's handbook, and follow cooking instructions on packaged foods.
● **Avoiding metal** Do not use metal dishes, dishes that have metal decoration, or kitchen foil in a microwave.
● **Supervising cooking** Always avoid letting foods cook unattended, since some high-sugar foods may catch fire.
● **Cooking and reheating** Make sure that microwaved food is thoroughly and evenly cooked before serving.

Safety boxes give tips on cooking and storing food safely, and preventing accidents in the kitchen

MAKING A SAFE, EFFICIENT KITCHEN

The kitchen is one of the most important rooms in any household, and is often the center of the home, where meals are not only prepared, cooked, and eaten, but where family and friends often gather together. Bear this in mind, whether you are planning a completely new kitchen or making improvements to an existing one. Start by listing your requirements, and then draw up a plan of the kitchen that would suit your needs. Include labor-saving equipment such as food processors whenever possible to reduce your workload and save time. Ensure that kitchen appliances are running efficiently by checking them regularly. Use a thermometer to check refrigerators and freezers, for example, to ensure that they are working at the correct temperatures for storing food safely.

Using a food processor
If you use a food processor often, invest in an extra bowl so that you can process more than one ingredient at a time without having to repeatedly wash one bowl.

Organizing a cabinet
To make sure everything is easily accessible in a cabinet, arrange small jars and regularly used items at the front, and put larger, less frequently used items at the back or on the higher shelves.

STOCKING A HEALTHY PANTRY

There is such a wide choice of foods to choose from today that keeping a good supply of healthy foods on hand should not present a problem. Aim to have a few healthy staples to rely on as a basis for all kinds of meals, such as bulgur wheat, brown rice, lentils, split peas, and dry pasta shapes. Make use of canned or dried foods for quick meals when time is short, or to cook for an unexpected guest. Rotate the foods you are storing to make sure that each is consumed before its use-by date. Do not forget that the freezer can provide you with a supply of fresh food all year round, and can act as a "storage cellar" for inexpensive, seasonal gluts of fruits and vegetables. Clearly label and date all packed food before you put it in the freezer so that it is easy to identify. Alternatively, keep a freezer logbook so you have a handy record of all the contents and their details. You can even keep it in the freezer in a plastic bag.

GETTING THE MOST FROM FRESH FOODS

Even if you are a novice in the kitchen, once you have mastered a few basic food-preparation techniques and cooking skills, you will find it easy to make a delicious, healthy meal. Start by shopping for the freshest ingredients possible, and watch for fresh foods that are at the peak of their season, when they will be at the lowest price and of the best quality. Choose low-fat cooking methods whenever possible, and cook vegetables lightly to retain flavor and nutrients, using methods such as stir-frying or steaming.

Stir-frying in a wok
Use a wok to keep fat levels low and retain flavor and nutrients in fresh food.

Using pesto as a glaze
Before grilling low-fat meats such as turkey or chicken breast fillets, brush with pesto sauce to keep moist.

ADDING VARIETY TO EVERYDAY MEALS

If you cook every day of the week, it is easy to run out of ideas that are simple, quick, and healthy, but with the wide choice of foods available and a wealth of suggestions for healthy eating to inspire you, you can always find different ways of serving even the most familiar foods. Pep up a plain roast chicken by tucking a few fresh herbs under the skin, or use flavored marinades or glazes to keep meats moist and add flavor when grilling or barbecuing. Add a topping of crumpled phyllo dough to transform simple stewed fruits into a pie in minutes, or introduce texture and extra nutrients to cooked vegetables by scattering them with nuts or seeds before serving.

ENTERTAINING WITHOUT STRESS

Successful entertaining has as much to do with advance planning and creative presentation as culinary skill. The greatest compliment you can pay someone is to invite him or her into your home and offer food, however simple. Make large celebrations less of a chore by planning in advance. Make lists and timetables to organize the tasks to be done, and you will then be able to relax on the day with your guests. There is no need to cook elaborate dishes; simple finishing touches and creative presentation can make food look special.

Using a mirror tile
The simplest presentation ideas are often the most effective. Use a plain mirror tile instead of a plate for serving canapés with drinks.

9

KITCHEN EQUIPMENT

A GOOD COOK CAN PRODUCE MEALS with limited equipment, but a well-organized, fully equipped kitchen will improve your efficiency and reduce the time you spend cooking. The kitchen is the most difficult room in the house to plan, so you should take time to consider your requirements. Shop around and see what is available before making decisions about equipment, whether you are choosing major appliances or small utensils.

ORGANIZING A KITCHEN

The number of cabinets and appliances in a kitchen will be dictated largely by space. The quality and layout of your kitchen, both of which affect efficiency, are under your control. If you are planning to design a kitchen from scratch, get the advice of a professional.

PLANNING A KITCHEN
● **Working on paper** When you start to plan your kitchen, draw the walls and doors to scale on graph paper. Make cardboard cutouts, to scale, of all kitchen appliances to be used, and experiment with their positions. Draw up several plans before making decisions or spending money.
● **Determining a basic shape** Depending on the space available, plan your kitchen in a U-shape, L-shape, or galley shape. These are the best layouts for moving around efficiently while you work.
● **Keeping surfaces level** Try to plan an unbroken run of counters, built over and between kitchen appliances, to make efficient use of space and to facilitate cleaning.
● **Anticipating traffic flow** Plan a kitchen so that people passing through do not cross the work area, especially that between the sink and stove.

PLANNING FOR AN EASY WORK FLOW
● **Minimizing walking** Keep the total distance between the sink, storage area, and stove to no more than approximately 23 ft (7 m) in order to minimize the amount of walking around you will do while cooking.

● **Placing work surfaces** Link areas between appliances with counters so that there will be a work surface wherever you need it. This will allow you to prepare and cook food near the appropriate appliances.

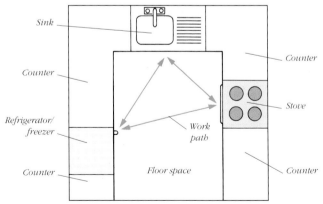

Sink · Counter · Refrigerator/freezer · Counter · Floor space · Counter · Counter · Stove · Work path

Creating a work triangle
If you are planning the design of a kitchen from scratch, try to arrange the positions of appliances so that you create a work path linking the refrigerator, sink, and stove. This will facilitate an easy flow of work that minimizes inefficient activity in the kitchen.

KITCHEN IMPROVEMENTS

IF YOU ARE PLANNING TO UPDATE OR IMPROVE an existing kitchen, there are many inexpensive adjustments to consider. Change the style of the kitchen by replacing cabinet doors, or improve existing doors with a new paint finish.

WORK SURFACES

Counters should be installed at a height that is comfortable to work at. A recommended, standard working height may not be suitable for you. Choose a hard-wearing material that is heat resistant, does not scratch, chip, or stain easily, and is easy to maintain and keep clean.

CREATING SURFACES

Covering a sink
To create a work surface that you can use if space becomes tight, cut a piece of wood to fit neatly over a sink. When the sink is not in use, put the wood in place.

MAKING PAN RESTS

Using tiles
Make sure that there is always a stable, heatproof surface on which to place hot pans by keeping two sturdy kitchen tiles on the counter next to the stove.

LIGHTING WORK SURFACES

● **Using spotlights** Choose flexible spotlights so that you can direct the lighting. Recess them into the ceiling, or place on top of wall cabinets.
● **Avoiding glare** Eliminate glare by positioning diffusers over low-level lights.
● **Reducing heat** Reduce the heat generated in a kitchen by installing fluorescent lights.
● **Locating switches** For flexibility, install separate switches for each area, such as a counter or an eating area.

PLANNING AHEAD

● **Positioning counters** Make sure that there is a surface near the entrance on which to place shopping or garden produce when you enter the kitchen.
● **Adding insets** Consider having a marble or wooden inset put into a counter for chopping and pastry making. This should extend the whole depth of the counter to avoid creating dirt traps, and the front edge should match that of the counter.
● **Avoiding dirt traps** Avoid seams in countertops, since they may trap dirt and become a health risk. Seal unavoidable seams with kitchen sealant.
● **Preventing dripping** Look for a counter with a ridged front edge to prevent spilled liquids from dripping over the edge.

USING DEAD SPACE

● **Storing in corners** Make use of counter space in corners for storing small appliances, such as food processors.

Installing a knife slot
Store sharp knives in a slot cut into the rear part of the counter behind a drawer. Check carefully before cutting the slot to make sure that the knives will not block the drawer.

SAVING SPACE

● **Folding items away** In a small kitchen, install a hinged counter or a table that will fold away while not in use.

Using a rack
To help keep work surfaces clear, hang regularly used, small utensils from a rack between two wall cabinets, within easy reach of the area where you will need them.

CABINETS AND SHELVES

There is a wide range of kitchen cabinets to choose from today, and they are available in many different styles. Since cabinets last for years, do not be influenced by the latest fashion. If your budget is tight, use plain white cabinets, which are inexpensive and practical.

KEEPING CABINETS CLEAN

Using plastic coving
To prevent dust and dirt from collecting beneath a floor-mounted cabinet, put coving along the edge of the plinth. Lay flexible flooring, such as vinyl, to cover the coving, and tuck it into the corner where the cabinet meets the plinth.

Cabinet unit

Cabinet door

Plinth

Flexible flooring *Coving*

Solid floor

● **Sealing wood** To protect natural wooden cabinets with a hard-wearing, water-repellent finish, coat with polyurethane. Seal hardwood cabinets with oil where appropriate, and reapply the seal frequently.

● **Cleaning interiors** Choose cabinets lined with laminated coatings and drawers lined with heavy-duty plastic, so that you will easily be able to wipe up spills and the sticky residues left by food containers.

CHOOSING & POSITIONING CABINETS

● **Positioning cabinets** If possible, attach a cabinet to a shaded, outside wall if it is to be used for storing food, since this will be cooler than an internal wall. Try to be aware of the temperature inside a cabinet – the cooler the better for food storage.

● **Checking stability** Ask a builder to check that a wall is structurally sound enough to take the weight of cabinets before installing wall units. You may find that a partition wall is unable to support the weight.

● **Making a partition** Divide kitchen and dining areas in the same room by installing a peninsula. This will provide extra storage space while permitting easy access from one area to another.

● **Selecting cabinet doors** Consider installing cabinets that have sliding doors, or doors that slide up and over.

● **Making a wine rack** To adapt a floor cabinet for storing bottles of wine, first remove any existing shelves. Then make an X-shaped shelf for the bottles using two pieces of plywood slotted together to fit the cabinet from corner to corner.

Making a dish drainer
Remove the bottom of a wall-mounted cabinet above the sink, and put a dish rack inside. Wet dishes can then drain into the sink, and you can close the doors to hide it away.

PLANNING STORAGE

● **Adjusting shelves** Choose cabinets with adjustable shelves or racks on runners, so that the heights can be adjusted to suit your needs.

● **Using corner space** Install a corner unit with revolving shelves to make use of an otherwise inaccessible corner.

● **Disposing of waste** Put a flip-top garbage pail in a cabinet beneath the sink or in the area where most of the food is prepared, so that trash can be disposed of easily.

● **Using wall space** Use the space beneath wall cabinets to hang a paper-towel holder or utensil rack. This will help to keep work surfaces clear.

KEEPING SHELVES CLEAN

● **Covering with a blind** Fit a fireproof roller blind over shelves built into a recess so that dust and grease do not settle on the shelves' contents.

● **Using open shelves** Dust settles easily on open shelves, so use them for items that are used and washed daily.

SAFETY

● **Choosing cabinets** Select units with rounded corners and recessed handles. Sharp corners and protruding knobs are likely to cause injury.

● **Placing wall cabinets** Avoid placing cabinets on a wall above a stove; reaching over a hot burner to gain access to a cabinet is dangerous.

● **Siting for height** Position wall cabinets so that the top shelves are easily accessible without necessitating a climb onto a chair or stepladder.

SPACE-SAVING DEVICES

Many home kitchens are quite small, with limited storage space, so creative use of space is essential for the efficient organization of a kitchen. Make use of corners by inserting corner shelves, and hang small items from racks on the wall if you run out of cabinet space.

SAVING CABINET SPACE

Hanging a rack
Suspend a wooden or metal rack from the kitchen ceiling, and hang pots and pans using butchers' hooks. Do not hang the rack too low, and check the length of chain needed to bring the pots and pans to an accessible height.

FILLING EMPTY SPACES

Filling gaps
Position a pull-out towel rack in a gap between two cabinets or appliances to keep dish towels tidy and accessible. Alternatively, use gaps between units for storing cookie sheets and trays, freeing cabinet space for other items.

BRIGHT IDEA

Using window space
If your kitchen window has an unattractive view, or no view at all, put safety glass shelves across the window. Use them for storing attractive glass jars and bottles, plants, or pots of fresh herbs.

COOKBOOKS AND RECIPES

Most cooks have a collection of favorite cookbooks, and inevitably these books become well worn. Buy a cookbook stand, or use the tips below to protect your books while cooking. Also make sure that you keep your favorite recipe clippings in good condition.

PROTECTING & STORING COOKBOOKS

● **Using a plastic bag** To protect the pages of a cookbook, slip the opened book inside a clear plastic bag to prevent it from being splashed during food preparation.
● **Keeping books dry** Attach a narrow wooden shelf with a rim to the wall above a work surface, and use it as a book rest. It will help keep books out of the way of food splashes.
● **Storing books** Place a bookshelf on top of a chest of drawers to create a kitchen dresser in which you can keep your cookbooks, display attractive pieces of china, and store kitchen equipment.

Adding an extra shelf
Hang a narrow shelf between a counter and a wall cabinet to create storage space for cookbooks. This will give you quick access to them, and save space on the counter.

KEEPING CLIPPINGS

● **Color-coding recipes** Store different categories of recipe clippings in differently colored photograph albums with peel-back plastic pages. Use blue for fish dishes, for example.
● **Using a scrapbook** Paste recipe cuttings into a scrapbook so that you can write notes next to them if necessary.
● **Making clever clippings** Store favorite, frequently used recipe clippings in a decorative way by pasting them onto a board or tray to make a collage. Paint over or spray with waterproof varnish so that any splashes of food or grease can be wiped off.

COOKING APPLIANCES

STOVES REQUIRE MAJOR FINANCIAL INVESTMENT and should therefore be chosen for long-term use. Everyone has different requirements when selecting a stove, and there is a huge variety from which to choose.

CHOOSING A STOVE

When choosing an oven or a stovetop, consider your cooking needs, bearing in mind the advantages and availability of different fuels, and any space limitations in the kitchen. Look for a design that is attractive and practical, with few dirt traps so that cleaning will be easy.

CHOOSING AN OVEN

When buying an oven, decide which features will be most useful, bearing in mind your lifestyle. Below are some features to consider first.

● **Capacity** Choose a large or a double oven to give you flexibility, especially if you cook for a lot of people.
● **Cleaning facilities** Choose an oven that is self-cleaning, or that has stay-clean features.
● **Timer** Consider a timer to control cooking for you while you are busy.
● **Convection** To encourage even cooking and reduce cooking times, choose a fan-assisted convection oven that circulates heat evenly.

SELECTING BURNER SURFACE & FUEL TYPE

● **Choosing burners** Select burners that will be easy to clean. Consider ceramic burners, which also use electricity efficiently. When not in use, the cool surface can be used as a work surface for rolling out pastry or dough.

● **Combining fuels** If you are able to combine fuels, consider two gas burners and two electric rings. The mix combines the safety advantages of electricity with the easy heat adjustment of gas burners, and is useful in a power failure.

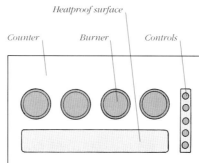

Heatproof surface

Counter   *Burner*   *Controls*

Placing burners

If you are planning a new kitchen, consider setting burners in a line, rather than a square formation, and set them well back from the front edge. Install a heatproof surface for resting hot saucepans in front of the burners.

CONSIDERING DETAILS

● **Catalytic liners** Reduce oven cleaning by choosing an oven with a catalytic oven lining that carbonizes food spills. Alternatively, select a pyrolytic oven, which has a high-temperature, self-cleaning cycle.
● **Built-in ovens** Choose a built-in oven, which is usually mounted at waist height, for convenient positioning.
● **Eye-level grills** Choose an oven with the grill positioned at eye level if you want to check food frequently during cooking. The grill pan should have a support and stops to prevent it from being pulled out too far.

USING OVEN DOORS

Resting a hot dish

Choose an oven with a strong door that pulls down rather than opening sideways. The door will provide a useful surface for hot casseroles or cookie sheets as they come out of the oven.

CONSIDERING SAFETY

● **Choosing warning lights** Pick a stove with controls that light up and warn you when the burners are hot, even if they are not glowing.
● **Checking safety** Make sure that, if a gas stovetop has a lid for covering burners when not in use, the stovetop has a cutoff switch, and the lid is made of heatproof glass.
● **Avoiding accidents** If you have young children, install a stove guard to deter them from touching hot pots and pans. Turn saucepan handles inward to prevent children from pulling them down.

USING A STOVE

Whatever type of cooking you do most often, it is a good idea to be aware of your oven's rate of energy consumption, and to check regularly that it is running efficiently. Refer to the manufacturer's handbook for tips on how to make good use of special functions.

CHECKING TEMPERATURE

Using a thermometer
Check the accuracy of your oven regularly by placing an oven thermometer in the center of the middle shelf. Heat the oven to 350°F (180°C), then compare with the thermometer reading.

COOKING EFFICIENTLY

● **Saving energy** Turn solid-element burners off a few minutes before you finish cooking. The food will continue to cook on the residual heat.
● **Preheating the oven** Allow at least 10 minutes for an oven to preheat. Arrange the oven shelves before turning on the oven to avoid losing heat or burning yourself.
● **Setting a timer** Avoid opening the oven door, which lowers the oven temperature, to check if food is done. Use a timer to monitor cooking times.
● **Avoiding scratches** Prevent damage to ceramic burners by lifting pans off rather than sliding them across.

SAVING FUEL

Cooking a complete meal
Use fuel economically by cooking a complete meal in the oven at the same time. Place dishes that need the highest temperatures at the top of the oven, and other dishes on the lower shelves.

CLEANING A STOVE

Wipe up cooking spills on a burner or inside an oven immediately after they have occurred. Once they harden or burn onto the surface, you will have to use a commercial cleaner to remove them. Switch off the power before cleaning an electric oven or burner.

CLEANING EFFICIENTLY

● **Reducing cleaning** Stand pies and casseroles on a cookie sheet in an oven to catch spills.
● **Wiping a ceramic surface** Wipe up fruit juice, sugar, and acidic food spills on ceramic burners immediately, since they may cause etching or pitting on the surface.
● **Cleaning shelves** Wash oven racks in the dishwasher, remove them before the drying cycle, and wipe over with a cloth. Alternatively, place them on an old towel in the tub, and soak in a solution of ammonia and hot water to loosen food deposits.
● **Saving energy** Start a self-cleaning cycle when the oven is still warm to save energy.

REMOVING BURNED FOOD

Using a damp cloth
If food burns onto a burner surround, turn the heat off, let cool, and cover with a cloth wrung out in a solution of water and dishwashing liquid. Let stand for two hours, then wipe clean.

MONEY-SAVING TIP

Cleaning chrome trim
To clean rust from chrome trim, rub it with a piece of aluminum foil wrapped around your finger, shiny side out. Buff up with a cloth dipped in rubbing alcohol.

USING A MICROWAVE

Cooking in a microwave is quick, easy, and economical. However many people you cook for, a microwave can be an invaluable addition to the kitchen, saving time and energy. If you have never used a microwave before, you will need to adapt your cooking methods.

CHOOSING A MICROWAVE

Many microwaves have useful features that you should consider before buying.

- **Power** Most full-power ovens use 650–750 watts. The higher the wattage, the shorter the cooking times.
- **Controls** Digital controls will give more accurate timings than dial controls.
- **Turntables** Ensure that the oven has a turntable. If it does not, the food will have to be turned manually.
- **Browning option** This will add a rich, golden color and crispness to food.
- **Cleaning** Look for self-cleaning interior panels on combination ovens.
- **Compact models** If kitchen space is limited, choose an under-cabinet model.

LEARNING BASIC SKILLS

- **Adapting recipes** To adapt a conventional recipe for the microwave, reduce the cooking time by about two thirds.
- **Adjusting cooking times** When doubling recipe amounts for the microwave, increase the cooking time by one quarter to one third. When halving recipe amounts, reduce the cooking time by approximately one third.
- **Checking temperature** Use a microwave thermometer to check that food is thoroughly cooked. Frozen dinners should reach 158°F (70°C).
- **Adding color** To enhance the color of food cooked in a microwave, top savory dishes with toasted nuts or a sprinkling of paprika, and top sweet dishes with toasted nuts, brown sugar, or ground spices.

INCREASING CAPACITY

- **Stacking plates** Use plate-stacking rings to cook two portions of food at once, and increase the cooking time by 1½ minutes. Move the plates around halfway through.

Using shelves
Buy shelves and trivets, both of which are available as microwave accessories, so that you can cook more than one item at a time. Alternatively, choose a microwave with a shelf.

MICROWAVING SAFELY

Follow a few basic guidelines to ensure that you use a microwave safely, choose suitable containers, and cook food thoroughly. Used correctly, a microwave is a versatile appliance, cooking and reheating food in a fraction of the time that it would take in a conventional oven.

COOKING THOROUGHLY

Place narrowest part of food inward

Arranging food
For safety, make sure food is cooked thoroughly. Distribute it evenly in a dish, and cook wedge-shaped items, such as pears or fish fillets, with the narrow ends pointing to the center of the dish.

CHOOSING DISHES

Checking heat resistance
To ensure that a dish will not overheat, place it in a microwave with a cup of cold water on High for two minutes. The water should heat up and warm the cup, while the dish should remain cold.

SAFETY

- **Following instructions** Read the manufacturer's handbook, and follow cooking instructions on packaged foods.
- **Avoiding metal** Do not use metal dishes, dishes that have metal decoration, or kitchen foil in a microwave.
- **Supervising cooking** Always avoid letting foods cook unattended, since some high-sugar foods may catch fire.
- **Cooking and reheating** Make sure that microwaved food is thoroughly and evenly cooked before serving.

COLD STORAGE

REFRIGERATORS AND FREEZERS ARE INVALUABLE ITEMS of equipment in the kitchen. Both of these appliances ensure that we have a wide choice of safe, fresh food at any time of the year, and they can help us create a varied, healthy diet.

CHOOSING APPLIANCES

When you are selecting a refrigerator or a freezer, consider carefully the needs of your household. Decide on the capacity that you require, taking into account the space available and the foods you store most often, such as garden produce or convenience foods.

ADDING STORAGE

Using baskets
Add extra storage baskets to a chest freezer. They will make it much easier to find and organize the contents of the freezer. Extra storage baskets can usually be ordered from the manufacturer.

KEEPING TRACK

Using drawer markers
If you choose an upright freezer, look for a model that has contents cards on the front of the drawers. These will help you keep track of items stored. List the foods in each drawer on the attached card.

LOOKING FOR FEATURES
● **Checking temperature** When choosing a freezer, look for one with a built-in temperature indicator on the outside. This will allow you to check that the appliance is running efficiently without opening the door.
● **Moving easily** If your house has solid floors, choose a refrigerator or freezer with casters, since they will make the appliance reasonably easy to move. Casters may damage soft flooring such as vinyl.
● **Lighting the interior** Check whether a freezer has an interior light, which is especially useful in a chest freezer. If not, keep a battery-operated clip-on light handy so that you can see the contents easily.

BUYING A FREEZER
● **Assessing capacity** Allow 2 cu ft (57 liters) of freezer space for each person in your household, together with an extra 2 cu ft (57 liters) if you do a lot of entertaining.
● **Fitting the space** If space is tight, choose an upright freezer, which will take up less floor space than a chest freezer.
● **Positioning a freezer** Check that there is enough space to open the freezer door or lid. The door of an upright freezer may need to open through an angle of more than 90° so that the drawers can be pulled out.

BUYING A REFRIGERATOR
● **Assessing capacity** Make sure that your refrigerator is large enough for your needs. Allow 8 cu ft (228 liters) for the first two people in the household, then another 1 cu ft (28 liters) for each additional person.
● **Reducing workload** For easy maintenance, it is best to choose a frost-free refrigerator-freezer, since these do not need to be defrosted.
● **Selecting shelves** Make sure that refrigerator shelves are adjustable in order to accomodate large items.

INSTALLING APPLIANCES

● **Adjusting height** Make sure that a refrigerator or freezer is stable. Use a level to check whether the appliance is level, and adjust the legs or casters accordingly.
● **Moving easily** To move an appliance without casters, slip an old piece of carpet under the foot to help it slide.
● **Avoiding dampness** To allow the air to circulate all around a freezer that is stored in a garage, raise the appliance 2 in (5 cm) off the ground by placing it on blocks.

USING APPLIANCES EFFECTIVELY

To maintain food stored in a refrigerator or freezer in the best condition, you must keep these appliances running efficiently. Regulating the temperature is important, since too high a temperature will cause food to deteriorate, and too low will cause energy to be wasted.

PREVENTING DEPOSITS
● **Wiping bases** When packing items into a refrigerator or a freezer, keep a clean, damp cloth handy to wipe the bases of messy containers. This will prevent food spills from transferring onto the shelves.

Lining with foil
Prevent ice-cube trays or frozen-foods spills from sticking to the base of a freezer or freezer compartment by lining with a layer of foil. Replace the foil regularly with a clean piece.

CHECKING TEMPERATURES

For safe and efficient running of refrigerators and freezers, check the internal temperature regularly with a thermometer.

● **Refrigerators** Run a refrigerator at 40°F (5°C) or below. The coolest section of the refrigerator should be 34°F (1°C). To check the temperature, place a thermometer in the center of the top shelf, and leave overnight. In summer, adjust the refrigerator's thermostat.
● **Freezers** Keep a freezer at 0°F (−18°C) or below. Check the temperature by placing a thermometer on the top shelf or the upper edge of the top basket, and leave overnight.

REDUCING FUEL USAGE
● **Positioning** Place freezers and refrigerators in a cool site away from direct sunlight and appliances that generate heat.

Filling spaces
If possible, keep your freezer full, since it is not energy-efficient to run it half empty. Fill large spaces with loaves of bread, or use crumpled newsprint to prevent air from circulating.

PREVENTING PROBLEMS
● **Labeling switches** To ensure that a freezer is not turned off by mistake, place tape over the switch, or label the plug clearly with the word "freezer."
● **Avoiding stale smells** To prevent an unpleasant odor from developing while a refrigerator or freezer is in storage, clean and dry it thoroughly, then prop the door open with a block of wood and secure it in place with strips of masking tape.
● **Moving house** Before moving a refrigerator or freezer, turn it off 24 hours in advance. Clean thoroughly, remove loose parts, and secure the door. Always keep a refrigerator or freezer in an upright position during transportation.

FREEZING EFFICIENTLY
● **Cooling foods** Cool foods completely before storing in a refrigerator or freezer. To cool hot food quickly, sit the base of the container in a sink half-filled with cold water.
● **Limiting amounts** To avoid raising the temperature of a freezer, freeze no more than one-tenth of the appliance's capacity of food at one time.

STORING SUCCESSFULLY
● **Arranging foods** When placing foods in a refrigerator, leave some space around each item so that air can circulate and chill the food evenly.
● **Avoiding "freezer burn"** Always wrap foods tightly before freezing to exclude air. This will prevent moisture from being drawn out of the foods, which results in loss of nutrients and dehydration.

MONEY-SAVING TIP

Checking a door seal
Make sure that the door seals on a refrigerator, freezer compartment, or freezer are working efficiently by closing the door on a piece of paper. If the paper can be pulled out easily, the seal is worn and should be replaced.

CLEANING REFRIGERATORS AND FREEZERS

Regular cleaning of refrigerators and freezers will help keep them as safe environments in which to store food. In addition to cleaning the insides, maintain the outer surfaces, since these are subject to daily wear and tear, and sometimes the damaging effects of steam.

PROTECTING SURFACES

● **Preventing rust** If a freezer or refrigerator is prone to condensation on the outside, protect the outer surface by rubbing it with silicone polish applied with a soft cloth.

● **Using glycerin** After defrosting a freezer, wipe the interior with glycerin. Next time you defrost it, the ice will be easier to remove, eliminating the need for scraping.

● **Cleaning doors** If someone uses permanent markers on the refrigerator door, remove marks by rubbing with lighter fluid applied with a soft cloth (test or ask manufacurer first). Wash with detergent, rinse, and dry.

RETOUCHING SCRATCHES

Using enamel paint
Cover a scratch on a refrigerator or freezer door with enamel paint. First, clean with detergent and wipe dry with a clean cloth. Test the color on an unseen area, and retouch with a fine brush.

CLEANING INTERIORS

● **Wiping spills** Always wipe up spills in the refrigerator as soon as they occur to avoid contamination or odors.

● **Removing odors** Remove lingering smells from the interior of a refrigerator or freezer by wiping with a cloth rinsed in a solution of 1 tbsp (15 ml) baking soda to 1 quart (1 liter) warm water.

● **Unpacking foods** Remove all foods from a refrigerator or freezer before cleaning or defrosting. Pack ice cream into a cooler, and stack chilled or frozen foods tightly together, covering them with a blanket for insulation.

DEFROSTING FREEZERS

The most convenient time to defrost a freezer is when stocks of food are at their lowest, for instance, after holiday seasons during which supplies are depleted, or in early summer before you stock up with garden produce. Remember to turn off and unplug the freezer before defrosting.

DEALING WITH A BREAKDOWN

If your freezer breaks down, or if there is an unexpected power outage, follow these simple emergency rules:

● **Check the electrics** Make sure that the wiring, plug, or fuse is not at fault before calling in a repair person.

● **Keep doors closed** Avoid opening the freezer. If it is full, the contents should stay frozen for at least 12 hours.

● **Save food** If the problem is long-term, ask neighbors or friends if they have spare freezer space you can use.

● **Use thawed food** Cook or use up thawed food quickly. Never refreeze food, since this can cause food poisoning.

DEFROSTING EFFICIENTLY

● **Lining with foil** Line the shelves of a freezer with foil when defrosting. Make a hole in the center of each layer to enable you to funnel water into a bowl underneath.

● **Lining with a towel** Before scraping ice from the sides of a freezer, lay a towel in the bottom to collect ice.

● **Cleaning up** If you have a wet-dry vacuum cleaner, use it to suck up ice debris and water during defrosting.

● **Drying thoroughly** Before switching the freezer back on after defrosting, wipe around the inside with a baking-soda solution, and dry thoroughly with paper towels. Let run for one hour after switching on before replacing contents.

SAVING TIME

● **Adding hot water** To defrost a freezer quickly, place bowls of hot water inside. Scrape off the ice as soon as it loosens.

Using a hair dryer
If time is short, blow warm air from a small hair dryer over the ice in a freezer, moving the dryer to avoid overheating one area. Make sure your hands are dry, and keep the dryer moisture-free.

POTS AND PANS

WHEN YOU SET OUT TO BUY POTS AND PANS, you will find a wide range of styles and materials from which to choose. Prolong their durability by buying the best quality you can afford, protecting their linings, and cleaning them carefully.

CHOOSING POTS AND PANS

Your choice of pots and pans will affect the success of your cooking. The material they are made of should be suitable for the type of stove you have and the kind of cooking you do. Select good-quality pots and pans, and they will give you reliable service for many years.

POT AND PAN MATERIALS

Choose cast iron pots and pans for gas, electric, or solid-element burners, but make sure that they have enamel bases for ceramic or halogen burners. Steel or aluminum can be used on gas or electric burners, but if you have a ceramic, halogen, or solid burner, choose copper-based steel or heavy-based aluminum pots and pans. Glass can be used on electric, gas, ceramic, or halogen burners. Copper and earthenware perform best on electric or gas burners.

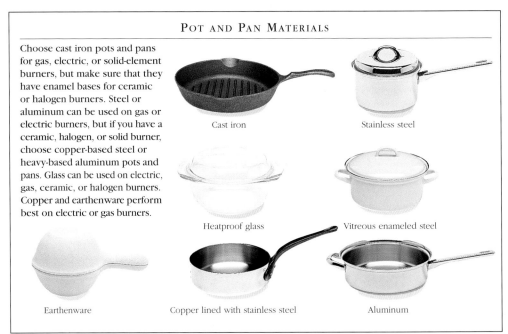

Cast iron

Stainless steel

Heatproof glass

Vitreous enameled steel

Earthenware

Copper lined with stainless steel

Aluminum

BUYING POTS & PANS

● **Cast iron** Buy the heaviest gauge of cast iron for the best results. Choose pots and pans with two handles, so that they will be easy to pick up when full. Look for wooden handles, which will remain cool.

● **Copper** Choose copper pots and pans lined with stainless steel. Although expensive, they are more durable than those that are lined with tin.

● **Heatproof glass** Buy heatproof-glass pots and pans for versatility, since they can be used to cook, freeze, reheat, microwave, and serve food.

IMPROVISING SPECIALTY PANS

Foil will hold asparagus in position

Steaming vegetables
To steam vegetables without a steamer, use a metal sieve and a wide saucepan. Place the sieve just inside the rim, above boiling water. Add the food, and cover.

Cooking asparagus
To make an asparagus steamer, use a deep saucepan and insert a ring of foil. The foil will ensure that the asparagus tips stay above water while they are cooking.

PROTECTING POTS AND PANS

Routine care of pots and pans will ensure that you get the best performance out of them. Whichever materials pots and pans are made of, their surfaces must be protected from damage, which can cause food to stick. Use nonmetal tools during cooking to minimize wear and tear.

PREPARING NEW POTS
● **Copper** Immerse new copper pans in boiling water, and let soak until cold to remove the lacquer coating.
● **Cast iron** To prevent sticking and protect the surface, season cast iron before use. Brush with vegetable oil. Pour in a little more oil, and place on a low burner for one hour. Cool, and wipe with a paper towel.
● **Enamel** Brush the inner surface of the enamel with oil, then place in a cool oven for one hour. Let cool 12 hours, and wipe clean.

PROTECTING COATINGS

Paper towel protects lining

Caring for nonstick pans
To prevent nonstick linings from becoming damaged by bumps and scratches, place paper towels between pans when stacking them together for storage.

CARING FOR CAST IRON

Preventing rusting
To prevent rusting during storage, dry uncoated cast iron pans well after washing. Rub all surfaces with a paper towel dipped in a little vegetable oil.

CLEANING POTS AND PANS

There are a few basic rules worth following when cleaning pots and pans. They will help maintain their performance during cooking. Techniques for cleaning different materials vary, so it is always advisable to read manufacturers' instructions before cleaning new pots and pans.

REMOVING STAINS
● **Bleaching enamel** To clean a badly stained enameled pan, fill it with a weak solution of about 2 tsp (10 ml) bleach to 2½ cups (600 ml) water. Let soak for a maximum of two hours to avoid damaging the surface of the enamel.

Brightening aluminum
To remove dark stains from an aluminum pot or pan, fill it with water, add the juice of one lemon, and simmer gently until the aluminum brightens.

CLEANING COPPER
● **Using half a lemon** To brighten up and remove stains from tarnished pots and pans made of copper, dip a cut half of lemon into table salt, then rub it gently over the stained copper surface. Rinse and dry thoroughly before use.

Using a vinegar paste
Make a thick paste from roughly equal parts of vinegar and flour. Dip a soft cloth into the paste, and rub it over the copper until clean. Rinse in hot water, and dry.

PREVENTING PROBLEMS
● **Protecting surfaces** Soak pots and pans in hot, soapy water to remove stuck-on foods. Soak pans coated with sugary substances in cold water.
● **Soaking earthenware** To prevent an earthenware pot from absorbing fat, fill it with boiling water, and let stand one hour before use. The pot will absorb water during soaking, keeping out fat and helping to create steam during cooking.
● **Cleaning handles** Wash wooden pan handles quickly in warm water, since soaking may cause them to crack.
● **Caring for steel** Make sure you wash stainless steel soon after cooking salty food, since salt causes surface pitting.
● **Drying pans** Always dry aluminum or polished steel pans immediately to prevent watermarks from forming.

BAKEWARE

A GOOD BASIC SELECTION OF BAKEWARE will be useful in any kitchen. Your choice of items will depend on the type of cooking you do. If you bake regularly, it is a good idea to collect a wide selection of pans in different shapes and sizes.

CHOOSING BAKEWARE

Bakeware is usually of a light or medium weight so that it can conduct heat quickly and efficiently. Traditional, uncoated pans are best for baking light sponge cakes, since they produce golden brown crusts. Nonstick surfaces tend to produce cakes with slightly dark, thick crusts.

BAKING EQUIPMENT

The equipment illustrated below makes up a useful collection of bakeware that would be suitable for most people's needs. Springform pans with removable bases allow for the easy removal of molded foods and facilitate cleaning, especially in the case of deep cake pans and flan pans. Include in your collection some cookie sheets that have a rim for baking mixtures that tend to spread, and some that have a rim on three sides only to allow you to slide off delicate items such as pastry easily. Whatever you bake, a large cooling rack is essential for cooling baked items after cooking.

Springform pan

Bundt pan

Large, loose-based flan pan

Individual flan pan

Deep cake tin

Cake pans

Loaf pan

Muffin tin

Jelly-roll pan

Ovenproof dish

Microwave-proof dish

Cookie sheet

Cooling rack

UTENSILS

Each cook will choose a unique range of utensils for the kitchen. However, many utensils can fulfil several functions, and a few well-made, good-quality tools are all that you need. Special gadgets are useful, but can be expensive.

CHOOSING KNIVES

The advice to buy the best equipment you can afford applies most especially to the purchase of kitchen knives. A good-quality set will save you time and energy, and should last a lifetime. Start with a selection for everyday cooking, which you can add to in the future.

SELECTING MATERIALS

● **Choosing blades** Make sure that the metal is of good quality. High-carbon stainless steel is expensive, but it is the most practical for cutting all kinds of food. It sharpens easily and does not discolor.

● **Choosing knife handles** Look for wooden knife handles that are sealed with heat-resistant plastic. These handles are hard-wearing and easy to clean.

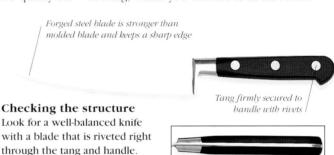

Forged steel blade is stronger than molded blade and keeps a sharp edge

Tang firmly secured to handle with rivets

Checking the structure

Look for a well-balanced knife with a blade that is riveted right through the tang and handle. The base of the blade should have a firm heel or shank to protect fingers and reinforce the blade.

Blade continuous with tang, which extends full length of handle

---

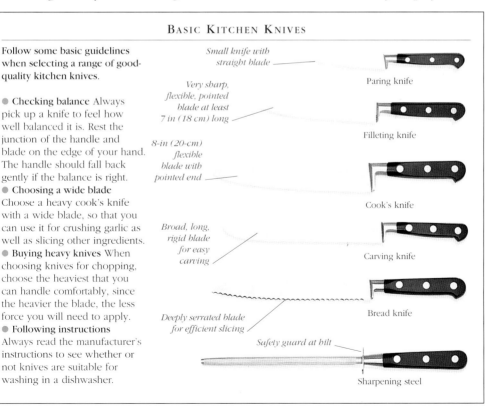

BASIC KITCHEN KNIVES

Follow some basic guidelines when selecting a range of good-quality kitchen knives.

● **Checking balance** Always pick up a knife to feel how well balanced it is. Rest the junction of the handle and blade on the edge of your hand. The handle should fall back gently if the balance is right.

● **Choosing a wide blade** Choose a heavy cook's knife with a wide blade, so that you can use it for crushing garlic as well as slicing other ingredients.

● **Buying heavy knives** When choosing knives for chopping, choose the heaviest that you can handle comfortably, since the heavier the blade, the less force you will need to apply.

● **Following instructions** Always read the manufacturer's instructions to see whether or not knives are suitable for washing in a dishwasher.

Small knife with straight blade

Paring knife

Very sharp, flexible, pointed blade at least 7 in (18 cm) long

Filleting knife

8-in (20-cm) flexible blade with pointed end

Cook's knife

Broad, long, rigid blade for easy carving

Carving knife

Bread knife

Deeply serrated blade for efficient slicing

Safety guard at hilt

Sharpening steel

CARING FOR KNIVES

After you have selected the best knives you can afford, it makes sense to store them safely and keep them in good condition. The safest way to store knives is to keep them in a knife block or on a magnetic rack. These will help prevent accidents and protect the blades.

SAFETY

- **Carrying** Always carry knives at your side with the blades pointing downward.
- **Dropping** If you lose your grip on a knife, allow it to drop to the floor. This is much safer than trying to break its fall, which could result in serious injury.
- **Sharpening** Keep knives sharp, since a blunt knife is more likely to slip and cut you than a sharp one.
- **Washing** Avoid washing knives together with other items, or leaving knives soaking. They may not be visible beneath the soap suds and could therefore be a danger to anyone putting his or her hands in the water.

PROTECTING POINTS

Hold cork firmly on counter and insert knife point carefully

Using corks

If you do not have a knife block or magnetic rack, prevent the fine points of sharp knives from becoming damaged in a cutlery drawer by placing a wine cork securely on each knife tip.

PROTECTING BLADES

- **Choosing a cutting board** Use a polypropylene or a wooden cutting board, since these do not blunt blades.
- **Restricting use** Keep good kitchen knives exclusively for preparing food. Do not use them to cut string or paper.
- **Washing knives** Wash carbon steel knives by hand immediately after use to avoid staining them. Remove any stubborn stains by rubbing the blade with a wet cork dipped in scouring powder.
- **Storing knives** Protect knife blades by using plastic paper binders, which are available from office supply stores. Slide a blade into a holder, and push it in as far as it will go.

SHARPENING KNIVES

It takes only a little time and trouble to sharpen knives. If you get into the habit of sharpening them every time you use them, they will perform well for years. If necessary, have your knives sharpened professionally every two or three years if the blades lose their edge.

USING SHARPENERS

- **Soaking in oil** Soak a whetstone in vegetable oil for smooth sharpening.
- **Sharpening regularly** Try to sharpen kitchen knives every time you use them so that they will be maintained in peak condition. Put them once through an electric or manual sharpener, or stroke them three or four times with a steel prior to use.
- **Protecting serrations** Take knives that have serrated edges to a professional knife sharpener, or do not sharpen them at all, since their serrations can be damaged easily during sharpening if extreme care is not taken.

USING ALTERNATIVE METHODS OF SHARPENING

Hold upside-down mug firmly by handle

Using a mug

If you do not have a steel or a special knife sharpener, use the base of an unglazed earthenware mug. Run the blade across it away from your hand and at a slight angle. Repeat several times.

Hammer in small tacks to secure paper to wood

Using fine sandpaper

To make a sharpening block, wrap a piece of wood in fine sandpaper, turn the edges underneath, and secure with tacks. Firmly run knives across the surface of the paper to sharpen the blades.

CHOOSING USEFUL TOOLS

Kitchenware stores are packed with a huge array of useful gadgets for tackling all kinds of kitchen jobs. Many tools are designed specifically with one task in mind, but some of them are very versatile and can be invaluable tools that may be used for a variety of purposes.

CHOOSING THE BASICS

● **Peeling vegetables** Use a swivel-bladed peeler for peeling vegetables, since it will peel much more thinly than a knife. This tool can also be used for shaving curls of fresh Parmesan cheese, and for making decorative curls from fresh coconut.

● **Lifting delicate foods** Buy a fish server for lifting foods without breaking them. Use two servers together for moving large, delicate quiches or cakes onto serving plates. Slide them underneath the item from opposite sides.

● **Removing zest** Use a zester to remove the zest without the pith from citrus fruits.

● **Whisking foods** Choose a balloon whisk – a good all-purpose whisk – for a variety of tasks, from making meringue to smoothing lumpy sauce.

CHOPPING TOMATOES

Using kitchen scissors
Save money by buying cans of whole rather than chopped tomatoes for cooking. Then chop the whole tomatoes in the opened can using a pair of sharp kitchen scissors.

USING TOOLS FOR A VARIETY OF PURPOSES

● **Using a canelle knife** Decorate tall tumblers for serving cool summer drinks with long strips of cucumber peel that have been cut lengthwise from a cucumber with a canelle knife.

Banding new potatoes
Run a canelle knife quickly around the middle of new potatoes before cooking them whole in their skins. This will prevent the skins from splitting and improve their appearance.

FINDING ALTERNATIVES

● **Squeezing juice** If you do not have a citrus squeezer, place a halved lemon or lime over the prongs of a fork, and twist to extract the juice.

● **Making a funnel** To fill jars without spills, make a funnel by improvising with an empty plastic dishwashing liquid bottle. Remove the lid, and cut the top part off the bottle at the shoulder. Wash it thoroughly, and dry before use.

● **Cracking nuts** To crack nuts easily without a nutcracker, use a pair of pliers instead.

● **Removing corks** To uncork a bottle of wine without a corkscrew, screw a large metal hook into the cork, place a wooden spoon handle through the hook, and pull the cork out.

● **Using a melon baller** Instead of using a large ice-cream scoop for serving sorbet, use a melon baller to make tiny scoops. Pile these up in serving dishes for an unusual and attractive presentation.

Cleaning an artichoke
Use a melon baller to scrape out the hairy choke from inside a cooked globe artichoke. Pull out the inner leaves to expose the choke, then scrape it out with the edge of the baller.

BRIGHT IDEA

Cleaning a work surface
Use the edge of a fish server to scrape up pastry or dough that has stuck to a work surface during rolling out. Push the fish server firmly along the surface so that its edge dislodges any stubborn leftovers. Wipe over the entire area with a damp cloth to remove any remaining flour or pastry crumbs.

USING OTHER UTENSILS

A number of other utensils are useful in the kitchen, and a carefully selected assortment of items will help you tackle most everyday tasks confidently and efficiently. As with other kitchen equipment, buy the best you can afford, since the best-quality tools will last the longest.

USING SIEVES

Use wooden spoon to press fruit

Puréeing acidic fruits
When pressing acidic foods such as raspberries to make a purée or remove seeds, use a flexible nylon sieve. Metal sieves may react with the acid and can discolor a purée.

MOLDING DOUGH

● **Measuring thickness** To roll out dough to a precise depth, use pieces of wood or rulers of the required thickness. Place one on either side of the dough, and roll the pin along the wood and over the dough, using the wood as a guide.
● **Molding shortbread** To shape shortbread without the aid of an expensive wooden mold, press the dough into a fluted metal flan pan placed on a cookie sheet.

USING MIXING BOWLS

● **Cooking in heatproof bowls** Choose heatproof mixing bowls so that they can be used for cooking food in a microwave or for stirring mixtures over a pan of boiling water if necessary.
● **Preventing slipping** To stop a bowl from slipping on a counter while stirring, place it on a dampened cloth.

MARKING UTENSILS

Paint tip of spoon handle

Color-coding spoons
To avoid transferring flavors, mark wooden spoon handles with colored enamel paints so that they can be identified easily. Keep one spoon for stirring onions, one for fruit, and so on.

USING PASTRY BRUSHES

● **Buying colored brushes** Look in kitchenware stores for pastry brushes with colored bristles to use for different foods. For example, choose a red-bristled brush for meat.

Position brush in lid so that bristles are just touching base of jar

Making an oil jar
Make sure you always have a brush handy for greasing baking pans by attaching a pastry brush through a hole in the lid of a screw-top jar. Keep a shallow depth of oil inside the jar.

USING METAL EQUIPMENT

● **Lining molds** Line metal molds with plastic wrap before filling with acidic foods, such as fruit-based gelatin molds. This will prevent a reaction between the acid and the metal, which could affect the taste and appearance of the food.
● **Choosing colanders** When buying a colander, remember that a metal one will be more versatile than a plastic one. It can be placed over a pan as an improvised steamer.
● **Heating cups** When measuring sticky foods in metal cups, warm the cup first by rinsing in boiling water; the food will slide off easily.

HANDLING MEAT

● **Using tongs** When turning meat during cooking, use food tongs to lift and then turn it. Piercing with a knife or fork will result in a loss of juices.
● **Basting roasts** Use a syringe-type, bulb-shaped baster to baste roasts during cooking. This will save you from having to lift a heavy pan from the oven to baste the meat.

Hold hot skewer with thick pot holder

Branding foods
To create a decorative, branded effect on grilled poultry, meat, or fish, heat a metal skewer until red hot in a gas flame or on an electric burner, then press it onto the food to mark it.

MAINTAINING UTENSILS

If you maintain kitchen utensils well, they will give many years of service. Items made from modern materials such as plastic are easily maintained, but wooden utensils need to be of good quality, cleaned carefully, and checked regularly for cracks to remain efficient and safe.

SOLVING PROBLEMS

● **Releasing stuck pans** If pans or bowls become stuck inside each other, fill the inner pan with iced water to make it contract, and dip the outer one in hot water to expand it. Pull apart to separate.

● **Removing verdigris** Soak copper utensils for 2–3 hours in a solution of washing soda in warm water. Rub with a soft cloth, rinse, and dry well.

● **Removing tannin** Clean a teapot by filling it with boiling water and adding a handful of household borax. Let stand overnight, and wash well before use. Clean chrome-plated teapots with a cloth dipped in vinegar and salt.

REMOVING ODORS

Rubbing with lemon
After using a cutting board for preparing strong-smelling foods such as fish or onions, wash it, then rub the surface with a cut half of lemon. Use a lemon in the same way to remove strong smells from your hands.

CLEANING PRESSES

Bristles clean inside holes

Using a toothbrush
If a garlic press becomes clogged with pulp after use, clean out the holes using a toothbrush. For the best results, clean the garlic press immediately after you have used it, rather than letting the garlic residue dry out.

FINDING ALTERNATIVES

Although a very well-equipped kitchen may be the ideal, it is possible to manage with surprisingly few utensils. If you do certain kinds of cooking only occasionally, improvise with a range of basic items rather than investing in specialized equipment that will be used rarely.

ROLLING PASTRY

● **Dredging flour** To flour a countertop if you do not have a shaker, sprinkle flour through a sifter or fine sieve.

Rolling pastry
Use a straight-sided bottle to roll out pastry if you do not have a rolling pin. To keep the pastry cool and easy to handle, fill an empty bottle with water, and chill before using in this way.

MAKING FUNNELS

Using a piping bag
To fill a narrow-necked jar or bottle without a funnel, use a piping bag. Place the narrow end of the bag into the neck, then pour in the food or liquid carefully to avoid spills.

INVENTING SUBSTITUTES

● **Making a cookie sheet** Turn a large roasting pan upside down to make an extra cookie sheet. Alternatively, use a double thickness of foil, and turn it up at the edges to make a rim.

● **Creating a counter space** If you need a temporary extra work surface in the kitchen, place a cutting board over an open kitchen drawer. Use it only for lightweight jobs such as chopping or slicing.

● **Improvising lids** Make a tight-fitting lid for a large casserole or pan by placing a cookie sheet over the top of it. Alternatively, fit a piece of crumpled foil inside the top of the pan, and press it against the sides to enclose the steam.

SMALL APPLIANCES

Today there is a wide choice of electrical kitchen appliances that you can use to save time and energy when performing everyday kitchen tasks. Decide which appliances will benefit you most according to the kind of cooking you do.

USING SMALL APPLIANCES

Make maximum use of each appliance by reading the manual before you start to use it. This will tell you which tasks the appliance will tackle and how to get the best performance out of it. Keep regularly used items, such as toasters, close at hand on or near a counter.

SELECTING APPLIANCES
● **Checking ease of cleaning**
Before buying, check that small appliances can be dismantled for cleaning, and whether or not parts are dishwasher-proof.
● **Storing cords** When selecting an appliance for countertop use, such as a toaster, mixer, or food processor, look for a model that stores the cord inside the appliance, or one that has a self-retracting cord.
● **Preventing slipping** For safety, buy small appliances that have nonskid feet.
● **Buying a small bowl** If you need to purée small amounts of food for a baby, consider a food processor made for the task, or buy a smaller bowl to fit your large processor.

USING BLENDERS

Dish towel protects hand from steam

Covering the lid
When puréeing hot foods in a blender, let them cool for a few minutes before blending. While blending, hold the lid in place with a folded dish towel in case the steam pushes it off.

MAINTAINING MIXERS

Use pointed dropper to insert oil into holes

Oiling a mixer
If the beaters of your mixer become stiff and difficult to remove, place a drop of light household oil into each of the holes into which the beaters fit. Insert the beaters, and switch on.

USING PROCESSORS

Using an extra bowl
If you use a food processor often for a variety of tasks, it is worth buying an extra bowl and blades so that you can prepare different foods in rapid succession. Spares are available from most suppliers.

PROCESSING EFFICIENTLY
● **Creating a pulse-switch effect**
If your food processor does not have an automatic pulse switch, alternately press the High and Off switches to achieve the same effect.
● **Preventing "walking"** If your food processor "walks" around on the counter while in use, or if it is noisy, place it on a rubberized or soft plastic mat.
● **Warming working parts**
Before mixing or kneading bread dough in a food processor, warm the bowl and blade by rinsing them in hot water before use. This will help the yeast rise.

CARING FOR SMALL APPLIANCES

Good-quality electrical appliances are built to withstand reasonable domestic use but will benefit from regular care and maintenance. Keep electrical appliances away from burners to prevent heat damage, and check cords regularly for wear, which could make them dangerous.

PREVENTING WEAR
● **Selecting speed** Use the correct speed on a food processor to avoid straining the motor. Check the manual to find the appropriate setting for the job to be done.
● **Changing speed** If a mixer or food processor motor strains during mixing, switch it onto High, or mix small quantities in separate batches. If a recipe recommends processing in batches, do so.
● **Correcting faults** If a blender or food processor stops, switch it off, and check that nothing is jamming the blade. Let it rest for a few seconds before turning it on again.

EASING SEALED LIDS

Spray oil inside lid

Using spray oil
Occasionally spray the inside edge of a food-processor lid with spray-on vegetable oil to ease the lid's fit within the rim of the bowl. Avoid spraying the bowl, since this may affect some foods.

STORING APPLIANCES
● **Hanging beaters** Rather than storing mixer beaters in a drawer, hang them on a small hook. This will help prevent them from becoming damaged and make them easy to find.
● **Storing blades** Store sharp appliance blades in a special rack or box instead of leaving them in a drawer with other utensils. Alternatively, cut slots in a piece of styrofoam from the appliance packaging. Keep blades in slots.
● **Covering appliances** Use a plastic cover to protect a food processor and keep it clean if the appliance is usually stored on a crowded counter.

CLEANING SMALL APPLIANCES

Kitchen appliances that are in everyday use will benefit from regular cleaning. Read the manufacturer's instruction booklet for special instructions before doing this. Always unplug electrical items before you clean them, and do not immerse electrical parts in water.

REMOVING DEBRIS
● **Using tongs** Keep wooden food tongs or two chopsticks near a toaster to remove foods that have become stuck inside.

Direct air spray into each compartment

Blowing out crumbs
Use a compressed air spray to expel crumbs through the bottom of a toaster. These sprays are available from photographic equipment suppliers. Unplug the toaster before cleaning.

REMOVING DEPOSITS
● **Clearing greasy deposits** If your garbage disposal unit becomes clogged with greasy food, drop a handful of ice cubes into it, then switch on for a few seconds. The ice will set the fat so that it can be ground up and disposed of.
● **Clearing clogged filters** Remove mineral deposits from a blocked coffee maker by filling the tank with equal parts distilled vinegar and water. Switch on and brew once, then brew again with clear water before use.
● **Using detergents** To clean a blender container after use, half-fill it with a solution of dishwashing liquid and warm water. Run it for a few seconds to remove food deposits.

PURIFYING GRINDERS

Using bread
If you have used a coffee grinder or mill for grinding spices, remove all traces of spice odor and flavor that may taint coffee by grinding a few pieces of bread before it is used again.

PREPARED INGREDIENTS

*G*ATHERING TOGETHER A RELIABLE, *varied supply of prepared ingredients is essential to the smooth running of any kitchen. With such a stock, you will have the ingredients on hand to rustle up some tasty meals in minutes, without having to shop specifically for them. A versatile collection of staples and standbys is the key. Include a selection of good convenience foods in your supplies. Used with fresh foods, they have a valuable place in the kitchen.*

PANTRIES

It is important to remember when choosing where to store dry foods that they need cool, dry, and preferably dark conditions. The best place for them is in a cabinet or hutch in the coolest part of the kitchen. Alternatively, store dry foods in a basement larder.

ORGANIZING CABINETS

Large containers, cake pans, and boxes of UHT milk (for emergencies)

Narrow shelf makes it easy to see what is stored

Canisters and packs of dry ingredients such as flour, sugar, and dried fruits

Tall bottles behind smaller ones

Heavy items in regular use, pickles, preserves, and small herb and spice jars

PLANNING STORAGE

● **Siting cabinets** When choosing cabinets for food storage, bear in mind that they should be cool and dry. A cold outside wall is better than an internal one – ideally it should be at a temperature of about 50°F (10°C).
● **Choosing shelves** Where possible, store foods on narrow shelves, so that you can see and reach items easily. An ideal width for a shelf is about 5 in (13 cm).
● **Lining shelves** Before filling cabinets with food, line the shelves with a wipe-clean surface such as plastic laminate, spongeable shelf-lining paper, or aluminum foil.

Arranging ingredients

Ideally, you should aim to store large, lightweight foods such as cereals on the top shelves. Heavy bottles and cans are easy to remove if stored on lower shelves. Small spice jars should be located at the front of a shelf.

DRY STORAGE

THE WARM AND OFTEN STEAMY CONDITIONS of many kitchens are not ideal for storing dry ingredients. Careful storage and the appropriate choice of containers can help keep moisture and heat from damaging stored foods.

STORAGE CONTAINERS

Take a look at the storage facilities already available in your kitchen before buying expensive extra shelving or elaborate storage containers. Economical, space-saving ideas and recycled containers, such as coffee cans, can provide efficient food storage at little cost.

MAKING MAXIMUM USE OF CABINET SPACE

● **Stacking containers** When you are choosing containers for storage where space is limited, make sure that they stack easily. Containers can then be arranged in two layers to make the fullest use of the space between shelves.

Stuff tube with plastic bags for tidy storage

Storing plastic bags
To store plastic grocery bags for reuse, make a fabric tube about 8 x 20 in (20 x 50 cm), gather the ends, and secure them with elastic. Hang the tube from a hook inside a broom closet door.

Creating hanging space
To keep small packs of herbs, spices, and nuts organized, and to save on shelf space, use a clear plastic shoe organizer. Hang it from a hook inside a food pantry door for easy access.

Hanging racks
Keep frequently used small items and condiments on racks hung inside cabinet doors to save on shelf space. Put the items on butcher's hooks and in clip-on baskets attached to the racks.

REUSING CONTAINERS
● **Recycling screw-top jars** Store dry goods in containers such as thoroughly washed coffee cans, which are airtight.
● **Making an airtight seal** To make sure that storage jars are airtight, wrap a strip of masking tape around the lids.
● **Coping without containers** If you do not have any airtight storage containers, place a whole package of a dry ingredient such as flour into a zip-top plastic bag.

INVENTING SHELF SPACE

Height of shelf is determined by items to be stored

Making an extra shelf
Make maximum use of deep shelving by adding an extra shelf for storing small items between two existing shelves. A simple, wipe-clean wooden shelf built with two sides about 6 in (17 cm) high will be the most useful. Improvise with a quick, temporary version by resting a narrow length of wood on cans placed at either end of a shelf. Use the extra space for storing small cans and jars.

CLEANING AND LABELING CONTAINERS

To make the best use of dry ingredients, it is important to store them correctly. Make a note of use-by dates, and always finish the contents of a container before refilling it so that you do not mix old and new ingredients. Wash and dry containers regularly to prevent odors.

CLEANING CONTAINERS

● **Removing odors** To rid a container of lingering odors, fill it with hot water, and add 1 tbsp (15 ml) baking soda. Let stand overnight, then rinse and dry before use.

LABELING CONTAINERS

● **Using package labels** When transferring food from a package into a storage jar, cut out the name and cooking instructions on the package, and tape them to the jar.

Dried fruits

Stackable container

Food can be identified through translucent container

Lid firmly screwed on

Shake well

Use colored lids to identify contents

Loosening debris

Fill a dirty bottle or jar with warm water and a few drops of detergent. Add a ½-in (1-cm) layer of dried beans or rice, then shake to loosen the debris.

Using color-coded containers

Instead of labeling individual containers, use color-coded plastic containers to store different types of ingredients. For example, use blue for beans and green for dried fruits, so that you can identify ingredients at a glance.

OPENING TIGHTLY SEALED JARS AND BOTTLES

Food jars and bottles are often difficult to open when food becomes stuck between the jar or bottle and the lid. To loosen, use a firm grip, tap the lid upside down on a flat surface, or try one of the methods below.

● **Loosening metal lids** Hold a metal lid under hot water to expand the metal. If the jar or bottle has been chilled, start with lukewarm water, and increase the heat gradually to prevent the glass from cracking.
● **Preventing sticky lids** Before resealing a jar or bottle with sticky food, wipe the rim and lid with a paper towel that has been dampened with hot water.

Twist off lid

Hold jar firmly

Lid protected with soft cloth

Apply gentle pressure

Loosening a tightly sealed jar

If a jar or bottle lid is difficult to twist open with a normal grip, wear a rubber glove to give you a firm hold on the lid. Or grip with a rubber band, a piece of sandpaper, or a damp cloth.

Using pliers

To loosen a tight lid on a bottle or jar with a narrow neck, use pliers or a nutcracker, but do not exert too much pressure. Place a cloth over plastic lids to prevent them from being damaged.

PANTRY STAPLES

N O KITCHEN IS COMPLETE without basic staple ingredients such as pasta, rice, flours, sugars, oils, and flavorings. These items provide the basis for almost every type of cooking, and combine well with fresh ingredients.

DRIED PASTA

T here are more than one hundred different pasta shapes. Most of them are versatile and are suitable for serving with a wide variety of dishes, but many shapes were designed with a particular sauce or type of food in mind. Dried pasta keeps well in a pantry or cabinet.

CHOOSING AND USING PASTA		
BASIC SHAPES	EXAMPLES	COOKING SUGGESTIONS
LONG, ROUND PASTA Capelli d'angelo Spaghetti	Long, round pasta is available in many thicknesses and includes types such as spaghetti, long macaroni, and buccatini (a thick, hollow spaghetti). Vermicelli (little worms), capellini (fine hair), and capelli d'angelo (angel hair) are very fine pastas that are traditionally dried and packed in curls that resemble birds' nests.	● Use olive-oil-based sauces such as pesto to keep the strands slippery and separate. ● Use rich tomato, cheese, and meat sauces with spaghetti or buccatini. These are firm pastas that will not be weighed down by the sauce. ● Choose light tomato, butter, or cream sauces for serving with vermicelli-type pastas to keep the delicate strands intact.
LONG, FLAT PASTA Tagliatelle Lasagne	Lasagne is a broad, flat pasta, and may be smooth, ridged, or wavy-edged; lasagnette is a narrow type of lasagne. Tagliatelle and pappardelle are wide, flat pastas; tagliarini, linguine (little tongues), and trenette are narrower versions. Fettuccine, traditionally made with egg, is narrower and thicker than tagliatelle.	● Use no-boil lasagne in baked lasagne recipes to shorten preparation time. You may need to increase the liquid content of the recipe; consult the package directions. ● Choose thick, ribbon pastas for egg-based carbonara sauces, since the large surface area helps cook the sauce quickly. ● Toss cooked tagliatelle in a sauce or oil immediately after draining to separate the strands.
SHORT, SHAPED PASTA Penne Farfalle Fusilli	There is a seemingly endless choice of short pasta shapes, the most popular being penne (pens or quills), farfalle (butterflies or bows), fusilli and fusilli bucatti (spirals or springs), conchiglie (shells), orichiette (ears), lumache (snails), and ditali (fingers of glove or thimbles). Pastina is a general term for tiny pasta shapes such as farfallini, lumachine, stelline, and ditalini.	● Use penne, fusilli, lumache, and conchiglie with chunky tomato or meat sauces, or with ragù, which will penetrate into the pasta hollows. ● Make a pasta pie from leftover cooked short pasta. Layer with a savory sauce, top with cheese, and bake. ● To make a soup more substantial, sprinkle in a handful of any type of pastina near the end of cooking.

STORING AND USING PASTA

Pasta is available fresh or dried in a variety of shapes, and all types are an excellent source of fiber and carbohydrate. Dried pasta stores well and is a useful standby ingredient for everyday meals and last-minute entertaining. Whole-grain pasta is a healthy option.

STORING PASTA

● **Keeping long pasta** Keep several types of long pasta in one container, but tie each type into a bundle with raffia to avoid mixing them.

USING LEFTOVER PASTA

● **Using up pasta** If just a small amount of pasta is left in the package, cook all the pasta, and use the leftovers in salads, soups, and omelet fillings.

SERVING PASTA SHAPES

● **Encouraging children** Make meals more fun for children by using alphabet or animal shapes, or other pasta shapes in a variety of everyday meals.

Move dryer in circular motion to dry thoroughly

Add farfalle to fusilli

Drying a spaghetti tin
Always wash a spaghetti tin or jar with a mild detergent before refilling it. Dry with a cloth, and use a hair dryer to finish drying the inside thoroughly. Then fill with a fresh supply of pasta.

Making a pasta mix
Keep leftover pasta shapes that have similar cooking times together in an airtight container. Farfalle, fusilli, and conchiglie can be mixed together and used in everyday pasta dishes.

HEALTHY TIP

Using whole-grain pasta
Choose whole-grain pasta for high-fiber, healthy pasta dishes. If you find that whole-grain pasta is too heavy to eat on its own, mix it half-and-half with refined pasta that is the same shape.

TYPES OF ORIENTAL NOODLE

Rice noodles
Rice noodles, made from rice, are available in different thicknesses and shapes. They are usually dried and should be soaked in warm water for 15 minutes before cooking. Use in soups and stir-fries.

Cellophane noodles
Also called bean-thread or pea starch noodles, these are made from mung beans. They are fine and white and are available dried in neat bundles. Soak for five minutes before adding to soups or braised dishes.

Wheat and egg noodles
These noodles are usually made from wheat or buckwheat flour and egg. Choose flat noodles for use in soups and rounded noodles for stir-fries, or cook them on their own and serve as a side dish with vegetables.

USING NOODLES

● **Bulking out salads** Keep some fine-thread Chinese or Japanese noodles in your pantry. Soak in hot water for 5–10 minutes, then drain and toss into salads to make them more substantial.

● **Frying noodles** If you are frying cellophane noodles, there is no need to soak them first. Just add the noodles straight from the package to hot oil, and fry until crisp.

● **Substituting in special diets** Many types of noodle, such as rice and cellophane noodles, are suitable for people on a wheat-free diet. Substitute these noodles in recipes that specify wheat pasta.

CHOOSING AND USING GRAINS

Grains are one of the world's most nutritious staple foods. They are a good source of protein and carbohydrate, and contain valuable minerals. Whole grains are high in fiber. Keep a variety of whole and refined grains in your pantry to use in different dishes.

STORING GRAINS

● **Storing white rice** Keep white rice in an airtight container stored in a cool, dark place. Whole, polished rice will store well for about one year if kept at room temperature. Ground rice will keep for up to six months.
● **Storing whole grains** Store whole grains for a maximum of six months before use. After this time, the oil content of unrefined grain turns rancid from exposure to heat, light, and moisture.
● **Mixing grains** Brown rice and wild rice can be stored and cooked together. They require similar cooking times, and they look interesting when mixed together in risotto- and pilaf-style dishes.

MEASURING & STORING RICE

Use lid as measuring tool

Pour rice into measured container

Marking quantities
Store rice in a clear, straight-sided container that is marked off in ½ cup (125 g) measures. Use the measure as a guide to pour out the correct amount of rice. Cook white rice with twice its volume of water – 1 cup (250 ml) water for every ½ cup (125 g) rice.

Measuring a portion
Containers such as coffee jars can be used to store rice or other types of grain. Choose a container with a lid that holds approximately ¼ cup (55 g) of rice, and which will therefore enable you to measure out rice portions quickly for cooking.

COMMON TYPES OF GRAIN

Grains form the basis of many main-course dishes, and can be served as a nutritious side dish. Check the instructions on the packet before cooking.

● **Long-grain rice** This may be brown or white, and it has a slim, long grain.
● **Short-grain rice** Short-grain rice is soft when cooked. It is ideal for rice pudding.
● **Basmati rice** This is a very flavorful, long-grain rice.
● **Glutinous rice** Used mainly in Chinese dishes, this round-grain rice has a sticky texture.
● **Arborio rice** This medium-grain rice absorbs more liquid than other types of rice.
● **Wild rice** This grain is the seed of a wild aquatic grass.
● **Cracked wheat** A processed wheat, this is also called bulgur.
● **Couscous** This is a processed grain made from semolina.

White long-grain rice   Brown long-grain rice   Short-grain rice

Basmati rice   Glutinous rice   Arborio rice

Wild rice   Cracked wheat   Couscous

FLOURS AND OTHER GRAINS

As long as your pantry is clean, dry, and cool, storing flours and other grain products should not be a problem. Products that are bought in paper packaging will keep best if they are transferred to clean, dry, airtight containers as soon as they are opened.

MAKING A SHAKER

Using a screw-top jar
To make a homemade flour shaker, make several holes in the metal lid of a screw-top jar by hammering a nail through it while resting it on a wooden board. Fill the jar with flour.

STORING FLOUR
● **Keeping fresh** Store all-purpose white flour in a cool, dry place for up to six months; store self-rising flour for up to three months. Whole-wheat and other flours have a higher fat content; buy small amounts and use within two months.
● **Storing in a cool place** If the temperature is above 75°F (24°C), or if humidity is high, wrap flour in a heavy plastic bag and refrigerate to prevent infestation and mold.
● **Using chilled flours** If flour has been stored in a cool place, bring it to room temperature before baking to avoid a heavy texture in the finished products.

FLOUR SUBSTITUTES

Each type of flour has different properties. Sometimes one type can be substituted for another.

● **Making self-rising flour** Sift 1½ tsp (7.5 ml) baking powder and ½ tsp (2.5 ml) salt with 1 cup (225 g) all-purpose flour. Use as store-bought self-rising flour.
● **Adding texture** Grind oats in a food processor, and use the resulting flour to replace up to one third of the white flour in bread recipes to provide texture and flavor.
● **Using cornstarch** If using cornstarch instead of white flour as a thickening agent, use half the amount given in the recipe.

DRIED FRUITS AND NUTS

Both dried fruits and nuts are useful for adding texture, flavor, and nutritive value to sweet and savory dishes. Keep a good selection on hand, but use them up or replace them regularly, since dried fruits can overdry and harden, and nuts quickly become rancid.

BUYING & STORING
● **Tasting before buying** If possible, taste nuts before you buy them to make sure that they are not rancid.
● **Buying nuts in their shells** Buy unshelled nuts, which keep twice as long as shelled nuts, as long as they are fresh when you buy them.
● **Choosing for freshness** Avoid shelled nuts that are shriveled or discolored. If they are in plastic bags, break one nut through the wrapping: if it is fresh it will snap apart rather than bend.
● **Storing at low temperature** Pack large quantities of fresh nuts in sealed bags, and store in the freezer for up to eight months. They will keep in the refrigerator for half that time.

STORING IN ALCOHOL

Cover fruits with brandy

Soaking fruits in brandy
Fill a canning jar with dried fruits such as prunes, apricots, bananas, and figs, and add brandy or a liqueur to cover. Use the plump, tasty fruits for making luxurious desserts.

ADDING VARIETY

Put flaked nuts in airtight container

Using a food processor
Make sliced hazelnuts in a food processor to use as an alternative to sliced almonds. Use whole, unskinned hazelnuts; the fine slicing blade of the processor will slice them finely.

LEGUMES

Legumes, including beans, peas, and lentils, are an excellent source of proteins, minerals, and carbohydrates. They can be used whole in salads, puréed in soups, or ground for dips. Legumes are inexpensive and store well, but buy in small quantities, since they toughen with age.

STORING UNCOOKED LEGUMES

● **Using glass jars** Store packages of legumes in airtight jars, and make a note of soaking and cooking times and purchase dates on the lids.

● **Rotating stock** Use up any old stock of legumes before adding newly bought ones to a jar. Cooking times may vary between old and new.

STORING COOKED BEANS

● **Refrigerating** If covered, cooked beans will store well in a refrigerator for several days. Alternatively, they can be frozen for up to three months.

Cannellini beans can be mixed with red kidney beans

Making a bean mix
Make up your own colorful mixture of dried beans, and store in a jar ready to add to soups and casseroles. Combine types of beans with the same cooking time.

Lay whole chilies on top of legumes

Deterring insects
To protect legumes from insect damage during storage, put a few dried chilies in the storage jars with them. Replace the lids tightly, and store as usual.

TRADITIONAL TIP

Checking beans
Put dried beans in a bowl of cold water, and discard any that float to the surface, since this is an indication of insect or mold damage.

VARIETIES OF LENTIL

Lentils are richer in protein than any other legumes except soybeans. Most do not need soaking before cooking.

● **Brown lentils** These are the most common type, flattish in shape, and green or brown in color. Brown lentils retain their shape well when cooked.
● **Split orange or red lentils** These quick-cooking lentils are useful for thickening curries or casseroles.
● **Puy lentils** Greenish gray in color, these are considered to have the best flavor. They complement smoked meats.
● **Yellow lentils** Also known as yellow dal, these lentils are often served as a side dish in Indian cooking.

CHECKING & CLEANING

● **Inspecting carefully** Before storage, check legumes and their packaging for signs of insect infestation. Discard any that are shriveled, discolored, or otherwise damaged.

Sift lentils with fingertips

Sifting out dirt
Spread legumes onto a shallow tray before use, and sift through them lightly to pick out any traces of dirt. Watch for damaged ones at the same time.

USING LEGUMES

● **Cooking dried peas** If you are short of time, use split dried peas rather than whole ones: split peas do not need to be soaked before cooking.
● **Combining proteins** Mix beans or lentils with cereals such as rice or pasta. These combinations provide a more nutritionally complete meal, so they are particularly useful foods in vegetarian diets.
● **Saving time** Cook a larger batch of beans than you need, and freeze half for later use to save time and fuel costs.
● **Pie weights** Save old and stale beans to use as pie weights when you make a pie shell. Store the beans in a separate jar and label clearly, since they will not be edible.

SUGARS AND SWEET FLAVORINGS

SUGARS AND SWEET FLAVORINGS play a very important role in our enjoyment of food. Their appearance, texture, taste, and versatility can be utilized in many ways to enhance cakes and pastries, fruit desserts, and even savory dishes.

SUGARS

There is little difference in the calorie counts of white and brown sugars, but the flavors are very different. Some of the darkest sugars add a particularly rich flavor and color to both sweet and savory dishes, and they are often specified in recipes for desserts and cakes.

SOFTENING & STORING BROWN SUGAR

Softening in a microwave
To soften brown sugar, place in a microwave-proof dish and add a wedge of apple. Cover tightly, and microwave on High for 30 seconds. Remove apple and stir.

Storing brown sugar
Keep brown sugar moist by storing in an airtight container with one or two wedges of apple. Alternatively, use a whole citrus fruit, or a piece of fresh bread.

TRADITIONAL TIP

Making vanilla sugar
Bury two vanilla beans in a jar of sugar, and let stand at least one week. Stir occasionally. Use this vanilla-flavored sugar in sweet dishes.

FLAVORED SUGAR

Pare citrus zest thinly to remove long strip

Adding a citrus flavor
To add subtle flavor to sweet dishes, desserts, cakes, and cookies, flavor the sugar used. To impart a citrus flavor to sugar, pare long, thin strips of zest from an orange, lemon, or lime. Bury the strips of zest in a container of sugar, and store for at least three days before using.

● **Making scented sugar** Add two sprigs of fresh lavender or rosemary to a container of sugar, and shake well. Let stand 24 hours, then shake again, before leaving for one week. Use to sweeten milk-based puddings and fresh fruit desserts.

STORING & USING

● **Preventing lumps** To keep packages of brown sugar from absorbing moisture and forming lumps during storage, place them in a thick plastic bag in a cool, dry place.
● **Making superfine sugar** If you run out of superfine sugar, make your own from granulated sugar. Place it in a food processor with a metal blade, and process for a few seconds for a fine consistency.
● **Keeping a thermos fresh** Add a sugar cube or a teaspoonful of white sugar to a dry, empty thermos bottle before storing it away. This will prevent stale smells from developing inside.

HONEY, SYRUPS, JAMS, AND JELLIES

Like most natural products, honey is affected by light and heat and does not respond well to wide fluctuations in temperature. Processed syrups, jams, and jellies are more stable, but they will also deteriorate if exposed to air and heat. Once opened, keep them in a refrigerator.

RESTORING HONEY

Reliquefying in hot water
If clear honey becomes crystallized during storage, reliquefy it by standing the jar in a bowl of hot water for five minutes. Then rotate the jar a couple of times until the honey becomes clear and liquid.

MEASURING HONEY

● **Using a heated spoon** To measure amounts of set honey and syrups easily, use a metal spoon that has been dipped in hot water. Honey and syrup will not stick to a heated spoon.

USING SUBSTITUTES

● **Using blended honey** Choose blended types of honey for cooking, since these have a robust flavor. The delicate flavors of more expensive flower honeys are destroyed by heat during cooking.
● **Substituting syrup** Honey and corn syrup contain 20 percent water, so reduce the liquid content of recipes when using instead of sugar.

JAMS AND JELLIES

Making an apricot glaze
Gently warm some apricot jam with a squeeze of lemon juice, then push through a sieve. Store in a screw-top jar in the refrigerator for a ready-made sweet glaze.

● **Keeping preserves fresh**
Buy preserves that have a minimum of 60 percent sugar content, which prevents mold.

CHOCOLATE

Chocolate is available in several different forms. In general, the better the quality of the chocolate, the better the flavor will be, since inexpensive chocolate contains fewer cocoa solids and more sugar. Chocolate is damaged by moisture and heat, so store it carefully.

FREEZING CHOCOLATE

Press firmly against grater

Fine curls

Storing grated chocolate
Grate chilled chocolate on a food grater to make fine curls. Store in a plastic bag in the freezer so that you can remove just the amount you need for cooking or decorating.

STORING CHOCOLATE

● **Cooling to keep fresh** Wrap chocolate tightly and store at a low temperature, ideally around 60°F (15°C).
● **Preventing bloom** Seal in flavor and keep out moisture by storing chocolate wrapped in baking parchment, then overwrapped with foil.
● **Storing chocolate chips** Keep chocolate chips in a storage jar, ready to put into doughs and batters. They are low in cocoa solids, so they are less sensitive to temperature changes than other chocolate.
● **Preventing lumpy cocoa** Cocoa absorbs moisture easily, so store it in a container with a tight lid. Remove any lumps by sifting before using.

BRIGHT IDEA

Enriching meat dishes
Use chocolate to enrich the flavor of spicy meat or game casseroles. Add 1 oz (25 g) of dark chocolate for every four portions of chili con carne, for example, during cooking to enhance its flavor.

HERBS, SPICES, AND SEASONINGS

I T IS WELL WORTH WHILE HAVING A GOOD SELECTION of dried herbs and spices on hand to add flavor to all kinds of everyday dishes. Bear in mind that many dried herbs have a limited shelf life and should be used within six months.

═══ DRIED HERBS ═══

M ost herbs store successfully in dried form, and there is a wide range of commercially dried herbs to choose from. Freeze-dried herbs retain their color and are therefore visually more attractive than traditionally dried herbs, but they are usually a little more expensive.

BUYING DRIED HERBS

● **Choosing jars** When buying herbs packed in jars, choose jars that have a good, airtight seal. Herbs retain their flavor best if stored in either screw-top or flip-top jars, both of which are more securely airtight than jars with corks.
● **Buying whole-leaf herbs** If possible, choose whole-leaf dried herbs such as rosemary or bay. Dried herbs that have been crushed or ground are likely to lose their flavor much more quickly than those whose leaves are left whole.

STORING HERB JARS FOR EASY ACCESS

Place jars on their sides so that contents are clearly visible

Using drawer space
Herbs and spices are best stored in a dark place such as a cool kitchen drawer. Keep small jars flat and tidy; the herbs and spices will be easy to select since you can see the contents or labels of each jar at a glance.

DRYING & STORING HERBS

1 When drying herbs such as sage, thyme, or parsley, keep the leaves on the stems until completely dry. Rub the stems gently between your fingertips, crumbling the leaves into a small bowl. Discard stems, or use to flavor stocks.

2 Put some of the crumbled leaves into small containers such as test tubes, using a piece of paper to funnel the herbs in gently. Keep the containers in a rack ready to use in cooking. Store any remaining herbs for future use.

STORING DRIED HERBS

● **Keeping light out** Store dried herbs in airtight glass containers, and keep them in as dark a place as possible.
● **Extending storage life** To prolong the lives of dried herbs, wrap them tightly in plastic bags. Keep the herbs in the refrigerator for three months, or freeze for up to six months.
● **Noting storage times** Write the purchase dates of dried herbs on pieces of masking tape, and stick these on the bases of the containers. Alternatively, use a felt-tip pen to write the dates on the jars.
● **Arranging alphabetically** If you have a large selection of herb containers, arrange them in alphabetical order so that you can find the herbs you need quickly and easily.

SPICES

Spices, like herbs, need careful storage away from light and heat, both of which shorten their shelf lives. Spices keep their flavor best when stored whole, so it is best to grind them as you need them, or to store ground spices in small amounts and use them within a short time.

USEFUL SPICES

Ground nutmeg

Keep a selection of basic spices in your cabinet.

- **Black peppercorns** Crush coarsely for spiced coatings.
- **Nutmeg** Always grate fresh nutmeg since the ground spice loses flavor quickly.
- **Cinnamon** Keep cinnamon sticks and the ground spice for versatility in your cooking.
- **Coriander and cumin** These are useful ground spices to add to many ethnic dishes.

CHOOSING WHOLE SPICES

- **Selecting seeds** Check that whole seeds such as caraway or coriander have a uniform shape and consistent color, with no stem or chaff content.
- **Checking cardamom** Buy whole cardamom pods that are pale green, plump, and unblemished. The seeds inside should be black or brown, and slightly sticky.
- **Buying cinnamon** Choose slim cinnamon sticks with an even, pale, soft brown color.
- **Choosing cloves** Look for whole cloves that are large, plump, and oily, with a warm, reddish brown color.
- **Testing beans for freshness** Bend vanilla beans: they should be supple and resilient.

USING MUSTARDS

- **Mustard powder** Add a little mustard powder, which acts as a preservative, to mayonnaise and other dressings to prolong their shelf lives, and to add a sharp flavor to the dressings.

Making mustard
Crush white and black mustard seeds together, and mix to a paste with wine vinegar. Add honey and flavorings such as chilies to taste. Keep in a screw-top jar.

PREPARING SPICE MIXES

- **Making cinnamon sugar** Mix 1 cup (225 g) superfine sugar with 1½ tbsp (25 ml) cinnamon. Store in a shaker, and sprinkle on warm buttered toast.

Making pie spice
Make your own favorite mixture of spices, such as sweet mixed spice for harvest-time baking. Grind together whole cinnamon, nutmeg, and cloves, or allspice; add a pinch of ginger. Store the mixture in a small, screw-top jar.

GRINDING WHOLE SPICES

Put whole spices into grinder

Using a coffee grinder
Grind your own whole spices in an electric coffee grinder to make a spice blend in seconds. Use a pastry brush or paper towel to clean the grinder thoroughly immediately after use, removing any lingering spice flavors.

KEEPING FLAVORS

- **Using spices quickly** Ground spices lose their flavor and aroma quickly, so buy only a small quantity at a time, and make sure that you use it up within six months.
- **Choosing chilies** Choose red chilies, which are simply ripened green chilies, rather than green chilies if you want a sweeter flavor. Select yellow caribe chilies for a sweet, mild flavor; green jalapeño chilies, which are the most common type, for average heat; and orange habanero chilies for a hot and distinctive fruity flavor. Experiment with other varieties to find your favorites.
- **Toasting whole spices** To get the most intense flavor from spices, toast them whole in a heavy, dry frying pan. Shake the pan over fairly high heat for a minute or two, and use immediately.

OILS, VINEGARS, AND SEASONINGS

Oils are fats that are in liquid form at room temperature. Exposure to light and air can cause them to deteriorate, so keep them in airtight containers in a cool place along with vinegars, salt, and seasonings, all of which require similar storage conditions for long life.

FLAVORING OILS & VINEGARS

White wine vinegar with fresh herbs

Cider vinegar with honey, lemon, and mint

Olive oil with garlic and lime wedges

Extra-virgin olive oil with orange zest and coriander seeds

White wine vinegar with skewered ginger and garlic

Red wine vinegar with cumin, cinnamon, and cloves

Creating unique flavors
Flavored oils and vinegars are easy to make at home. Immerse clean, fresh herbs, spices, fruits, or edible flowers in oil or vinegar in sterilized screw-top bottles. Refrigerate for about two weeks before filtering and using.

INFUSING FLAVORS
● **Bruising ingredients** Lightly bruise fresh herbs before steeping in vinegar to help release their flavor. Cloves of garlic and shallots also benefit from being lightly crushed.
● **Infusing quickly** To infuse flavors into vinegar quickly, heat the vinegar gently until almost boiling. Pour it onto your chosen flavoring, cool, then seal in bottles.
● **Flavoring with fruits** Use fresh raspberries, strawberries, blackberries, blueberries, or slices of lemon or orange to make delicately flavored fruit vinegars, which can be used to add mellow flavors to savory dishes and drinks.
● **Storing fruit vinegars** To keep fruit vinegars for longer than about one week, strain and then discard the fruits before transferring the vinegar into clean bottles.

USING OILS
● **Nut oils** Oils that are made from nuts, such as walnut or hazelnut, have rich, intense flavors, making them ideal · for use in salads or flavoring savory dishes. Once opened, store them in the refrigerator, since they deteriorate quickly.
● **Olive oil** Save the best-quality extra-virgin olive oil for lightly cooked dishes and salads, since too much heat will destroy the fine flavor and aroma of the oil.
● **Healthy oils** Use oils labeled monounsaturated, such as olive oil, or polyunsaturated, such as sunflower oil, for a healthy diet. These do not increase blood cholesterol levels, unlike saturated animal fats.

STORING OILS

Storing bottles of oil
To help keep cabinet shelves clean, stand bottles of oil on a tray that can easily be wiped clean. Use a tray that has deep sides to reduce the risk of the bottles being knocked over.

TRADITIONAL TIP

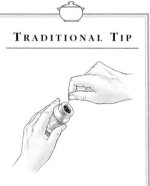

Storing free-running salt
To make sure salt stays dry, and therefore runs freely from the salt shaker, add a few grains of rice to the shaker. Replace the rice every few months – not every time you refill the shaker.

CONVENIENCE FOODS

MOST PEOPLE RELY ON CONVENIENCE FOODS from time to time, usually when they are unable to shop for and cook fresh ingredients. Fast food need not necessarily mean junk food, and there is a vast range to choose from.

STOCKING AND USING CONVENIENCE FOODS		
TYPES OF FOOD	EXAMPLES OF FOOD	GENERAL USES
CANNED, SAVORY FOODS	Keep a supply of whole and chopped plum tomatoes and beans; vegetables such as corn, asparagus, and artichoke hearts; tuna; cooked ham; sauces; condensed and ready-to-heat soups; peanut and other nut butters.	● Add chopped tomatoes to casseroles and pizza toppings. ● Fold whipped egg whites into condensed soup for an easy soufflé.
CANNED, SWEET FOODS	Store canned fruits such as pineapple and pear rings and chunks and peach halves or slices; exotic fruits such as litchis and guavas; fruit pie fillings; applesauce; and fruit cocktail.	● Layer fruits and rice pudding in tall glasses. Stir puréed fruits or jam into plain yogurt for quick ambrosia. ● Use ready-made fruit pie fillings as quick cheesecake toppings.
DRY FOODS AND PACKAGED MIXES	Stock sauce and gravy mixes; dried vegetables; instant mashed potatoes, pasta and rice mixes; instant desserts; dried milk and gelatin powder; bread, pastry, batter, and cake mixes.	● Enrich instant mashed potatoes with single cream and mixed dried herbs. ● Transform a simple cake mix by sprinkling with brandy, then filling with cream and canned fruits.
BOTTLED FOODS AND PRESERVES	Keep jams and jellies; fruits in brandy; ready-made meals such as chili or baked beans; pesto; olives; sun-dried tomatoes; and antipasto.	● Spread pesto on Italian bread; toast to make bruscetta. ● Add ricotta or feta cheese to sun-dried tomatoes for an easy appetizer.
PREPARED FOODS	Stock up with partly baked breads and pastries; prepared ready-to-serve meals and pasta dishes; milk, cream, and whipped desserts.	● Use partly baked breads and pastries to create a homemade effect. ● Make a dessert by filling a ready-made pastry shell with canned fruits.
REFRIGERATED FOODS	Chill prepared meals; fresh pasta; soups; sweet and savory sauces; fruit salad; prepared mixed salads and dressings; fresh pastry; pâtés; and dips.	● Add chopped herbs and crunchy croutons to prepared soups. ● Prepare salads in advance and chill while you prepare the rest of the meal.
FROZEN, SAVORY FOODS	Freeze vegetables and stir-fry mixes; French fries; cooked rice; pizza bases; prepared fish and shellfish; meat and poultry; pastry, pies, and quiches.	● Fill an omelet with a stir-fry mix. ● Use prerolled pastry sheets or sheets of phyllo dough to make a quick base for a flan or tart.
FROZEN, SWEET FOODS	Freeze prepared fruits, especially raspberries and seasonal soft-fruit mixes; melon balls; ices, sorbets, and iced desserts; cakes; and fruit juices.	● Make summer desserts in winter with frozen soft fruits. ● Purée frozen fruits with confectioners' sugar to make a sauce.

FRESH INGREDIENTS

IF YOU ARE ABLE TO SHOP FOR FOOD on a daily basis, keeping perishable ingredients fresh is not a problem. For most people, though, this is not a practical option, and they have to buy large amounts of fresh foods less frequently. Good planning, sensible shopping, and careful storage will ensure that perishable foods remain fresh, flavorful, and safe.

SHOPPING

Food shopping must begin in the kitchen if it is to be successful. Making a detailed list of everything you need can be an ongoing task, and every member of the household can help. Plan several days' menus in advance, and use them as a basis for fresh-food shopping.

BUYING WISELY
● **Making the most of bargains** Watch for seasonal best buys, and plan your menus around foods that are in season.
● **Avoiding waste** You should buy only what you can store. Bulk buying is usually a false economy if you cannot use the food while it is fresh.

MAKING LISTS
● **Listing in order** Organize items on your shopping list into groups and, if possible, arrange the groups so that they follow the layout of the supermarket. This will make shopping quick and easy, and you will be less likely to miss items that are on the list.

USING REMINDERS
● **Noting dates** Note use-by dates on perishable foods, and keep these in mind when planning meals and shopping in advance. It may be possible to freeze certain items for a few days to extend their shelf lives, but check the package labels for refrigeration details.

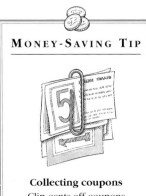

MONEY-SAVING TIP

Collecting coupons
Clip cents-off coupons together with a large paper clip, and attach it to a kitchen bulletin board. The coupons will be easy to find when you are ready to go shopping.

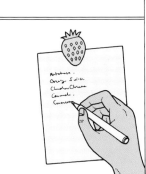

Keeping a list handy
Keep a current shopping list attached to the refrigerator door with a magnet. Each time an item of food is used up, add it to the list as a reminder to replace your stock of ingredients.

Clipping to a cart
When you go shopping, take a large clip or a clothes pin with you to attach your shopping list to the cart so that the list does not get lost. It will also help you to read the list at a glance.

PACKING

The priority on any food shopping trip is to keep the food cool and fresh until you get home. If possible, shop for perishable items last, and avoid leaving them in a warm car. Invest in cooler bags with ice packs if you cannot get food into a refrigerator quickly.

PACKING SHOPPING TO KEEP IT COOL

Keep foods cool with ice cubes

Using a cooler bag
If the weather is warm, pack perishable food into an insulated cooler bag. Put a tightly closed jar filled with ice cubes or several ice packs inside the bag.

Lining a shopping basket
Make your own improvised cooler bag by insulating an ordinary shopping bag or basket with a layer or two of crumpled newspaper or bubble wrap.

MAKING PACKING EASY
● **Starting with heavy items** When packing at the check-out, always begin by placing heavy items at the bottoms of bags or boxes. Lighter, more delicate items should be placed on top to avoid damage.
● **Keeping a spare bag** Always keep a string bag or folded shopping bag on hand, ready for any unexpected shopping.
● **Keeping foods separate** Pack chilled and frozen foods separately from your other shopping and, if you are traveling by car, load frozen foods last. You can then unload them first, and freeze them immediately.

STORING

Storing food safely is largely a matter of common sense. It is worth following some simple guidelines to avoid health risks. Check use-by dates when buying food, and adhere to them; always keep highly perishable foods cold; and keep raw and cooked foods separate.

STORING FOOD SAFELY
● **Finding the coldest zone** To identify the coldest zone of a refrigerator, check the manufacturer's handbook, since the location varies according to make and type. Frost-free refrigerators have an even temperature throughout.
● **Keeping opened canned foods** Empty the contents of an opened can of food into a bowl, cover, and refrigerate.
● **Avoiding contamination** Always store raw meats and foods to be defrosted beneath any cooked foods to prevent drips from raw foods from contaminating cooked foods.
● **Removing packaging** Leave foods wrapped unless their packaging recommends that you do otherwise.

ORGANIZING A REFRIGERATOR	
AREA	**FOODS TO BE STORED**
Cool zone: middle to lower shelves beneath freezer compartment	Milk, yogurt, fruit juices, hard cheeses, eggs, butter, margarine, low-fat spreads, and cooking fats.
Cold zone: shelf below freezer compartment, or bottom shelf of storage refrigerator	Precooked chilled foods, cooked meats, soft cheeses, prepared salads, home-prepared dishes and leftovers; raw meats and fish (a meat drawer is ideal).
Salad drawers or bins	Vegetables and fruits suitable for low-temperature storage, and salad items such as unwashed lettuce, whole tomatoes, radishes, cucumbers, and celery.
Refrigerator door and compartments	Milk, soft drinks, fruit juices, opened bottles and jars of sauces, preserves, and salad dressings.

VEGETABLES, FRUITS, AND HERBS

FOR A HEALTHY, WELL-BALANCED DIET, it is essential to include a wide range of vegetables and fruits that are rich in vitamins, minerals, and fiber. Fresh or dried herbs help add color and a distinctive flavor to every meal.

CHOOSING VEGETABLES

Each vegetable has particular indicators of quality, but in general crispness and a bright color are very good signs to look for. Choose vegetables in season for the best value. Out-of-season produce adds variety and interest to meals, but may cost more than locally grown vegetables.

CHECKING VEGETABLES FOR QUALITY & FRESHNESS

Press center gently

Apply light pressure to snap

Check for insects or decay under florets

Checking a cabbage
Before buying a cabbage, check that the heart is firm by pressing the center with your thumb. Avoid those that have soft or discolored outer leaves, and brown or damaged patches.

Snapping a bean
To make sure that green beans are fresh, hold a bean between your forefinger and thumb, and bend it gently. If it is fresh, the bean will snap in two – not bend – under light pressure.

Checking a cauliflower
Always pull back the outer leaves of a cauliflower, and look carefully between the florets to ensure that there are no insects or signs of decay. The florets should be firm and white.

SHOPPING WISELY
● **Selecting shape and size**
When buying vegetables such as Brussels sprouts, choose those of a uniform size and shape so that they cook evenly.
● **Testing avocados** Test an avocado by cupping it lightly in your hand and squeezing very gently. If it gives slightly, it is ready to eat. Pressing with fingertips will cause bruising.
● **Buying garlic** Buy plump garlic with tightly packed cloves and dry skin. Avoid any bulbs with soft, shriveled cloves or green shoots.
● **Selecting chilies** Choose chili peppers according to your taste. In general, the smaller the chili, the hotter it will be.

SALAD AND FRUIT VEGETABLES

Ripening tomatoes
If you need to speed up the ripening of green tomatoes, place them in a paper bag with an apple or a ripe, red tomato. Place the bag in a warm, dark place, and leave it there for a couple of days until the tomatoes ripen and turn red.

● **Lettuces** Choose lettuces that are firm and crisp, with bright, undamaged leaves. Avoid any that have discolored or yellow outer leaves.
● **Peppers** Red, yellow, and orange peppers have a sweeter flavor than green peppers and are more suitable for salads.
● **Cucumbers** Select cucumbers that are large, straight, and firm with fresh, shiny skin.
● **Other vegetables** Some vegetables, such as zucchini, cauliflower, and mushrooms, that are usually served cooked, make delicious salad ingredients. Use them raw or cooked to add extra texture to salads.

STORING VEGETABLES

Most vegetables have a limited storage time. Green vegetables should ideally be used within two days, but some root vegetables can be stored for several weeks in a cool, dark, airy place. All vegetables lose nutrients as soon as they are cut, so prepare them just before use.

STORING GARLIC

Garlic should be completely covered with oil

Storing in oil
To store garlic, peel a whole head of garlic, place the cloves in a jar, cover with olive oil, and refrigerate. The oil will preserve the garlic, and the garlic will flavor the oil, making it delicious for salad dressings. Refrigerate the flavored oil for up to two weeks.

COLD STORAGE

Most vegetables can be stored in a cool, dark, well-ventilated place. Vegetables that perish quickly should be stored in the refrigerator. However, low refrigeration temperatures can bring about changes to the flavor and texture of some vegetables, such as potatoes.

● **Mushrooms** Store fresh mushrooms in a paper bag at the bottom of the refrigerator.
● **Cabbage and celery** Keep cabbage and celery in the salad drawer of the refrigerator in order to retain flavor and texture.
● **Tomatoes** Avoid storing tomatoes in the refrigerator; low temperatures change their texture and can spoil the ripening process.

REVIVING CELERY

Add drops of lemon juice

Iced water

Maintaining crispness
Revive wilted celery sticks by placing them in a bowl of iced water for at least one hour. Add a squeeze of fresh lemon juice to improve the flavor. To revive a whole head of celery, cut a thin slice from the root end, and stand the head in iced water.

STORING ONIONS
● **Saving pieces of onion** Leave the skin, and try to retain the root end on the piece of onion that you wish to keep. Wrap in plastic wrap, and store in a refrigerator for up to three days.

Place onion inside stocking

Knot prevents onions from touching

Stringing onions
Onions and garlic are best stored hung up in strings. Put the onions or garlic bulbs in a nylon stocking. Tie a knot between each onion or garlic bulb, then hang in a dry place.

BRIGHT IDEA

Making a garlic pot
Keep garlic fresh by allowing air to circulate around it. Instead of buying a specially made garlic pot, use an upturned terra-cotta pot that has a drainage hole in its base. Place the garlic on a small saucer, and cover with the terra-cotta pot.

KEEPING CHILIES
● **Freezing in freshness** Chilies freeze very successfully and can be used straight from the freezer, without thawing first. Freeze fresh, whole chilies in a freezer bag.

Thread through top of chili, not stem

Making a garland
String fresh chilies in a garland to dry and store. Using strong cotton or nylon thread and a clean needle, string them, knot the thread ends together, then hang the chilies to air-dry.

SHOPPING FOR FRUITS

Methods of testing ripeness vary from one fruit to another, but plumpness, firmness, and a good fragrance are usually good, general indicators of freshness in most types of fruit. Farm stands and greenmarkets offer the freshest produce, and often feature unusual items.

ENSURING FRESHNESS

● **Grapes** Before buying grapes, shake the bunch gently. The grapes should stay on the stem. If a few fall off, the branch is not fresh.

● **Citrus fruits** Citrus fruits such as lemons, oranges, and grapefruits should feel heavy for their size if they are juicy.

● **Banana skins** The skins of bananas become slightly flecked with brown when ripe. Slightly green, underripe bananas will ripen at room temperature in a few days.

● **Berries** These should be plump, not shriveled or moldy, with good color. If the hulls are still attached, the berries were picked when underripe, and they will be flavorless.

CHECKING FRUITS FOR QUALITY & RIPENESS

Gently press with both thumbs

Checking a melon
To determine whether or not a melon is ripe, hold it firmly in both hands. Lightly press the area immediately around the tip of the melon, at the opposite end from the stem end; the surface should give slightly. A ripe melon will also have a pleasantly sweet scent.

Pull leaf out from top of pineapple

Checking a pineapple
To check whether a whole pineapple is ripe and ready to eat, pull gently at a leaf at the top of the pineapple. If the leaf pulls out easily, the fruit is ripe. Like melons, pineapples have a sweet scent when ripe. Soft, dark patches indicate bruising.

STORING FRUITS

Most fruits should be consumed quickly, when they are at their best and most nutritious. If it is necessary to store fruits, the correct conditions will help preserve their flavors and vitamin content. Remove tight packaging unless the label states otherwise.

COLD STORAGE

Wrapping fruits
To store citrus or hard fruits for longer than one week, wipe each fruit dry, and wrap in newspaper. Pack in a plastic bag or a box, and store in a cool, dry place.

● **Storing long-term** Store pears for up to six months at 30°F (–0.5°C). Store in single layers to avoid bruising.

STORING BERRIES

Preventing damage
To store soft berries, invert the container onto a cookie sheet lined with paper towels. Arrange berries in a single layer. Discard any damaged or moldy berries, and cover lightly with more paper towels before chilling.

KEEPING FRUITS

● **Storing grapes** Wrap bunches of grapes loosely in newsprint, and keep them in the dark. For a tasty treat, freeze whole grapes and snack on them straight from the freezer.

● **Getting the most juice** Citrus fruits such as oranges, lemons, and limes will yield the most juice if they are stored at room temperature. If they have been stored in a refrigerator, warm each one in the microwave on High for about five seconds.

● **Freezing bananas** Freeze whole bananas in their skins, wrapped in plastic wrap, for up to six months. Eat them while slightly frozen, or mash them and use in baking or drinks.

MAINTAINING A SUPPLY OF HERBS

Herbs make such a wonderful difference in even the simplest everyday dishes that it is worthwhile ensuring that you always have a supply of both fresh and dried versions. Even in winter, you can have a choice of fragrant leaves for both cooking and garnishing.

HARVESTING HERBS

● **Using potted herbs** Herbs in pots bought from a farm stand often have a limited life, but if you use just a few top shoots at a time, they will thrive longer.

● **Managing growth** Allow herbs to become established before harvesting them regularly, and pick evenly to keep them in good shape.

● **Growing herbs closeby** Grow your herbs on a kitchen window ledge or by the kitchen door so that they are always within easy reach, even when it is dark or raining.

● **Letting herbs flower** Allow a few herbs, such as borage, rosemary, or chives, to flower, and use as a pretty garnish.

CHOOSING & GROWING HERBS

Oregano has a spicy aroma and enhances tomatoes and meats

Chives have a mild onion flavor

Sage is strongly flavored and is used in stuffings

Tender flat-leaved parsley can be served whole in salads

Trailing silver thyme is pretty

Golden lemon thyme complements fish and chicken well

Growing herbs for cooking

Grow a variety of herbs together on your kitchen window ledge. Herbs that will grow well together for culinary use are parsley (the Italian flat-leaved variety is best), chives, thyme, oregano, and sage.

STORING HERBS

Once herbs are cut, they have a short life, and their aroma and flavor soon diminish. With careful storage, however, herbs can be kept fresh for several days. Tender-leaved herbs such as basil, chervil, and coriander wilt quickly, so they should be used up as soon as possible.

PREPARING DELICATE HERBS FOR STORAGE

Cut stems diagonally

Be careful not to crush herbs with bag

1 Before storing delicate herbs, cut the ends off the stems with a sharp knife. Place the herbs in a tall glass of cold water covering at least 1 in (2.5 cm) of the stems. Add a pinch of sugar to the water.

2 Place a plastic bag loosely over the herbs and glass, and secure the bag with a rubber band. Store in a cool place or in the refrigerator. Change the water and trim the stems every one or two days.

REVIVING HERBS

Use plant mister

Reviving limp herbs
To refresh fresh sprigs of delicate herbs that have wilted, place them on paper towels and moisten them with a fine mist of water. Chill briefly in the refrigerator before use.

DAIRY FOODS

Dairy products are highly nutritious foods, but they are often high in fat and should therefore be used in moderate quantities. The refrigerator is the best place for storage, although many dairy products also freeze well.

EGGS

Eggs are an excellent source of both protein and vitamins. They are an extremely versatile food and can be boiled, fried, poached, or used to thicken, emulsify, coat, bind, or glaze. Eggs are sensitive to temperature changes and should be warmed to room temperature before use.

MARKING BOILED EGGS

Mark cross on eggshell

Using a pen
Use a food-coloring pen to mark a cross on hard-cooked eggs. The cross will distinguish them from uncooked eggs if stored together.

TESTING EGGS

Salt water

Checking for freshness
Dissolve 2 tbsp (30 ml) salt in 2 cups (500 ml) water. Place the eggs in the water. If an egg sinks, it is fresh; if it floats, it is stale.

BUYING & STORING

● **Checking for cracks** When buying eggs, move each egg gently in the carton to check that none are damaged.
● **Keeping freshness** Store eggs in a carton in the refrigerator to prevent them from losing moisture and absorbing odors through their shells from strongly flavored foods nearby. Avoid poor caddies.
● **Storing correctly** Always store eggs with the pointed end down, to center the yolk and keep the eggs fresh.

CREAM

There are several types of cream, each of which has different properties, depending on the butterfat content. The butterfat content also determines the cream's richness, flavor, and whipping characteristics. The more fat a cream contains, the less likely it is to curdle.

STORING CREAM

Pour cream into ice-cube tray

Freezing in an ice tray
Open-freeze heavy cream in an ice-cube tray, then put the cubes into freezer bags, and store in the freezer. The cubes can be added directly to hot soups, sauces, or casseroles.

USING CREAM

● **Heavy cream** Choose heavy cream when you need softly whipped cream for folding into mousse-type desserts, or for piping. Light cream will not hold the air as well and will lose its fluffiness quickly.
● **Low-fat alternative** Mix a few tablespoonfuls of plain yogurt or whipped cottage cheese into whipped heavy cream to lighten creamy desserts or cake fillings.
● **Crème fraîche** Use crème fraîche as a substitute for light or sour cream in hot sauces, since it can be heated to boiling without curdling.

BRIGHT IDEA

Making sour cream
To make sour cream, add 1 tsp (5 ml) lemon juice to ⅔ cup (150 ml) light cream. Stir, and let stand until thickened.

CHEESE

Cheese is a high-protein food and has many culinary uses. It can be used to add flavor to fillings and sauces, and forms the basis of some desserts. Most cheese is eaten uncooked in salads and sandwiches, or as part of a buffet. All cheese is best served at room temperature.

STORING SOFT CHEESE
● **Freezing cheese** Freeze cheese only if it contains more than 45 percent fat, since cheese with a lower fat content will separate.

Wrapping in grape leaves
Wrap pieces of soft cheese such as brie in blanched, fresh grape leaves, or in brine-packed leaves that have been rinsed. This will keep the cheese fresh for 3–4 days if stored in the refrigerator.

KEEPING FETA CHEESE

Add sprigs of herbs for flavor

Preserving in oil
Store cubes of feta cheese in a jar. Add sprigs of herbs, garlic cloves, or chilies for flavor. Fill the jar with good-quality olive oil and refrigerate. Use the oil for salad dressings.

TRADITIONAL TIP

Keeping cheese moist
To keep hard cheeses such as mature cheddar or Parmesan moist during storage, wrap in a clean piece of muslin or cotton cloth that has been dampened with beer. Place in an airtight container, and store in the refrigerator for 1–2 weeks.

BUTTER

Butter is a natural product that is made from cream. It can be salted or unsalted and is a valuable fat for use in baking, since it adds body and richness. Butter can be used for light sautéeing or, if mixed with herbs or other ingredients, as a flavoring.

STORING BUTTER
● **Keeping odors out** Always wrap butter well or store it in a closed container, since it easily picks up tastes from strongly flavored foods.
● **Storing at low temperature** Keep unsalted butter in the freezer for up to six months. Freeze salted butter for only three months, since changes in flavor can occur at very low temperatures.
● **Clarifying butter** To store butter for several weeks, heat it gently until frothing but not browned. Strain through cheesecloth to remove salt and moisture, then refrigerate.

PREPARING & STORING HERB-FLAVORED BUTTER

Blending with herbs
Make flavored butter by stirring chopped fresh herbs or garlic into softened butter. Use a fork to work the herbs in thoroughly. Serve with grilled meats and fish.

Cutting out shapes
To make shaped butter pats, roll out the butter on a sheet of waxed paper. Use a small cookie cutter to cut out shapes. Store in a container in the refrigerator.

MEAT AND POULTRY

MEAT OF ALL KINDS IS A GOOD SOURCE OF PROTEIN, B vitamins, and iron. Fat, which is present in varying degrees, is necessary for flavor and tenderness, but you should avoid eating high-fat cuts of meat too often.

BUYING

The most important rule to follow when you are buying fresh meat is to buy it from a reputable supplier. You must be able to rely on the butcher or grocery store to have hung and stored the meat properly, and perhaps to advise you correctly about cuts of meat and cooking.

SELECTING MEAT
● **Checking the color** Beef should be dark red with a slightly brownish tinge and a light marbling of fat. In the case of lamb, the darker the color, the older the animal.
● **Choosing the right cut** In general, the front part of an animal produces the toughest cuts of meat, suitable for slow cooking. Tender cuts come from the middle, which has the least-used muscles.
● **Buying quality cuts** Tough cuts may be inexpensive, but they take longer to cook, raising energy costs.

MONEY-SAVING TIP

Skinning chicken pieces
Chicken skin is high in fat, so it should be avoided in low-fat diets. If you need skinless chicken pieces, buy them with the skins on, and remove the skin yourself. Pull off the skin using your fingertips.

SERVING QUANTITIES PER PERSON	
CUTS OF MEAT OR POULTRY	**QUANTITIES**
Steaks without bone, such as beef, lamb, or pork fillet, lean beef sirloin, or pork loin.	4½–6 oz (125–175 g)
Steaks on the bone, such as T-bone steaks or leg-of-lamb steaks.	6–8 oz (175–225 g)
Lamb chops or cutlets on the bone, or boneless lamb chops.	2 small or 1 large
Pork chops with bone.	1 large
Cuts with a high proportion of bone, such as pork spare ribs, beef shanks, or oxtail.	14 oz–1 lb 2 oz (400–500 g)
Lean casserole meats, such as diced lamb shoulder, or stir-fry meats such as pork fillet.	4½–5½ oz (125–150 g)
Roasts on the bone, such as beef rib, leg or shoulder of lamb, or pork loin.	8–11 oz (225–300 g)
Roasts without bone, such as beef rib, rolled leg of lamb, or pork loin.	4½–6 oz (125–175 g)
Chicken pieces on the bone, such as drumsticks, thighs, wings, or quarters.	2 pieces or 1 quarter
Whole roast chicken or turkey on the bone.	12 oz (350 g) oven-ready
Whole roast duck or goose on the bone.	2 lb 4 oz (1 kg) oven-ready
Organ meats, such as liver, kidneys, or hearts.	3½–4½ oz (100–125 g)

STORING

The correct storage of meat and poultry is vitally important, since they can deteriorate quickly, especially if kept at warm temperatures. Refrigerate meat and poultry as soon as possible after buying. In warm weather, pack them in a cooler bag to transport them home.

FREEZING MEAT

Fold sheet of waxed paper around each chop

Separating meat pieces
When freezing hamburgers, chops, or steaks, which tend to stick together when frozen, separate them with pieces of waxed paper or freezer wrap. You will then be able to remove the quantity needed without thawing the whole batch.

FREEZING POULTRY

Grip bag tightly around straw

Expelling air
To remove excess air when packing whole poultry ready for freezing, place the bird in a plastic freezer bag, and gather up the opening, leaving a gap of about ¼ in (5 mm). Insert a straw through the gap, and suck out as much air as possible.

SAFETY

● **Keeping raw meats cold**
Always put fresh meat and poultry into the refrigerator as soon as you arrive home. Store in covered containers so that the meat cannot drip onto other foods.
● **Preventing contamination**
Keep different types of meat separate during storage. Always wash your hands and utensils after handling each type of raw meat and before preparing other types of meat or food.
● **Using thawed foods** Always use any thawed meat or poultry quickly, and do not be tempted to refreeze it, since this will increase the risk of food poisoning when the meat is eaten.

THAWING MEAT AND POULTRY

Immerse bird fully in water

Immersing in water
To speed up the thawing of a whole turkey or chicken, leave it in its freezer-proof wrapping, immerse it in a large basin of cold water, and place in the refrigerator. Change the water at frequent intervals until the poultry is completely thawed.

● **Allowing time** Allow plenty of time for meat and poultry to thaw. In a refrigerator, thawing may take several hours, or even two or three days in the case of large roasts or whole birds.

● **Preventing drips** Place meat or poultry on a large plate if thawing in a refrigerator. Lay paper towels underneath the meat or poultry to absorb the juices and prevent them from dripping onto other foods.
● **Thawing in the refrigerator** You may need to remove refrigerator shelves to fit a large bird into a small refrigerator. Leave the bird in its wrapping, but puncture the seal. Always use a drip tray.
● **Checking for ice** To ensure that whole poultry is completely thawed, feel inside the cavity, and check whether the legs and thigh joints move easily.
● **Using a skewer** To make sure that a large roast is completely thawed, push a skewer through the thickest part of the meat. You should be able to feel with the skewer if there is any ice remaining.

REFRIGERATING MEATS
● **Storing raw meat** Raw meat and poultry should ideally be stored on the bottom shelf of a refrigerator in a pan. This will ensure that their juices do not drip onto other foods.
● **Arranging meats** Keep fresh, ready-to-eat foods on the top shelf, and cooked meats on the middle shelf above raw meats.
● **Removing wrappings** If you purchase meat that is wrapped in paper, discard the paper and transfer the meat to a covered dish before storing it in the refrigerator. However, if meat is packed in a sealed tray, you can keep it safely in the tray for storage.
● **Using plastic wrap** Place meat or poultry in a deep dish for storing, and cover the dish tightly with plastic wrap. Make sure that the plastic wrap does not touch the food's surface.

FISH AND SHELLFISH

THE MOST IMPORTANT THING TO REMEMBER about using fish and shellfish is that they must be totally fresh. They deteriorate quickly, so to enjoy them at their best, buy only what you need, store it with care, and use it as soon as possible.

FISH

Fish is a very important part of a healthy diet. There are so many varieties from which to choose, suitable for all cooking methods, that you will find one that is appropriate for any occasion. If you prefer not to have to bone fish, ask the supplier to fillet it for you.

CHECKING FOR SIGNS OF FRESHNESS

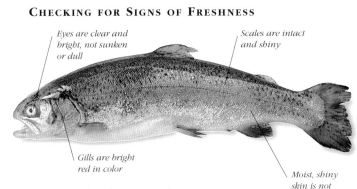

Eyes are clear and bright, not sunken or dull

Scales are intact and shiny

Gills are bright red in color

Moist, shiny skin is not slimy and has no abrasions

Looking closely for freshness
Look for clear, bright eyes and moist, shiny skin. The gills, if present, should be bright red, and the scales should be difficult to remove. When pressed with a fingertip, the flesh should spring back easily. The fish should smell fresh and clean.

CHOOSING FISH

● **Round, white fish** Large round fish, such as cod, are usually sold cut into steaks, cutlets, or fillets, with or without the skin.
● **Flat fish** Large flat fish, such as halibut or turbot, are sold whole or in fillets or steaks. Small fish such as flounder are sold whole or in fillets.
● **Oily fish** These include salmon, herring, mackerel, trout, and sardines, and are sold whole or in fillets. Oily fish are an important source of omega-3 fatty acids, said to help prevent heart disease.

REFRESHING FISH

Immerse fillet completely in iced water

"Crimping" a fillet
If a fish fillet becomes slightly limp on the way home from shopping, revive it in the way that anglers do, by "crimping" it. Add 1 tbsp (15 ml) sea salt to 4 cups (1 liter) iced water in a bowl. Soak the fish in the icy salt water for about 15 minutes.

REFRIGERATING FISH

Pack ice cubes closely around sides of fish to chill it quickly

Packing with ice
Speed up the chilling of fresh fish in the refrigerator by placing ice cubes or crushed ice around it. Alternatively, fill two plastic bags with ice and seal, then place the fish between them. Make sure that you remove the bags before the ice has melted.

FREEZING FISH

● **Glazing** To keep fish fillets moist in the freezer, first open-freeze the fish until solid, then dip briefly into iced water. A thin covering of ice will form over the fish. Whole fish can be dipped twice in order to produce a thicker ice layer. Then wrap the fish and freeze.
● **Labeling** Always clearly label fish packs before freezing with the date they were frozen. White fish has a storage life of 12 months; oily fish, six months. Cooked fish dishes keep for just three months in the freezer.
● **Refreezing** Check with the supplier that fish has not been previously frozen. It is not advisable to refreeze fish.

SHELLFISH

It is especially important with shellfish to make sure that you buy them from a reputable supplier. Avoid any that may be contaminated or not fresh, since they could cause serious illness. As in the case of fish, shellfish should not be kept for long before preparing and cooking.

BUYING SHELLFISH

● **Mussels and clams** When buying live mussels or clams, choose those with tightly closed shells. Avoid any that will not close if tapped, and those with broken shells, since they may be dead and could therefore cause food poisoning if eaten.

● **Mussels** When buying mussels, avoid those covered with sand, since large amounts will be difficult to remove.

● **Scallops** Buy scallops that are a creamy ivory; coral, if attached, should be bright orange. If they are too white, they may have been soaked in water to increase weight.

● **Lobster** When buying a lobster, choose one that is between 1 and 2 lb (0.5 and 1 kg) in weight. Small lobsters may have too little flesh inside, while very large ones can be coarse, chewy, and dry.

BUYING CRAB

● **Choosing** If you like the white meat from the claws, buy a male crab. For the rich pink coral from inside the body shell, choose a female.

Hold crab by front claws, and shake gently

Checking the weight

When buying a cooked whole crab, hold it firmly by the claws, and shake it gently. The crab should feel heavy for its size. If it feels light or rattles, it is of poor quality and has water inside.

REFRIGERATING PRAWNS

● **Rinsing** Before storing fresh, raw shrimp in the refrigerator, rinse in cold water and drain well. Use within two days.

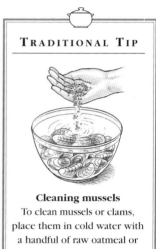

TRADITIONAL TIP

Cleaning mussels
To clean mussels or clams, place them in cold water with a handful of raw oatmeal or cornmeal. Let stand for two hours. Mussels and clams will expel dirt as they feed.

STORING OYSTERS

Place curved side of shells downward in deep tray

Cover with clean dish towel dampened with cold water

Preventing loss of juices

Store live oysters curved side down to prevent loss of juices. Arrange in an open tray, cover with a damp cloth, and store in the bottom of the refrigerator. Use as quickly as possible, within 24 hours of purchase.

STORING LIVE SHELLFISH

Keep flow of cold water constant

Keeping crayfish alive

If you buy live crayfish, lobsters, or crabs, keep them alive until you are ready to cook them. Place the crayfish in as large and deep a bowl as possible in the sink, and keep the cold-water tap running continuously into it.

OCTOPUS & SQUID

● **Checking the weight** Avoid buying octopus that is more than 2 lb (1 kg) in weight, since it is likely to be tough.

● **Choosing for freshness** Choose octopus or squid with a good color, a slippery appearance, and a fresh, salty smell. Avoid any with broken outer skins or those lying in puddles of ink.

● **Saving the ink** If you can, buy squid that has not already been cleaned and still has its ink sac, and clean it at home. Use the ink to add flavor and color to a sauce.

● **Cleaning** Clean octopus or squid before storing them. Put in the refrigerator in a bowl covered with plastic wrap.

BAKED GOODS

Whether you bake bread and cakes yourself or buy them ready-made, smart storage will enable you to keep baked goods fresh and appetizing for as long as possible. Bread and most cakes can also be frozen successfully.

BREAD

You may not always be able to buy fresh bread every day, but it is possible to keep bread fresh for several days if you follow a few commonsense rules. Good air circulation is necessary to prevent bread from becoming stale or moldy in storage, or from drying out.

REVIVING STALE LOAVES OF BREAD

Adding garlic butter
Cut a stale French loaf in thick slices almost to the base, then spread garlic butter between the slices. Wrap in foil, and bake in a hot oven for 8-10 minutes.

Steaming in a pan
Place a slightly stale loaf of bread in a colander over a pan holding a small amount of boiling water. Cover with the pan lid until the bread is warmed by the steam.

PREVENTING STALENESS
● **Adding fat** For moist, home-baked bread that will keep well, add 1 tbsp (15 g) fat to every 4 cups (500 g) flour.
● **Cooling bread** Always cool freshly baked bread before storing because condensation would encourage mold.
● **Allowing air circulation** Stand a bread crock on a triangular wooden pot stand or brick to increase air circulation.
● **Scalding a bread crock** If you always store bread in an earthenware bread crock or metal bread box, scald the crock or box regularly with boiling water to kill any mold spores, then dry thoroughly.

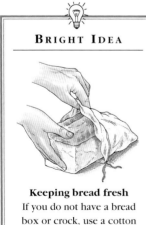

BRIGHT IDEA

Keeping bread fresh
If you do not have a bread box or crock, use a cotton drawstring bag to store a loaf of bread. Wash and dry the bag between uses, to prevent mold from developing.

FREEZING BREAD
● **Separating slices** Before freezing sliced bread, place waxed paper between the slices so that you can remove them without having to thaw the whole loaf.
● **Keeping crust** Freeze crusty bread such as French baguettes for no longer than 7–10 days. If it is frozen longer, the crust will begin to flake off.
● **Freezing dough** Freeze unrisen bread dough for up to one month and thaw for about six hours at room temperature, let rise, and bake.
● **Thawing** Thaw bread loaves and rolls in a warm oven, and they will be crisp and fragrant, like freshly baked bread.

STORING BREAD
Bowl must be big enough to cover loaf completely

Making a bread crock
If you have nowhere to store a loaf of bread, place the loaf on a wooden bread board, and cover with an upturned earthenware bowl. Alternatively, wrap the loaf in a clean, dry dish towel.

BREAD CRUMBS

Bread crumbs are a valuable pantry ingredient, whether in their fresh form or dried for longer storage. Keep both white and whole-wheat bread crumbs for use in stuffings, coatings, or toppings. Bread crumbs add texture and interest to both sweet and savory dishes.

PREPARING BREAD CRUMBS FOR STORAGE

Bag keeps crumbs tidily in one place

Mix in herbs for savory bread crumbs

Making dry bread crumbs

Dry leftover bread to make into bread crumbs. Arrange slices on a baking sheet, and bake at 300°F (150°C) or until completely dry and lightly browned. Place in a plastic bag and crush with a rolling pin.

Seasoning bread crumbs

Add seasonings to fresh or dried bread crumbs to coat fish and chicken, or to use as toppings for baked and grilled dishes. Stir in crumbled dried herbs, finely grated Parmesan cheese, spices, salt, and pepper to taste.

MAKING & STORING

● **Using a food processor** To make fine fresh or dried bread crumbs quickly, drop pieces or slices of fresh bread or toast into the moving blade of a food processor.

● **Making small amounts** If you only need a small amount of bread crumbs, use a clean coffee grinder to grind small pieces of toast into crumbs.

● **Freezing crumbs** Keep freshly made bread crumbs in a plastic freezer bag in the freezer for up to six months.

● **Storing in a jar** Use a screw-top jar to store dried bread crumbs for about a month. The crumbs must be completely dry before storing.

CAKES AND MUFFINS

Most people enjoy eating cakes, whether their choice is a simple cupcake or a luxurious layer cake. The very many different kinds of cake present a range of storage problems. The longest-keeping cakes are rich fruit cakes and sponge cakes made with honey. Most cakes freeze well.

STORING & USING CAKES

● **Slicing in half** Improve the storage life of a large fruit cake by cutting it in half across the middle, taking slices from the inside of the cake, then sliding the two halves back together. Store in an airtight container.

● **Placing on lid** Store an iced cake on the lid of a cookie tin with the inverted tin over it. You can then slice and remove pieces without risking damage.

● **Making trifle** Crumble leftover stale sponge cake in a dish, sprinkle with liqueur, and top with fruit and whipped cream to make a quick, triflelike dessert.

● **Topping desserts** Make dry cake into crumbs, and sprinkle over desserts and ices.

FREEZING CAKES

Wrap sides of each slice in one piece of paper

Storing cake slices

When freezing a large cake, cut it into slices before freezing, and interleave each slice with a piece of waxed paper. Reassemble the cake, and freeze as usual. You can then remove as many slices as you need without thawing the whole cake first.

REFRESHING MUFFINS

Moistening muffins

If muffins or cupcakes have become a little dry in storage, refresh them by brushing with milk and placing them in a warm oven for 6–8 minutes, or until warmed thoroughly. If they are very dry, dip them in milk before placing them in the oven.

PREPARING INGREDIENTS

ONCE YOU HAVE PLANNED a menu and shopped carefully, you will need to begin preparing the ingredients. All good cooks will agree that sound skills in basic preparation methods are very important, whatever the type of food you are cooking, and whatever the occasion. Learn the correct way to prepare ingredients and you will save time and effort in the kitchen.

PREPARATION BASICS

The use of good-quality utensils is important even for basic food preparation – not only for the sake of efficiency, but also to make the task more pleasant. A sharp knife, for example, will make chopping and slicing quick and safe. As your skills improve, try new techniques.

CUTTING UP FOODS

Slicing safely
When slicing vegetables, use your knuckles to guide the knife and prevent it from cutting too close to your fingertips. Keep fingertips tucked in, and slice downward and forward.

CHOPPING EFFECTIVELY
● **Chopping finely** To chop food finely, use your knife like a pivot. Hold the tip down, and use a rocking action to chop.
● **Dicing foods** First, square one end of the vegetable or fruit. Cut into slices, stack, and cut lengthwise into sticks. Cut crosswise for diced pieces.

SLICING THINLY

Cutting julienne strips
To produce extra-thin julienne strips of vegetables, use a vegetable peeler to slice very fine ribbons. Then stack these together, and slice lengthwise as thinly as possible.

PREPARING STRIPS
● **Trimming vegetables** Before cutting julienne strips from vegetables such as carrots or cucumber, trim the vegetables into neat, rectangular blocks.
● **Cutting cabbage** To slice cabbage into thin strips, roll each leaf firmly like a jelly roll. Slice with a sharp knife.

DICING FRUITS

Lemon juice

Preventing discoloration
Sprinkle your cutting board with lemon juice before you dice apples or pears, then squeeze lemon juice on the cut fruits. This will keep the fruit from browning during preparation.

USING DICED FRUITS
● **Preventing sticking** If the blade of your knife becomes sticky while dicing sugary ingredients, dip it from time to time into a deep cup of very hot water placed nearby.
● **Using color** Consider adding diced fruits to a salad for a colorful "confetti" effect.

VEGETABLES

WHEN PREPARING VEGETABLES FOR COOKING BY ANY METHOD, it is important to retain their color, flavor, and nutrients. Prepare vegetables just before you need them, since they deteriorate quickly once they are peeled or cut.

GREEN VEGETABLES

Green vegetables, especially those that have delicate leaves, such as spinach, lose vitamins quickly once cut. If possible, tear the leaves rather than cutting or slicing them; otherwise, use a very sharp knife to ensure that the leaves are damaged as little as possible.

TRIMMING SPINACH

Removing stalks
To remove the stalks from large spinach leaves without cutting, fold each leaf vertically, grasp both sides with one hand, and pull the stalk sharply away from the leaf with the other hand.

TRIMMING BROCCOLI

Using broccoli stalks
To make use of thick broccoli stalks instead of discarding them, trim and slice them horizontally into ⅕-in (5-mm) thick slices. Cook them for the same period of time as the tender florets.

PREPARING LEAVES
- **Cleaning leaves** To remove insects and dirt from green-leaved vegetables, wash leaves in a large bowl of cold, salted water before using.
- **Shredding leaves** Stack and tightly roll leaves of spinach, lettuce, or cabbage, and slice into coarse shreds to prepare for sautéeing or frying.
- **Using outer leaves** Save the tough outer leaves of a green cabbage for stuffing with a savory filling. To make the leaves flexible, blanch them in boiling water for one minute, then drain.

BULB VEGETABLES

Bulb vegetables include different varieties of onion, garlic, and leek, all of which are an invaluable source of flavor in savory dishes. They are also natural antibiotics. Onions and garlic seem to help lower blood cholesterol levels and therefore protect against heart disease.

AVOIDING ONION TEARS

- **Leaving roots intact** Leave the root end intact when slicing or dicing an onion. This will prevent the release of the strong juices and fumes that cause eyes to water.
- **Using vinegar** Sprinkle a little distilled white vinegar onto the cutting board. This will counteract the effects of the onion juices.
- **Burning a candle** Light a candle nearby when preparing onions to burn off the sulfuric fumes.

CRUSHING GARLIC

Using a garlic press
When using a garlic press, leave the peel on the garlic clove. The soft garlic flesh will still be pushed through the mesh, and the garlic press will be easy to clean out after using.

CLEANING LEEKS

Washing out dirt
To make sure you remove all the dirt between the leaves of a leek, slit it lengthwise, almost to the root end. Hold the leek under running water, fanning out the leaves to wash them thoroughly.

ROOT VEGETABLES

This category includes root vegetables such as carrots and turnips, as well as foods that are really tubers, the swollen roots of plants such as potatoes or yams. Root vegetables are good sources of vitamins and fiber, especially if the skins are not removed prior to cooking.

ADDING INTEREST
● **Keeping the tops** Trim all but ¾ in (2 cm) of the leafy tops from baby carrots and turnips, then cook and serve whole.

Making carrot flowers
Run a canelle knife or a fork crosswise down the length of a peeled carrot to make grooves. Then slice the carrot crosswise, producing flower shapes.

PREPARING ROOTS
● **Beets** Leave the roots and tops of whole beets untrimmed before boiling them, to prevent juices and color from leaking out.
● **Potatoes** To make crisp fries, rinse sliced potatoes in cold water to remove excess starch. Dry them thoroughly on paper towels before frying.
● **Jerusalem artichokes** To avoid annoying peeling, boil Jerusalem artichokes whole in their skins. The skins will rub off easily after cooking.
● **Young vegetables** Peel young root vegetables thinly or scrub them, because the peel is high in fiber and the flesh just under it is high in nutrients.

BRIGHT IDEA

Making hasselbacks
For really crisp, golden roast potatoes, make "hasselbacks." Peel the potatoes, then cut thin slices downward, not quite all the way through. Brush with oil, sprinkle with salt, and bake in a hot oven for 30–40 minutes until crisp and well browned.

SALAD VEGETABLES

Most salads need little preparation apart from the careful cleaning and trimming of all the ingredients to ensure that as many nutrients as possible are retained. To prevent loss of crispness, flavor, and vitamins, avoid preparing salad vegetables too far in advance.

PREPARING LEAVES
● **Tearing lettuce leaves** Always tear lettuce leaves, rather than cutting them with a knife, to make bite-sized pieces.
● **Removing the core** To take out the tough core from an iceberg lettuce, bang the lettuce firmly – core downward – on a countertop. Turn it over, and you should be able to twist and remove the core easily.
● **Drying the leaves** If you do not have a salad spinner, dry washed leaves by rolling them loosely in a clean dish towel. Hold both ends firmly, and shake the towel gently.
● **Refreshing a lettuce** To revive a limp head of lettuce, trim the stem and dip it into iced water for a few minutes.

STRINGING CELERY

Pull peeler blade down ridged outer edge of stem

Using a vegetable peeler
To remove the tough strings quickly from the outer sticks of celery, separate all the celery ribs, and lightly stroke a swivel-bladed vegetable peeler down the length of each one.

PREPARING CUCUMBER

Drag edge of melon baller down cucumber

Removing seeds
Use a melon baller to scoop out the seeds from a cucumber before dicing or slicing. Cut the cucumber in half lengthwise, and scrape the melon baller down the middle to remove the seeds.

FRUIT VEGETABLES

These include sun-ripened vegetables such as eggplants, sweet peppers, tomatoes, and avocados. With their bright colors and fresh, rich flavors, fruit vegetables play an important role in ensuring that our everyday diet is not only varied, but also appetizing and nutritious.

CUTTING EGGPLANTS
● **Scoring** Cut a diamond pattern in the flesh of eggplant halves before grilling or baking, to ensure even cooking throughout.

PEELING
● **Blanching** To peel tomatoes, place them in a pan of boiling water. Remove after one minute and place in cold water. The skins will peel off easily.

Removing bitter juices
To reduce the bitterness of an eggplant, lay slices in a colander, and sprinkle with salt. Drain for 30 minutes, rinse, and dry. This also reduces oil absorption.

Grilling peppers
To skin whole peppers, place on foil, and grill until the skins blacken, turning often. Wrap the foil over so that steam will loosen the skins, then remove them.

TIMESAVING TIP

Insert spoon at wide end

Peeling a ripe avocado
Instead of trying to peel a ripe avocado with a knife, cut the avocado in half, and scoop out the flesh from each half in one piece using a large metal spoon. Keep the spoon close to the peel.

OTHER VEGETABLES

All kinds of vegetables, from all over the world, can be found in supermarkets today. Many do not fit into traditional categories, and some are, strictly speaking, not vegetables at all. Mushrooms are edible fungi, but they can be prepared in ways similar to many vegetables.

CLEANING & TRIMMING
● **Corn on the cob** Use a clean nylon hairbrush to remove the silk threads from corncobs without damaging the kernels.
● **Okra** When trimming the stalks from okra, ensure that you do not pierce the central parts and so release the sticky juices from the insides.
● **Chilies** If you need to reduce the strength of chilies for a milder flavor, scrape out the seeds and membranes inside. Wash your hands well or wear rubber gloves while preparing chilies, since they can irritate eyes or skin.
● **Zucchinis** If you are grating a zucchini for a salad, stir-fry, or stuffing, leave the stem on to give you a grip as you work.

PURÉEING SQUASH

Fibrous strings catch around blades

Removing fibers
To make a really smooth purée of cooked squash, whip with an electric mixer. The blades will pick up any fibrous strings during the process, so that you can remove them easily.

MUSHROOMS

Cultivated mushrooms should not be peeled or washed, since this reduces their flavor and vitamin content.

● **Cleaning** Wipe mushrooms gently with damp paper towels to remove dirt.
● **Keeping color** To ensure that cultivated mushrooms stay white during cooking, sprinkle with lemon juice.
● **Retaining vitamins** When marinating raw mushrooms, cover tightly with plastic wrap to prevent contact with the air and loss of vitamins.
● **Refreshing** To plump up dried mushrooms before use, immerse in boiling water for one minute. Dry before use.

FRUITS AND NUTS

Fruits and nuts require a range of preparation skills so that they can be presented at their best. Whether you are cooking fruits or serving them raw, whenever possible retain the skins and juices, since these contain nutrients.

CITRUS FRUITS

Citrus fruits are very versatile and are used in both sweet and savory dishes. Make use of every part of these fruits, including their zest or peels, juice, and flesh, which can be sliced or cut into segments. Always wash wax-coated fruits before removing the zest or cooking whole.

JUICING CITRUS FRUITS
- **Warming fruits** If citrus fruits have been stored in the refrigerator, they will yield the most juice if allowed to come to room temperature first.
- **Using a microwave** Pierce the skins of the fruits and heat for 10 seconds on High to increase the juice yield.
- **Squeezing easily** To make a citrus fruit easy to squeeze, first roll it under the palm of your hand on a counter.
- **Zesting and juicing** If you need both juice and zest from a citrus fruit, remove the zest before squeezing the fruit.

GARNISHING WITH FRUITS
- **Decorating slices** Before slicing citrus fruits for garnish, score grooves in the peel with a canelle knife or a fork; this gives the slices rippled edges.

Twist ends in opposite directions

Twisting lemon and lime
Cut thin slices of lemon and lime. Place a lime slice on top of a lemon slice, and cut a slit halfway across the two. Twist the slices into a spiral, making an unusual fruit garnish.

CUTTING LEMON WEDGES

Removing pith
When making lemon wedges for garnishing, slice off the strip of pith running down the ridge of each wedge so that juice squeezes easily, without squirting.

PEELING & ZESTING
- **Removing pith** To peel an orange cleanly, immerse the whole fruit in boiling water for four minutes. Drain and cool, and the pith will come away with the zest.
- **Using a peeler** Pare citrus fruit rind with a vegetable peeler rather than a knife to avoid peeling the pith as well.
- **Saving zest** If you are squeezing fruit for juice but do not need the zest at the same time, remove it anyway, and freeze for later use.
- **Reusing skins** After squeezing citrus fruit halves, scrape the remaining flesh from inside the skins. Freeze the empty skins, and use as serving bowls for fruit salad, compote, or sorbet.

REMOVING SEGMENTS

Cut over bowl

Catching juice
Hold peeled citrus fruits such as oranges or grapefruit over a bowl when removing segments to catch excess juice. Add this juice to fruit salads or drinks.

USING LEFTOVER PEEL

Keep peel in canning jar, covered with alcohol

Flavoring vodka
Place strips of thinly pared orange, lemon, or lime zest in a canning jar, and pour vodka over to cover. Mature in a refrigerator for 6–8 months. Add the vodka to drinks, or stir a tablespoonful into desserts such as fruit salad, ice cream, or chocolate mousse.

FRUITS WITH PITS

Fruits with pits, such as peaches, apricots, and plums, usually need little preparation other than removing the pits. Occasionally, it is necessary to remove the skins to achieve a smooth texture. Fruits that have thick skins, such as mangoes, always need to be peeled.

PITTING & PEELING

● **Twisting fruits apart** Find the natural indentation in peaches or nectarines, and cut around each fruit along this line through to the pit. Then twist the two halves apart.

● **Pitting plums** Cut around the "waist" of a firm plum, across the indentation, then twist the two halves apart.

● **Blanching and peeling** Remove skins easily from plums or peaches by plunging them into boiling water for one minute, then into ice-cold water until they are cool. Drain, and peel off the skins.

PITTING & CUBING A MANGO

1 Remove a thick slice from both sides of the fruit, cutting as close to the pit as possible. Peel the skin and flesh around the pit with a sharp knife, and cube the flesh.

2 Score each thick slice into squares, cutting down to the skin but not through it. Push the skin out into a convex curve so that the cubes can be removed easily.

SOFT FRUITS

Luscious soft fruits are best served very simply, so preparation is usually minimal. The only essential task is to pick over the fruit thoroughly to remove damaged parts, hulls, and stems, as well as dirt. Always handle soft, ripe berries gently to prevent them from bruising.

PREPARING SOFT FRUITS

● **Washing berries** If delicate berry fruits need to be washed, place them in a colander and rinse under running water, shaking the colander gently. Place on a paper towel to dry.

● **Preparing gooseberries** Use scissors to snip off the tops and bottoms of gooseberries before cooking or serving.

● **Enhancing flavor** Add a squeeze of lemon juice to berry fruits such as blueberries or strawberries to bring out the flavor. For a special occasion, sprinkle the fruits lightly with rum or brandy.

● **Using overripe fruits** If soft fruits are slightly overripe and not looking their best, mash them lightly with a fork. Serve spooned over vanilla ice cream, or stir into plain yogurt to make a quick dessert.

HULLING SOFT FRUITS

● **Removing stems** To hull red- or blackcurrants easily, pull each stem gently through the prongs of a fork, and carefully push off the fruit.

Grip hull firmly with tweezers

Hulling a strawberry
Use flat-ended tweezers to grasp and remove the leafy hull from a fresh strawberry without damaging the fruit. This method will also prevent the juice from staining your fingers.

USING FROZEN FRUITS

● **Keeping shape** To make sure frozen strawberries stay in good shape when thawing, put them into a serving dish while frozen, thaw slowly in the refrigerator, and serve while still slightly chilled.

● **Decorating from frozen** Decorate desserts with soft fruits such as raspberries or blackberries straight from the freezer. Let them thaw in place for about 30 minutes.

● **Quick-thawing fruits** To thaw frozen fruit quickly without using a microwave, place the fruits in a container in a dish of warm water for 30 minutes.

● **Making sorbet** Whip up an instant sorbet by puréeing frozen raspberries in a food processor with confectioners' sugar to taste. Spoon into chilled glasses, and serve.

OTHER FRESH FRUITS

This section includes many exotic tropical fruits, some of which may need different methods of preparation than those required for familiar, home-grown fruits. Many tropical fruits are in fact best served simply to show off their vibrant colors and delicate, scented flesh.

PREPARING KIWI FRUIT

Cut large slice off top, then scoop out flesh

Removing flesh
Instead of peeling kiwi fruit, cut a slice from the top, and scoop out the flesh with a teaspoon as you would with a soft-boiled egg. For packed lunches or picnics, slice off the top, and wrap the whole fruit in plastic.

CORING PEARS

● **Coring a pear half** Cut a pear in half before removing the core, rather than coring it whole. This makes it easy to see the core, and will ensure that no flesh is wasted.

Scoop core out carefully from base of whole pear

Using a melon baller
If you plan to cook and serve pears whole, remove the cores from the underside of each fruit by scooping out with a small melon baller or the pointed tip of a vegetable peeler. This way, the pears will keep their shape.

SERVING FRUITS SIMPLY

● **Strawberries** Bring out the delicious flavor of fresh strawberries by tossing them together with fresh, juicy segments of pink grapefruit.
● **Figs** To serve figs whole, cut a deep cross about two-thirds of the way through the fruit from the stem end. Squeeze the fruits gently to open them out ready to eat.
● **Papaya** Present papaya simply, like an avocado, as an appetizer. Cut the papaya in half or in quarters, and scoop out the seeds with a teaspoon. Serve with a slice of lime. Alternatively, serve slices of papaya sprinkled with lime juice as an appetizer or dessert.

PREPARING MELON

● **Leveling the base** Before serving a melon half or slice, cut a thin slice from the base of the fruit so that it sits firmly on the serving plate, making the cutting steady and easy.

Conserving juice
When scooping out melon seeds, hold the melon above a sieve placed over a bowl so that none of the juice is wasted. Spoon the melon juice over the melon to serve. Alternatively, add it to fruit salads or drinks.

BRIGHT IDEA

Coring pineapple rings
Remove the hard central core, and trim the edges of fresh pineapple slices with metal cookie cutters. Use a small round cutter to stamp out the central core, and a larger one to trim the skin and remove "eyes" from the slice.

TRIMMING & PEELING

● **Star fruit** To remove the brown, damaged edges that can spoil the appearance of a ripe star fruit, run a vegetable peeler quickly down the point of each ridge before slicing and serving the fruit.
● **Pomegranate** Make slits in the skin of a pomegranate, dividing it into segments. Peel each segment back, and remove with the pith.
● **Dates** If dates have become dull in color, or if sugar has crystallized on the surfaces, rinse them quickly under hot water. Then dry the dates thoroughly before serving.
● **Tamarillos** Always peel tamarillos thinly before serving, since the peel has an unpleasant, bitter taste.
● **Kiwi fruit** If the skin of a kiwi fruit is difficult to peel, plunge the fruit into boiling water for about 30 seconds, then try peeling it again.

DRIED FRUITS

Dried fruits are a concentrated source of nutrients, with apricots and peaches in particular being rich in iron and vitamin A. Many are ready to eat, but some need soaking, which provides an opportunity to add flavor by using fruit juice, tea, brandy, or wine.

PREPARING FRUITS

● **Chilling fruits** Chop dried fruits easily by freezing them for one hour before use.

● **Making a breakfast compote** Place dried fruit in a thermos, and top off with boiling water. Cap, let stand overnight, and serve warm for breakfast.

● **Saving time** To speed up soaking, put fruits in a bowl and cover with water. Cover the bowl, and microwave on High for 90 seconds. Let stand five minutes before use.

● **Using a food processor** Chop dried fruit with a little granulated sugar so that the fruits do not stick to the blades.

SOAKING FRUITS

Plumping up with tea
To plump up dried fruit for adding to cakes or quick breads, soak in tea instead of water. Choose a tea with a distinctive flavor, such as Earl Grey.

CHOPPING FRUITS

Preventing sticking
To chop sticky dried fruits, such as apricots, without the fruits sticking to the blades, cut with kitchen scissors or a sharp knife dipped frequently in hot water.

NUTS

Nuts are a versatile, highly nutritious food, useful in both sweet and savory dishes. Use fresh, whole nuts, with or without shells, and take the time to crack, chop, blanch, or grind them before adding to a dish, since their flavor is far better than ready-prepared nuts.

USING HAZELNUTS

● **Grinding** Grind whole, fresh hazelnuts in a food processor, and use them as a lower-fat alternative to ground almonds.

Removing skins
To remove the fine skins from hazelnuts easily, toast them lightly under a hot broiler until they are pale golden, then pour onto a clean dish towel. Fold the towel over the nuts, and rub them firmly. The skins will fall off.

USING FRESH COCONUT

● **Extracting milk** Pierce two of the eyes at one end of a fresh coconut with a skewer, and pour out the milk.

Continue tapping by crack

Opening the shell
Crack a whole, fresh coconut by tapping around the widest part with a small hammer to find the nut's natural fault line. Once a crack appears in the shell, continue turning and tapping the coconut to make a clean break.

SHELLING & BLANCHING

● **Cracking brazil nuts** To make brazil-nut shells easy to crack, place the nuts in the freezer for about six hours, or bake them for 15 minutes at 400°F (200°C). Let them cool before cracking.

● **Preventing breakage** To keep nut kernels whole and undamaged, press the middle of each shell gently with a nutcracker, turning the nut so that it cracks evenly.

● **Slitting chestnut skins** Before roasting or toasting whole chestnuts, cut a cross in each skin with a sharp knife to prevent them from exploding.

● **Microwave blanching** To blanch almonds, place them in boiling water, and microwave on High for two minutes. Drain, and peel off the skins.

HERBS AND SPICES

Herbs and spices will contribute a wonderful variety of flavors to your cooking. Always add herbs and spices to a dish in small amounts, tasting the food after each addition, until you achieve the flavor you desire.

FRESH HERBS

Treat all herbs gently during preparation, since they contain volatile oils that can easily be lost. Soft-leaved herbs, such as basil, coriander, and chervil, are particularly delicate. Most herbs are best added toward the end of cooking to preserve their flavor and color.

MAXIMIZING FLAVOR

● **Washing herbs** Shake herbs quickly under cold running water. Dry on paper towels.
● **Using stems** After using the leaves of fresh herbs such as parsley or dill, chop the stems finely and use to flavor stocks, sauces, and stews.
● **Flavoring with sage** To add a rich, intense flavor to chicken or pork roasts, tuck whole sage leaves just under the skin of the chicken or into small slits cut into the fat of the pork before roasting.
● **Replacing chives** Scallion tops are similar in flavor and color to chives. Chop them and use as a substitute when chives are not available.

CHOPPING PARSLEY

Scissors cut herbs finely without mess

Using kitchen scissors
To chop parsley easily and quickly, remove the stems, wash and dry the sprigs, and place in a large cup. Use a pair of kitchen scissors to snip the parsley inside the cup.

PREPARING MINT

Releasing flavor
To obtain the maximum flavor from fresh mint leaves, bruise them first to release their volatile oils. Place them in a small bowl, and pound gently with the end of a rolling pin. Use immediately.

PREPARING BASIL

Use fingertips to tear gently

Tearing leaves
To avoid losing the flavor and color too quickly from delicate-leaved herbs such as basil, tear the leaves with your fingers instead of chopping them with a knife. Add to savory dishes at the end of the cooking period.

MAKING A BOUQUET GARNI

Orange zest

Adding citrus flavor
Introduce a delicate citrus flavor to a bouquet garni by adding a thinly pared strip of orange, lemon, or lime zest to the mixed herbs. Use to flavor soups, sauces, or casseroles.

● **Mixing flavors** Combine sprigs of rosemary, parsley, and thyme with a bay leaf and a stick of celery to flavor red-meat dishes and rich bean dishes.
● **Flavoring fish** Add delicate herbs such as parsley, chervil, or dill to a bouquet garni for dishes including white fish.
● **Adding tarragon** For a scented flavor in chicken or pork dishes with white-wine or cream sauces, add a sprig of tarragon to the bouquet-garni mix.
● **Using horseradish** Add a bruised root of horseradish to a bouquet garni to flavor stocks or sauces for beef dishes.

DRIED HERBS

Dried herbs are a convenient substitute if fresh herbs are not available. However, they have a much more concentrated flavor than fresh herbs, so you will need to reduce quantities. As a general rule, use about half the amount of dried herbs that you would of fresh.

USING DRIED HERBS
- **Thyme** To remove the leaves of dried thyme from their woody stems, place the sprigs on a clean paper towel, fold over, and rub the herbs vigorously. If using a small amount, rub the herb stems between your fingertips.
- **Bay leaves** Soak dried bay leaves in water for a few minutes before threading onto skewers between cubes of meat, chicken, or fish. The leaves will add flavor to the meat without burning.
- **Stalks** Scatter the stripped, dry stalks of thyme or rosemary onto the coals of a barbecue to give a smoky, herb flavor to the food that is being cooked.

PREPARING ROSEMARY

Stripping leaves
To strip the leaves quickly from the woody stems of rosemary, hold the tip of each sprig in one hand, and strip the leaves off with a finger and thumb, pushing against the direction of growth.

BRIGHT IDEA

Using a tea infuser
If you want to enhance the flavor of a dish without leaving bits of herb behind, put the herbs into a tea infuser, and stir them into the dish at the end of cooking.

SPICES

Most spices can be added directly to dishes during cooking. However, it is well worth spending a little time to crush, bruise, or toast them first to bring out as much flavor as possible. Once ground or bruised, spices should be used immediately to prevent loss of flavor.

USING VANILLA SEEDS

Use tip of knife to scrape seeds from inside opened pod

Use pan to crush ginger

Removing seeds
To obtain a really strong flavor from a vanilla bean, use the tiny, oily seeds rather than infusing the whole pod. To extract the seeds, cut the pod lengthwise using a sharp knife. Then add the seeds directly to sweet dishes.

BRUISING GINGER

Using a heavy pan
Bruise a whole piece of peeled, fresh ginger by placing it on a cutting board and hitting it with the flat base of a heavy pan. If bruised ginger is added to preserves or hot drinks, its flavor will be infused quickly.

CRUSHING & GRINDING
- **Avoiding mess** Crush whole spices by placing them in a small plastic bag and hitting them several times with a rolling pin or a meat mallet.
- **Mixing spices** Mix together 75 percent black or white peppercorns and 25 percent whole allspice. Keep in a peppermill ready to grind onto grilled meats or fish. You could also mix black, white, pink, and green peppercorns to spice up plain chicken.
- **Making chili powder** Roast four dried, red chilies at 400°F (200°C) for 10 minutes. Remove the stems and seeds, then use a mortar and pestle to grind the chilies into a ready-to-use powder.

DAIRY FOODS

THERE IS AN INCREASING CHOICE AMONG DAIRY PRODUCTS, and many of the new items offer a wide range of flavors and low-fat alternatives for good health. Some low-fat products are not stable if cooked, so heat them gently.

EGGS

Versatile and nutritious, eggs are the basis of countless sweet and savory dishes. Whole eggs are used for a range of cooked dishes, whites are used for adding volume and binding, and yolks are used for glazing and enriching. Extra yolks or whites can be stored.

SEPARATING EGGS

Using the eggshell
Crack the shell gently on the edge of a bowl, and carefully pull the two halves apart. Let the white run into the bowl, and pour the yolk several times from one half of the shell to the other.

MAKING MERINGUE

● **Whipping egg whites** Whip egg whites in a copper bowl if you have one; it will produce the greatest volume.
● **Using at room temperature** Remove egg whites from the refrigerator about an hour before needed; they whip best at room temperature.
● **Keeping whites** Egg whites whipped with sugar will keep their shape for several hours; plain whipped whites must be used directly after whipping.
● **Saving overwhipped whites** To rescue overbeaten egg whites, beat another white separately until frothy, then stir it into the mixture. Whip again to regain the bulk.

USING WHOLE EGGS
● **Glazing** To make a golden brown glaze for pastry, bread, or muffins, beat an egg with a pinch of salt, and brush over the food before baking.
● **Extending an egg glaze** Make eggs go further for glazing by beating 1 tbsp (15 ml) oil with each whole egg.
● **Making omelets** When mixing, beat in 1 tbsp (15 ml) of water to every two eggs for lighter results. Alternatively, separate the white and whip until stiff, then fold into the yolks for a soufflé omelet.
● **Scrambling eggs** Beat in a little milk with the eggs to make creamy scrambled eggs.

USING EGG WHITES

Wipe bowl with cut lemon

Removing traces of grease
Before whipping egg whites, make sure that your bowl is free of grease by wiping it with the cut surface of a fresh lemon. Alternatively, wipe with a paper towel moistened with vinegar.

REMOVING YOLK TRACES

Use edge of shell to pick up traces of yolk

Using a half shell
If you get even a trace of yolk in the white after separating an egg, remove it before whipping the white. The best way to do this is by scooping out the yolk with the edge of a halved eggshell.

USING SPARE YOLKS
● **Chilling egg yolks** Place left-over egg yolks in a small cup. Cover with cold water, and refrigerate for up to two days.
● **Freezing egg yolks** Beat spare yolks with either a pinch of salt for use in savory dishes, or a pinch of sugar for use in sweet dishes, then label and freeze for up to six months.
● **Enriching dishes** Spare egg yolks are useful for enriching many dishes. For invalids, add an extra yolk when making omelets, pancake batters, and custards to add nutrition.
● **Improving texture** Beat an egg yolk into a hot chocolate sauce or savory cream sauce for a smooth, glossy texture.

BUTTER AND CHEESE

Butter and cheese are rich sources of fat, so are best used in moderation, but both can bring richness and flavor to many dishes. Margarine can be substituted for butter where flavor is not critical, but low-fat spreads are most suitable for spreading, not cooking.

PREPARING BUTTER

● **Softening** Use a microwave to soften butter that has been refrigerated. Put the butter in a microwave-safe dish and cook on Defrost for about 30 seconds for each stick (100 g).

● **Clarifying** To make a really clear glaze for pâtés or vegetables, clarify butter by melting it with an equal quantity of water. Let set, then lift off the cleared butter, leaving the salts and other solids in the water.

● **Making perfect butter curls** Use firm, chilled butter, and dip the butter curler into warm water. Drop the curls into a bowl of iced water, and store in the refrigerator.

SHAVING HARD CHEESES

Using a peeler
Shave thin curls of Parmesan, pecorino, or other hard cheeses straight from the block with a vegetable peeler. Scatter the curls of cheese over hot pasta dishes, salads, or bruschetta.

MAKING LIGHT PASTRY

Grating butter
To make light shortcrust pastry without cutting in the butter, chill butter until hard, and grate it into the flour using a medium grater. Mix evenly with a fork before adding water to bind.

CREAM AND YOGURT

These foods enrich all kinds of sweet and savory dishes, and the lighter substitutes for cream make it possible to use dairy produce in almost any diet. Lower-fat forms of cream must be stabilized with cornstarch before cooking, so that they can be heated without curdling.

WHIPPING CREAM

● **Checking fat content** To maximize volume when whipping, use cream with a fat content of about 40 percent.

● **Increasing volume** Before whipping, chill the whisk and bowl as well as the cream.

● **Adding sugar** Whip 1 tsp (5 ml) confectioners' sugar into each ¾ cup (150 ml) of cream for a fluffy result that will hold its shape well.

● **Adding flavor** To produce an even texture, always add flavorings such as brandy to cream before whipping.

● **Whisking by hand** Use a balloon or spiral hand whisk, which will allow you to feel texture changes and to avoid overwhipping the cream.

USING EFFECTIVELY

● **Lightening a topping** Mix half plain yogurt with half whipped cream for a light, flavorful dessert topping.

● **Stabilizing** To keep plain yogurt from curdling in hot dishes, mix 1 tsp (5 ml) cornstarch into every ¾ cup (150 ml) yogurt before heating. Alternatively, add after cooking, without boiling.

● **Making crème fraîche** Mix together equal quantities of sour cream and heavy cream. Cover, and let the mixture stand at room temperature for two hours or until it thickens.

● **Whipped cream accents** Freeze dollops of whipped cream on a baking sheet, then use to top off Irish coffee.

BRIGHT IDEA

Making yogurt at home
Heat 2¼ cups (600 ml) pasteurized milk to 110°F (43°C). Stir in 1 tbsp (15 ml) plain yogurt and ¼ cup (50 g) powdered skim milk. Pour into a thermos and let stand for seven hours, then chill in a bowl until thickened.

MEAT AND POULTRY

CAREFUL PREPARATION OF MEAT AND POULTRY is essential to the success of all types of cooking. The skillful use of different cutting methods, marinades, and coatings can make even the most inexpensive cut look and taste delicious.

MAKING GENERAL PREPARATIONS

There are many ways of preparing meat and poultry to enhance their appearance, flavor, and tenderness. For healthy cooking, trim off excess fat and skin, keeping some fat for flavor and moisture. Retain bones and trimmings to make stock, and freeze for future use.

CUTTING MEAT

● **Slicing for tenderness** Slice meat across, not with, the grain for a tender result.

● **Dicing evenly** When dicing meat for casseroles or curries, make the cubes the same size so that they cook evenly.

● **Trimming kidneys** Use kitchen scissors instead of a knife to cut out and remove the tough cores from kidneys.

● **Cutting stir-fry strips** Freeze meat for 30 minutes before slicing for a stir-fry. This will make it easy to cut thinly.

● **Snipping edges** To prevent the edges of grilled or fried steaks, chops, or bacon from curling, make slits in the fat at ½-in (1-cm) intervals.

COATING CHICKEN

Seasoned flour in plastic bag

Shaking in a bag
To coat chicken pieces in seasoned flour or spices quickly and cleanly, place the coating mixture in a plastic bag, and add the poultry. Shake the bag until the contents are evenly coated. Remove the pieces and cook.

TENDERIZING MEAT

Puréed papaya

Marinating in papaya
To tenderize a tough cut of meat, purée fresh papaya and spread it over the surface of the meat. Alternatively, pour papaya or pineapple juice over the meat, cover, and refrigerate for three hours. Dry meat before cooking.

PREPARING DUCK

Scoring skin
To prepare duck breast for grilling or frying, score the skin deeply in a diamond pattern. This will help the meat cook evenly, keep its shape, and release excess fat during cooking.

PREPARING OFFAL

● **Soaking liver** For a milder flavor, soak strong-tasting liver, such as pig's liver, in milk for one hour prior to cooking.

● **Tenderizing liver** To make liver tender, pour tomato juice over it, and let soak three hours before cooking.

● **Cleaning hearts** Wash hearts thoroughly, then soak in lightly salted water for one hour to clean out any blood deposits.

● **Blanching sweetbreads** To keep sweetbreads firm, first blanch them for 20 minutes in salted, boiling water with the juice of half a lemon. Then drain, and press between two plates before cooking.

TIMESAVING TIP

Snipping bacon
To "chop" bacon quickly and easily, use a pair of kitchen scissors. Cut raw bacon slices straight into a pan. Snip cooked bacon over salads.

BONING

Most of the basic preparation of meat cuts is done before you buy them, but it is worth learning a few simple skills to get the best out of meat and poultry. Boning and trussing meat at home saves money, since prepared cuts are the most expensive.

PREPARING LAMB JOINTS
● **Protecting bones** Cover the bone ends of a rack of lamb with foil to prevent them from burning during cooking.

Use sharp knife to loosen bone

Loosening bone
For an easy-carving shoulder of lamb, loosen the blade bone from the flesh, but leave it in place. When roasted, the meat will shrink back, and the bone can then be pulled out easily.

TRUSSING POULTRY
● **Tying drumsticks** To truss a whole bird, tie only the drumsticks together, and the bird will keep its shape.

Using dental floss
To truss or sew meat or poultry unobtrusively, use some unwaxed dental floss. It is strong enough to hold the shape neatly and firmly, without spoiling the appearance of the dish.

SPLITTING FOR GRILLING
● **Pressing flat** To ensure that poultry lies as flat as possible when opened out for cooking, press firmly on the breastbone with the heel of your hand.

Using skewers
To hold a split Cornish hen in shape for cooking, push metal skewers through the thickest parts of the meat. They will allow the heat to penetrate and ensure thorough cooking.

SAFETY

Follow these few simple guidelines when handling meat to keep it free from bacterial contamination.

● **Washing hands** Wash before and after handling meat and poultry, and before preparing other foods.
● **Cleaning equipment** To avoid cross-contamination after preparing meat, thoroughly wash knives, surfaces, and cutting boards.
● **Keeping cool** Once meat is prepared and ready to cook, cook it immediately, or cover it with foil and store it in the refrigerator until it is needed.
● **Using stuffings** Always make sure cooked stuffings have cooled completely before using them to stuff raw meat.

USING CUT-UP POULTRY
● **Soaking duck pieces** Soak joints of wild duck in cold water for about an hour to remove any excess blood. Dry thoroughly on paper towels.
● **Cutting up whole birds** Buy a whole chicken, and cut it up yourself, since this is less expensive than buying precut pieces. Use the trimmings to make a stock for future use.
● **Adding flavors** Remove the skin from poultry pieces and slash the thickest parts of the flesh before coating in spices or marinades. This will allow the flavors to penetrate fully.
● **Using coatings** Use herb-flavored, packaged stuffing mix as a quick coating for chicken. Dip each piece in egg, and then into the stuffing mix before baking or frying.

FISH AND SHELLFISH

Most of the preparation of fish can be done before it reaches the kitchen. It is worth finding a supplier who will prepare the fish just as you want it. A few basic skills will help you get the most from this nutritious food.

FISH

Fresh fish needs little preparation, and if it is bought already filleted or skinned it can be considered a ready-to-cook convenience food. Frozen fish can usually be used as a substitute for fresh fish. If possible, cook straight from frozen to retain all the juices and flavor.

SCALING FISH
● **Rinsing under water** Hold fish under cold water while removing scales, washing them away as you scrape.

REMOVING BONES
● **Boning cooked fish** When flaking fish, check for small bones after cooking, when they can be removed easily.

FILLETING FISH
● **Filleting flat fish** Fillet flat fish without gutting it: there is no danger of the gut being pierced and contaminating the flesh.

Use sharp edge of scallop shell

Using a scallop shell
Remove all the scales from a whole fish with the edge of a scallop shell, scraping firmly down the length of the fish from the tail end toward the head.

Using tweezers
Use tweezers to pluck out stray bones left in fish fillets after filleting. Press gently with your fingertips to feel for the small bones under the surface.

Boning mackerel
To bone mackerel, slit open the belly, and place the fish skin side up. Press firmly with your thumbs down the backbone. Turn over, and lift out the bones.

CLEANING & SKINNING
● **Preventing mess** To scale a whole fish cleanly, place it in a large heavy plastic bag, and scrape off the scales inside it.
● **Using salt** Dip fingertips into salt before skinning fish to give a better grip. Also, rub salt inside the belly cavity to remove any residues, then rinse well before cooking.
● **Skinning frozen fish** Pull the skin from frozen fillets while still frozen. Use paper towels to help you grip the skin.
● **Removing fishy smells** Rub the cut surface of a lemon over hands, knife, and cutting board after preparing fish to counteract fishy odors.

PREPARING A WHOLE FISH

Trimming the tail
If you are preparing a whole fish, such as salmon or trout, to serve with its tail on, trim the thin edges of the tail with scissors to make a V shape. This will prevent the tail from curling up in the heat during cooking.

● **Trimming the fins** Use kitchen scissors to snip the fins off a whole fish before cooking.
● **Cleaning through the gills** To preserve the shape of fish that is to be served whole, remove the stomach contents of the fish through the gill flaps instead of slitting open the belly.
● **Removing the gills** If a fish is to be cooked and served with the head intact, snip out the gills with scissors first, since they can impart a bitter taste.
● **Removing the head** To remove the head from a whole fish, cut following the natural curve behind the gills.

SHELLFISH

Much of the fresh shellfish we eat is sold in the shell and is often live, so preparation must be done at home. Live shellfish, such as oysters, mussels, and clams, are best prepared just before you serve them to ensure maximum freshness and safety, as well as the best results.

CLEANING & SERVING

- **Debearding mussels** Remove beards from mussels just before cooking, since they die once the beards are removed.
- **Using crushed ice** Prepare a serving platter with crushed ice before opening oysters, so that the shells can be firmly nestled in and the juices remain in the shells.
- **Chilling shellfish** Put clams or oysters, unopened, in the freezer for 10 minutes before serving; they will open easily.
- **Serving in shells** When buying shelled scallops, ask for the curved shells so that you can use them as serving dishes. Scrub and boil to clean.

CRACKING CRAB CLAWS

Tap claw gently but firmly with hammer

Using a hammer
To crack a crab claw without shattering it, cup it in the palm of your hand, and tap with a small hammer until the shell cracks. Alternatively, crack the claw on a folded dish towel on a board.

OPENING OYSTERS

- **Using the oven** Place oysters in one layer on a cookie sheet, and put in a hot oven for 3–4 minutes until they open.

Rest shell in palm to retain juices

Using a can opener
Open oyster shells with the pointed tip of a can opener. Grasp each shell firmly in a cloth, holding the flat side upward, then insert the opener into the hinge and push down firmly.

CRUSTACEANS

Fresh shrimp, lobsters, and other crustaceans are usually sold in the shell, and a few simple skills are needed to prepare them. Do not be deterred by this preparation, which is speedy and worthwhile. The flavor of fresh crustaceans is better than peeled, frozen, or canned products.

DEVEINING SHRIMP

Use scissors to snip along back

Hold firmly between fingers and thumb

Using scissors
To devein large shrimp before cooking, cut along the back of each shell. It is easy to see the dark vein running down the back. Lift out the vein carefully, or scrape it out with a knife.

DEALING WITH SHELLS

- **Peeling easily** To peel cooked shrimp, grasp the head between finger and thumb, and twist to remove. Pull the legs to one side; as they break away, part of the shell should lift off. You will be able to peel it all off.
- **Cutting shells** Use kitchen scissors or poultry shears to cut lobster shells in half easily.
- **Wiping edges** After cutting lobster or crayfish shells in half for serving, wipe around the edges of the cut shells with a clean, damp cloth to remove small fragments.
- **Serving in shells** To serve lobster attractively in the shell, lift out the tail flesh from each half and replace it, rounded side up, in the opposite half.

USING SHELLS

Use shells to add color and flavor to stocks, sauces, and other accompaniments.

- **Making fish stock** After boiling lobster and scooping out the meat, return the shell pieces to the cooking liquid, and add a glass of white wine, a few onion slices, and a bouquet garni. Simmer for 20 minutes, then strain.
- **Making a fish sauce** Grind lobster shells in a food processor until smooth. Cook in a little butter, then add white wine and cream to make a rich sauce for white fish.
- **Making shrimp butter** Purée equal amounts of shrimp shells and butter with a little lemon juice in a food processor.

Cooking Methods

THE MAIN REASON for cooking food is to make it palatable and easily digestible. Different cooking methods have varying effects on foods, and it is important that you choose a suitable cooking method for each type of food. Rapid boiling, for instance, helps retain the color and texture of fresh vegetables, but tough cuts of meat need slow simmering to make them tender. Cooking methods may be combined, as in braising, in which quick frying and slow stewing brown and tenderize meat.

HEALTHY COOKING

The way in which food is cooked plays an important role in determining the food's nutritional contribution to our diet. Whenever possible, choose low-fat cooking methods, or cook with oils that are low in saturated fat, and use methods of cooking that retain nutrients.

STIR-FRYING
● **Adding in stages** When stir-frying mixtures of vegetables, place each vegetable in the pan separately to maintain the heat. Add the slowest-cooking first and the fastest-cooking last.

BOILING
● **Reusing cooking liquids** Refrigerate liquids that have been used for boiling food, since these contain flavor and nutrients. Add to gravies, sauces, soups, or stocks.

STEAMING
● **Cutting same-sized pieces** To ensure that pieces of food cook evenly and within the same period of time when steaming, cut them all to approximately the same size.

Stir constantly to seal food

Sealing food quickly
Use less oil or fat for stir-frying than you would normally use for shallow frying, so that the surface of the food seals quickly. Add just enough oil to the pan to coat the food lightly.

Conserving nutrients
To preserve the vitamins when boiling vegetables, bring the water to a rolling boil before adding the vegetables to the pan. Bring back to the boil quickly, and keep the heat high until done.

Wrap paper securely around food

Making a bundle
Retain the nutritious juices from steamed foods by wrapping food in bundles of baking parchment or aluminum foil before placing in a steamer. Pour the juices over the food to serve, or add to a sauce.

VEGETABLES

MOST VEGETABLES RETAIN THEIR COLOR, texture, and flavor best if they are cooked quickly and lightly. Many different cooking methods can be used. Vegetables taste best if served as soon as possible after they have been cooked.

POTATOES

Potatoes are very versatile and respond well to most cooking methods. To a great extent the variety of potato determines which cooking method you use. For instance, grainy-textured potatoes are good for baking, roasting, and mashing, while waxy types are best boiled.

ENSURING SUCCESS

● **Baked potatoes** To speed up the cooking of baked potatoes, push metal skewers through their centers to conduct the heat. Alternatively, parboil the potatoes for 15 minutes before baking.
● **Mashed potatoes** Add a little hot milk (not cold) to mashed potatoes to give them a really fluffy texture. Warm the milk in a microwave for speed.
● **Boiled potatoes** Prevent old potatoes from blackening by adding a squeeze of lemon juice or a teaspoonful of vinegar to the cooking liquid.

CRISPING POTATOES

Roughing up the surfaces
For crisp roast potatoes, cut the potatoes into chunks, parboil, and drain. Shake the covered pan to roughen the surfaces of the potatoes, then roast as usual.

KEEPING POTATOES HOT

Preventing soggy potatoes
Use a clean dish towel to cover mashed potatoes and keep them hot before serving. The towel will absorb excess moisture, keeping them fluffy and dry.

GREEN VEGETABLES

Most green vegetables are rich in vitamin C, and they should be cooked quickly in the minimum of liquid to retain this very important nutrient. If you boil greens, keep the cooking water and add to gravies or soups. Alternatively, use water-free methods such as stir-frying.

COOKING CABBAGE

Steaming wedges
Instead of shredding cabbage, cut it into slim, portion-sized wedges and steam the wedges until just tender. The wedges will retain more nutrients than shredded cabbage and look decorative.

COOKING ASPARAGUS

Add water to create steam

Using a microwave
Arrange asparagus spears in a wide, shallow dish with their pointed tips to the center. Add 3 tbsp (45 ml) water, cover, and cook on High for about 12–14 minutes per pound (500 g).

IMPROVING GREENS

● **Cabbage** Braise cabbage in a little stock instead of water. Shred finely, and cook with just enough stock to moisten, shaking the pan often.
● **Spinach** To remove excess moisture from cooked spinach, put spinach into a colander, and press with a potato masher, or press between two plates.
● **Napa cabbage** Shred the coarse outer leaves of Napa cabbage, and stir-fry. Save the tender leaves for salads.
● **Brussels sprouts** Cut crosses through the stems of Brussels sprouts for even cooking.

ENHANCING FLAVOR

Most vegetables are best cooked lightly to retain their flavor, color, and texture. By experimenting with different cooking methods and adding ingredients such as herbs, it is possible to add interest to, and enhance the flavor of, even the most ordinary vegetable.

USING ONIONS
● **Frying onions** To obtain a sweet, caramelized flavor, fry onions slowly in butter with a pinch of salt until they are a rich, golden-brown color.

USING FRUIT JUICES
● **Sprinkling lemon juice** Fresh lemon juice will pep up the flavor of most vegetables. Use it instead of adding salt for people on low-salt diets.

ADDING SPICES
● **Spicing leeks** Add a spicy pungency to leeks by gently sautéeing them until soft in a little butter with a pinch of ground coriander and cumin.

Add juice to other ingredients

Pour in orange juice to moisten carrots

Sprinkle with freshly grated nutmeg

Adding onion juice
To add the flavor of onion to savory dishes without including sliced or diced onion pieces, squeeze half an onion on a lemon squeezer to extract the juice. Add the liquid to the dish.

Flavoring carrots
Add a rich, sweet flavor to plain carrots by cooking in orange juice instead of water. Braise small, whole, new carrots until tender with just the juice of an orange and a pat of butter.

Using nutmeg
Sprinkle freshly grated nutmeg over cooked spinach, parsnips, or potatoes just before serving. The heat of the vegetables will bring out the full, warm, spicy aroma and flavor of the spice.

MAXIMIZING FLAVOR

● **Brussels sprouts** Instead of boiling Brussels sprouts, shred them finely, and stir-fry lightly in a little olive oil to retain flavor and crispness.
● **Beets** Wrap beets in foil, and bake instead of boiling to preserve flavor and color. Trim the tops of the beets, and wrap in buttered foil. Bake in a moderate oven for 1–2 hours.
● **Peas and snow peas** Add a sprig of fresh mint when boiling peas or snow peas.
● **Tomatoes** Add a pinch of sugar to cooked tomatoes and homemade tomato sauce.

USING LEFTOVERS
● **Grilling with cheese** Arrange vegetables in one layer in a heat dish. Cover with thin slices of Gruyère, and grill.
● **Making potato pancakes** Mix mashed potatoes with grated onion, then shallow-fry in cakes until golden.
● **Making fritters** Dip broccoli or cauliflower florets in batter. Then deep-fry in hot oil until they are a golden color.
● **Tossing salads** Dice cooked, mixed vegetables, and toss with mayonnaise and lemon juice. Serve cold as a salad.
● **Making soup** Purée cooked vegetables with leftover gravy, stock, or milk to taste.

TIMESAVING TIP

Making vegetable bundles
Wrap prepared vegetables in buttered foil, and cook in the oven in a roasting pan with roast meat for the final 30–40 minutes of cooking time. Add sprigs of fresh herbs to the bundles, and season with salt and pepper. Seal the bundles firmly to keep in the flavors.

ADDING VARIETY

Vegetables are versatile ingredients that will contribute significantly to a healthy diet, but if they are always cooked in the same way they lose their appeal. Be creative by combining vegetables with other ingredients in unusual ways and using different cooking methods.

VARYING PRESENTATION

Draw peeler along length of vegetable

Making vegetable ribbons
To serve carrots and zucchini in an unusual way, and to cook them quickly, slice them into thin ribbons by using a vegetable peeler instead of a knife. Steam or stir-fry the ribbons for 2–3 minutes or until they are tender.

COOKING CREATIVELY

● **Making "confetti"** Use the coarse shredder blade of a food processor to shred evenly vegetables such as carrots, peppers, zucchini, or celery root. Cook together in a quick "confetti" stir-fry.
● **Adding bacon** Transform cooked green beans into a dinner-party dish by tossing with crushed garlic, golden-fried crumbled bacon, and a chopped tomato.
● **Puréeing eggplants** Serve eggplants as a purée. Bake them whole in their skins for about 45 minutes in a moderate oven, or until tender. Scoop out the flesh, mash with a fork, and add salt, pepper, and olive oil to taste.

ADDING TEXTURE

Sunflower seeds

Sprinkling with seeds
To add an interesting texture to plain, cooked vegetables and increase their nutritive value, sprinkle with a few lightly toasted sunflower, pumpkin, or sesame seeds, or add chopped nuts just before cooking.

CORRECTING MISTAKES

If you have overcooked vegetables, there is no need to discard them, since they can usually be revived easily, or presented in a different way in order to disguise the mistake. You may even find that the end result is better than what you had originally intended.

PURÉEING VEGETABLES

Add heavy or light cream to taste

Mixing with cream
Rescue boiled carrots, spinach, or peas that have overcooked by serving them as a rich, creamy purée. Put the vegetables in a food processor, and purée until just smooth. Add a few tablespoonfuls of cream to taste.

REVIVING MASH

Rescuing soggy potatoes
If potatoes intended for mashing are overcooked or if they have collapsed, whip an egg white until stiff, and fold it carefully into the mashed potatoes. Pile the mixture into a dish, and bake in a hot oven until golden.

RESCUING DISASTERS

● **Counteracting salt** Rescue oversalted vegetables by pouring boiling water over them. If they are still too salty, stir them gently in a few tablespoonfuls of cream.
● **Reducing toughness** If mushrooms have become tough and dried out, add a few tablespoonfuls of red wine. Let the mushrooms soak for 10 minutes, then bring to a boil. Stir in a little cream.
● **Making soufflés** Mash overcooked cauliflower or broccoli, and mix in a can of condensed soup and three egg yolks. Fold in three whipped whites. Bake in ramekins in a hot oven for 20 minutes.

SALADS

Salads form an essential part of our diet, whether they are simple side dishes or substantial main courses. Fresh, nutritious ingredients, served raw or lightly cooked, make a colorful, attractive dish to stimulate the appetite.

USING BASIC INGREDIENTS

Be creative with salad ingredients, and use fresh flavors, colors, and textures to the fullest. Use a variety of greens to make the most of a simple salad, or create interesting main courses by combining lots of salad ingredients. Match ingredients with dressings to your taste.

DRAINING SALADS

Using a saucer
Place an upside-down saucer in the bottom of a salad bowl before adding the salad. Excess water and dressing will gather underneath the saucer, keeping the salad leaves crisp.

SPROUTING BEANS

Soaking beans in a jar
Sprout mung beans or other whole beans for use in salads. Put them in a large jar and soak overnight. Drain, cover the jar with cheesecloth, and rinse twice a day until the beans sprout.

MAKING RICE TIMBALES

Turn out compacted rice carefully

Shaping rice
Toss cooked rice in a dressing, then pack firmly into coffee or tea cups, or into a small bundt pan. Invert the cups onto a serving dish, and unmold for attractively shaped rice salads.

PRESENTING LEAVES

● **Using whole leaves** Use crisp, whole lettuce leaves, such as romaine or iceberg, as natural serving dishes.
● **Cutting wedges** To produce interesting shapes and texture in a green salad, thinly slice an iceberg lettuce into wedges.
● **Lifting out a core** To remove the central core from an iceberg lettuce while keeping the leaves whole, slam the lettuce firmly, stem end down, onto a countertop. The core should then be loose enough to be lifted out by hand.
● **Removing bitterness** To avoid a bitter flavor in chicory, cut out the core at the stem end.

IMPROVING INGREDIENTS

● **Cucumber** Before adding a sliced cucumber to salad, sprinkle the pieces with salt, and let drain for about 20 minutes to remove excess moisture. Rinse and dry.
● **Onions** To prevent the strong flavor of onions from dominating a salad, let the cut onion soak in cold water for one hour before use.
● **Tomatoes** Add interest to a tomato salad by mixing beefsteak, sun-dried, and cherry tomatoes. Sprinkle with olive oil as a dressing.
● **Celery** Keep leftover celery fresh for reuse by trimming and standing in chilled water.

FLAVORING WARM SALADS

● **Adding vinegar** Sprinkle warm salad ingredients with a few drops of an aged vinegar, such as balsamic or sherry vinegar. The warmth of the salad will bring out the full flavor of the vinegar.
● **Using sesame oil** Give a Far Eastern flavor to a warm salad by adding a teaspoon of sesame oil to the dressing.
● **Cooking shallots** Simmer finely chopped shallots slowly in a few tablespoonfuls of red wine vinegar until soft. Toss them into a potato or bean salad for a warm, rich flavor.

ADDING VARIETY

Combine common and unusual ingredients to make imaginative and appetizing salads. Mix crunchy ingredients, such as croutons and seeds, with soft textures, such as fresh and dried fruits. Contrast sharp flavors with mild ones, and use herbs to add a distinctive flavor.

ENHANCING SALADS
● **Adding anchovies** Stir a few finely chopped canned anchovies into a potato salad.
● **Using herbs** Scatter generous amounts of fresh, chopped herbs, such as parsley, chervil, or chives, into a plain green salad, or add arugula for a peppery bite.
● **Adding texture** To add a crunchy texture to a simple salad, stir in a handful of toasted sunflower or sesame seeds, flaked almonds, or even salted peanuts just before serving the salad.
● **Shaving Parmesan** Scatter curled shavings of Parmesan cheese onto a plain salad.

MAKING MIXED SALADS

Layering ingredients
Pour a dressing into a straight-sided bowl, and place layers of colorful mixed salad vegetables into it. Turn the filled bowl over onto a serving dish for a dressed salad.

ADDING GARNISHES

Use cutter to stamp shapes from bread

Making croutons
To add a crunchy garnish to a simple salad, use croutons. Cut shapes from sliced bread with a small cutter. Gently fry the shapes in oil until golden, toss with parsley, and add to salad.

MAKING DRESSINGS

A well-balanced, freshly made dressing can add a subtle or a distinctive flavor to a salad. Classic recipes, such as vinaigrette, are a good starting point, but imaginative dressings can be created using flavored vinegars and oils, fruit juices, herbs, spices, seeds, and zests.

COMBINING INGREDIENTS
● **Dressing warm ingredients** Dress rice or pasta salads while they are still slightly warm so that they absorb the flavors of the dressing.
● **Adding nut oils** Enhance salad dressings by using nut oils, such as walnut or hazelnut, for a rich flavor.
● **Lowering fat** Use plain yogurt or milk, instead of oil, as a basis for a low-fat dressing.
● **Sweetening dressings** If you find vinegar-based dressings too sharp, substitute apple or orange juice for the vinegar, or add a teaspoonful of honey.
● **Adding cheese** Use ripe Stilton or Roquefort for a blue-cheese dressing. Mash cheese with a fork, and stir into light cream or mayonnaise.

MAKING VINAIGRETTE

Using a screwtop jar
To make vinaigrette quickly, pour vinegar, or lemon juice, and oil into a straight-sided, screw-top jar. Use three parts oil to one part vinegar, or four or five parts oil to one part lemon juice. Shake the jar to mix the ingredients.

BRIGHT IDEA

Using a mustard jar
When a mustard jar is almost empty, leave the last scrapings in the jar, and use it to make a salad dressing. Measure the other ingredients into the jar, and shake well. The remaining mustard will flavor the dressing.

FRUITS

S OME FRUITS – EVEN SOFT SUMMER FRUITS – tend to be more palatable cooked than uncooked, but most require only light cooking to bring out their full flavor. Gentle poaching, grilling, or baking will maintain flavor, color, and shape.

BAKING FRUITS

F ruits can be baked just as they are, as in the case of baked apples, or wrapped in pastry bundles to cook gently and retain the flavor. Always prepare fruits just before baking, since most of them soon start to brown and lose vitamins when they are exposed to the air.

ADDING FLAVOR

● **Sprinkling spice** Mix ½ cup (60 g) dark brown sugar with 1 tsp (5 ml) ground cinnamon, and sprinkle over fruit for a sweet and spicy glaze.
● **Adding chocolate** Bake bananas until their skins turn black, then slit down one side and spoon in melted chocolate. Eat this delicious dessert right from the skins.
● **Baking peaches** To bring out the flavor of slightly underripe peaches, bake them in their skins, whole or in halves, in a hot oven for approximately 20 minutes. Slip off the skins of the fruits before serving.

BAKING WHOLE APPLES

Score lines vertically from top to bottom

Scoring skins
Use a canelle knife or an ordinary knife to score the skins of whole, cored apples before baking, so that the fruits cook without splitting. Sprinkle lemon juice on the apple to prevent browning.

BAKING WHOLE ORANGES

Gather foil, then twist to secure

Wrapping in foil
Remove the peel and pith from oranges, and slice into rings. Reassemble on foil squares, and add a pat of butter and a dash of liqueur. Wrap in foil and bake in a hot oven for 10 minutes.

QUICK APPLE FILLINGS

To bake apples with a tasty filling, remove the cores but leave them unpeeled. Pack the hollowed centers with a filling before baking.

● **Using almond paste** Chop almond paste and dried apricots, and pack into the centers of cored apples. Sprinkle with lemon juice.
● **Crumbling cookies** Lightly crush macaroons or gingersnaps, and mix them with chopped almonds or walnuts. Spoon into apples.
● **Stuffing with nuts and dates** Make a stuffing for apples from chopped dates and walnuts. Spoon maple syrup on top before baking.

MAKING PIE FILLINGS

Mix cornstarch thoroughly with fruits

Thickening juices
To thicken juices in fruit pie fillings, toss the prepared fruits in a little cornstarch. If sugar is to be added, mix it with the cornstarch before adding to the fruits to distribute it evenly.

WRAPPING FRUITS

● **Wrapping pears in pastry** Cut long, thin strips of puff or shortcrust pastry, and spiral around peeled pears, leaving the stems exposed. Brush with milk, and bake in a hot oven until the pastry is golden.
● **Topping apples** Bake whole apples until almost tender, peel off the skins from the top halves, spread stiff meringue over the peeled parts, then bake in a hot oven until the meringue is golden.
● **Making phyllo bundles** Halve and pit plums or apricots, then put a blanched almond in each cavity. Put halves back together, and wrap in phyllo dough. Brush with oil, and bake in a moderate oven until golden.

POACHING FRUITS

Fruits can be poached by cooking gently in syrup until they are just tender. Cook over low heat to retain flavor and prevent the fruits from falling apart. To make a purée, poach fruits until soft, and beat with a wooden spoon or prepare in a food processor until smooth.

ENHANCING FLAVORS

● **Counteracting acidity**
Reduce the acidity of rhubarb and improve its flavor by poaching it in orange juice or sprinkling it with ginger.
● **Using lemonade** Poach apple slices in leftover lemonade and white wine.
● **Adding tea** Use a scented tea such as Earl Grey for poaching dried fruits to make an exotic fruit compote. Add a few cardamom pods or star anise for a rich, spicy flavor.
● **Oven-poaching fruits** Allow the flavor of fruits to develop to their full intensity by poaching them in a tightly lidded dish in a cool oven for approximately one hour.

POACHING APRICOTS

Add enough liquid to moisten apricots

Using a microwave
Pour water or fruit liqueur and lemon juice over the apricots. Cover. Then cook on High 4-5 minutes, turning halfway through. Slip off the skins, and serve apricots in the juices.

SERVING POACHED PEARS

Slice up to, but not through, stem end

Slicing into a fan
Poach whole pears, peeled but with stems on, in wine or sugar syrup until tender. Drain and cut into very thin slices, almost through to the stem end. Press lightly to fan out the slices.

GRILLING AND BARBECUING FRUITS

Grilling fruits is an excellent way of bringing out their sweet, ripe flavors – and almost any fruits can be cooked using this method. The dying heat from a barbecue after cooking the main course is ideal for grilling fruits brushed with spicy glazes or wrapped in foil bundles.

GRILLING PEACH HALVES

● **Adding lemon juice** Sprinkle fresh peach halves with lemon juice before grilling to prevent the flesh from browning.

Adding a topping
Top fresh or canned peach halves with a spoonful of ricotta or mascarpone cheese, sprinkle with a sweet spice such as cinnamon, allspice, or anise, and grill until the cheese bubbles.

BARBECUING PINEAPPLE

● **Glazing** Brush pineapple pieces with a mixture of equal amounts of melted butter, rum, and brown sugar. Then grill.

Skewering wedges
Cut a pineapple lengthwise into quarters, remove the core, and cut between the skin and the flesh, leaving the flesh in position. Slice the flesh, secure with skewers, and barbecue.

GRILLING FRUITS

● **Using skewers** Thread strawberries onto bamboo skewers, brush with melted butter, and sprinkle with confectioners' sugar. Then grill.
● **Marinating fruits** Soak peach or apricot halves in brandy for 30 minutes before grilling.
● **Making exotic kebabs** Mix chunks of exotic fruits such as mangoes, kiwi fruits, guavas, and kumquats on skewers, brush with butter, then grill.
● **Using rum butter** Use leftover rum or brandy butter as a glaze for grilled fruits.
● **Serving with sweet toasts** Grill slices of fruit with slices of buttered brioche or raisin bread, and serve together, sprinkled with cinnamon.

EGGS

GGS ARE A VERSATILE COOKING INGREDIENT that can be used to thicken, aerate, enrich, bind, coat, or glaze sweet and savory foods. They can be enjoyed as a complete food in themselves, whether fried, boiled, poached, or baked.

FRYING EGGS

Fried eggs need not be unhealthy, especially if you choose a light, unsaturated oil for frying. If your frying pan is of good quality or has a nonstick surface, you will need only a minimal amount of oil. To remove excess fat, drain eggs on a paper towel before serving.

COOKING OMELETS

Carefully fold one-third of omelet over filling

Enclosing a filling
To make a filled omelet, fold over one side to the middle using a spatula. Tip the frying pan, and slide the omelet down, then flip the other side over neatly to enclose the filling.

SHAPING FRIED EGGS

Pour egg into cutter

Using cookie cutters
Heat shaped cutters in a frying pan with oil. Pour an egg into each cutter, holding the cutter if necessary with a spatula, and fry. Run a knife around the inside of the cutter to remove the egg.

PREVENTING EGGS FROM STICKING
● **Using a clean pan** Start with a clean pan when frying eggs. If the pan has been used to cook other foods, such as bacon, the eggs may stick.

● **Choosing oil** Use a good-quality, light oil for frying eggs, such as sunflower or corn oil. Heat the oil, and cook the eggs over moderate heat.

HEALTHY TIP

Reducing fat
To "fry" an egg without fat, place a heatproof plate over a pan of boiling water. When the plate is very hot, break an egg onto it. The egg should set in about eight minutes.

USING A MICROWAVE
● **Frying on a browning dish**
Preheat a browning dish according to the manufacturer's instructions, and lightly brush the surface with oil. Break an egg onto the browning dish; the heat will brown the base of the egg. Prick the yolk with a toothpick to prevent it from bursting, and cover with a paper towel. Cook on High for about one minute.
● **Allowing standing time**
When cooking scrambled eggs in a microwave, remove them just before they set. Stir, and let stand for one minute. The eggs will finish cooking in the residual heat and have an even, creamy consistency.

SCRAMBLING EGGS

● **Lightening** For scrambled eggs that are light and fluffy, beat in a little carbonated water just before cooking.
● **Enriching** Add a dash of dry sherry to the beaten egg mixture before cooking to give a rich flavor to scrambled eggs.
● **Extending** To make scrambled eggs go further, add 1 tbsp (15 ml) fresh whole-wheat or white bread crumbs to each egg.

● **Adding extras** Stir finely sliced strips of smoked salmon or smoked ham into scrambled eggs as they cook. Alternatively, add finely chopped chervil or chives for a fresh, herby flavor.
● **Making sandwich fillings** If you are short of time to hard-cook eggs for sandwich fillings, scramble the eggs instead, then cool, and mix with mayonnaise and seasoning to taste.

BOILING AND POACHING EGGS

Boiling and poaching are quick and simple methods of cooking eggs, requiring no extra fat. With careful timing, it is easy to cook eggs to perfection. Eggs should be at room temperature prior to boiling to avoid cracking, so remove them from the refrigerator 30 minutes before cooking.

PREVENTING PROBLEMS
● **Preventing black rings** To prevent dark rings from forming around the yolks of hard-cooked eggs, drain them as soon as they are cooked. Crack the shells, and run under cold water to cool quickly.
● **Adding vinegar** If eggshells crack during boiling, add a tablespoonful of vinegar to the water to set the white.

POACHING EGGS
● **Using fresh eggs** Use very fresh eggs for poaching so that the whites will cling to the yolks. Keep the water at a low simmer during cooking for a smooth, soft-textured result.

BOILING EGGS

Prick shell carefully

Hold egg rounded end up

Preventing cracking
Before boiling eggs, prick the rounded end with a pin to allow the expanding air to escape during cooking and thus reduce the risk of cracking. Lower into cold water, and bring to a boil.

MARBLING BOILED EGGS

Using tea bags
Boil eggs for two minutes, remove each one, and tap with a spoon to crack the shell. Return to the pan with six tea bags, simmer for one minute, then cool. Remove shells, and eggs will be marbled.

BAKING EGGS

Eggs can be baked simply in ramekins with nothing more than salt and pepper, or used in more elaborate baked dishes such as soufflés and custards. A moderate oven temperature, which will prevent egg whites from becoming tough, is best for most baked egg recipes.

MAKING SOUFFLÉS

Cut just inside edge

Creating a "top-hat" effect
When making a hot soufflé, use a sharp knife to cut the mixture around the edge just inside the dish before cooking. This will encourage the mixture to rise evenly, creating a "top-hat" effect when the soufflé is cooked.

BAKING IN POTATOES

Sprinkle cheese on top of egg

Scooping out the flesh
Bake a large potato until tender, and cut a slice from the top. Scoop out the flesh from the center, and break an egg into it. Season with salt and pepper, cover with cheese, and continue baking until the egg is set.

PREPARING SOUFFLÉS
● **Preparing ahead** To prepare a hot soufflé in advance, make the mixture, and spoon it into a dish ready for baking. Cover with plastic wrap, and chill for two hours before baking.
● **Ensuring even rising** To dislodge any large air pockets in a soufflé mixture, give the dish a sharp tap on a counter before putting it into the oven.
● **Adding bread crumbs** For a good rise and a crisp, golden crust, sprinkle a greased soufflé dish with fine bread crumbs before adding the mixture.
● **Making soufflé tomatoes** For an unusual appetizer, slice the tops from large tomatoes, and scoop out the centers. Fill each with cheese soufflé mixture. Bake in a hot oven until risen.

MEAT AND POULTRY

W HEN CHOOSING A COOKING METHOD FOR MEAT OR POULTRY, consider the cut you have chosen. If you use the appropriate cooking method, it is possible to make even the toughest cuts of meat and poultry tender and succulent.

FLAVORING MEAT AND POULTRY

E ven for everyday meals, it is worth making the most of meat dishes by adding extra flavor with coatings, glazes, or tasty stuffings. In many cases, an accompaniment that adds flavor, such as stuffing or a sauce served with roast meat, helps make the meat go further.

USING COATINGS

● Sprinkling with spices Brush poultry skin with oil, and sprinkle with curry spices to give a rich, spicy, crisp skin.
● Making a glaze Mix equal quantities of Worcestershire sauce and tomato paste to make a spicy glaze. Brush the mixture over beef, lamb steaks, chops, or chicken pieces before grilling.
● Coating with crumbs Toss fresh bread crumbs in olive oil. Add plenty of chopped fresh herbs, and cover the meat skin with the mixture for the last 30 minutes of roasting.

FLAVORING CHICKEN

Adding lemon slices
To add flavor and keep a whole chicken moist during roasting, gently lift the breast skin, and tuck slices of lemon or orange underneath. Brush with oil, season, and place in a hot oven. Use unwaxed lemons if possible.

ADDING STUFFING

● Using mango To give an exotic flavor to a whole turkey or chicken, and to moisten the flesh, tuck pieces of diced mango into the neck end. The fruit will cook to a purée, sweetening the poultry juices.
● Flavoring packaged stuffing Mix a few chopped nuts, some dried fruits, or grated Parmesan cheese into packaged stuffing to add flavor.
● Serving separately Press extra stuffing into oiled ramekins, bake for the last 20–25 minutes of roasting, and serve with the meat.

FLAVORING HAM

● Studding with cloves To give a spicy flavor and an attractive finish to roast ham, score the fat surface, and press a clove into each cut.

Glazing with mustard
For a quick, delicious glaze for roast ham or pork, mix equal amounts of powdered mustard and brown sugar. Sprinkle the mixture over the fat surface for the final 30 minutes of cooking.

FLAVORING PORK

● Adding herbs Before tying up a roast of boned pork for cooking, tuck a handful of fresh sage leaves inside it for a rich flavor. Roast as usual.

Stuffing a pork chop
To add a special taste to a plain pork chop, cut small slits along the fat edge, and open them out to make pockets. Tuck dried apricots or prunes inside, then grill, fry, or bake the chop.

FLAVORING RED MEAT

● Adding garlic To flavor lamb, cut deep slits in the surface with a knife, and tuck a sliver of garlic into each slit. This will infuse a subtle flavor to the meat as it cooks.
● Marinating meat Immerse lamb or beef steaks in a marinade of olive oil, garlic, red or white wine, and herbs. Keep in the refrigerator for 2–3 days, then grill lightly.
● Spreading with juniper For a rich flavor, crush juniper berries to a paste with a little red wine. Spread over the surface of venison steaks or roasts before cooking.
● Drawing out flavor Season meat with salt just before cooking, since salt draws out the juices from meat.

STEWING MEAT AND POULTRY

Stewing is a slow, gentle cooking method, usually in a covered pan, and with cooking liquids partially covering the food. This method is especially suitable for tough cuts of meat, such as beef shanks (*osso buco*), which can become tender and juicy after long cooking in a stew.

THICKENING STEWS

It is best to thicken at the end of cooking, since thickened stews tend to stick and burn during cooking. If a stew contains too much liquid, reduce or thicken it by one of the following methods.

● **Reducing liquid** Reduce liquid by boiling it rapidly without a lid until the correct consistency is reached.
● **Using cornstarch** Blend some cornstarch with enough stock, water, or wine to make a thin paste, then stir it into the hot juices. Bring to a boil, and stir for two minutes.
● **Adding bread crumbs** To thicken stews and casseroles quickly, stir in a few spoonfuls of fresh, white bread crumbs.

ENHANCING STEWS

● **Replacing water** Use wine, tea, or beer in stews instead of water. These liquids will help tenderize tough meat.
● **Adding beets** Add a slice or two of beets to meat stews and casseroles to deepen the color of the sauce to a rich, golden brown.
● **Using herbs** Add tender herbs such as parsley or basil to stews and casseroles at the end of the cooking period, so they do not disintegrate during the long cooking.
● **Adjusting saltiness** To save a too-salty stew, peel a potato, and cut it into chunks. Add it to the pan, simmer until soft, then remove. Alternatively, dilute the stew with cream or a can of unsalted tomatoes.

TRADITIONAL TIP

Cooking lamb in coffee
Instead of using stock or water for a lamb stew or casserole, try the traditional method of adding black coffee. Coffee complements lamb surprisingly well, and makes the meat juices rich, flavorful, and dark.

BRAISING MEAT AND POULTRY

Braising is a slow, gentle method of cooking that often uses a bed of vegetables and little or no added liquid. Braising is suitable for tough, mature, or dry cuts of meat and poultry. Pot roasting is a similar method by which whole pieces are braised with a little liquid.

USING VEGETABLES

Place meat on top of vegetables

Increasing flavor

Braise meat on a bed of vegetables such as onions, celery, leeks, turnips, or carrots, which may be precooked if preferred. Brown the meat first to hold in juices before adding to the vegetables.

RETAINING JUICES

Cut paper to size of pot

Covering with paper

Press a buttered circle of baking parchment onto the meat before covering the pot with a lid. This will concentrate the cooking juices and help to prevent the food from steaming.

PREPARING MEAT

● **Browning meat** When browning meat prior to braising, fry a few pieces at a time, so that they cook quickly and the juices are sealed in.
● **Marinating game** Marinate mature game birds in red wine before braising to ensure tenderness and richness. Braise on a bed of celery or lentils.
● **Adding paprika** Sprinkle a little paprika over meat for simple braising to add color to the finished dish.
● **Using pork rind** Place a roast for pot roasting on a piece of pork rind, which will add flavor and prevent the meat from sticking to the pan.

GRILLING AND BARBECUING

Both grilling and barbecuing are quick, simple, and healthy methods of cooking that are suitable for most meat, fish, vegetables, and fruits. In each case, seal in the juices by cooking initially at a high heat. Then lower the heat to ensure that the food cooks thoroughly.

MAKING A HINGED WIRE RACK FOR BARBECUING

Cut wire ¼ in (2 cm) larger than hanger

Place food on one side of rack, then fold other side over

Keep long sides of hangers parallel

1 Make a hinged wire rack to turn delicate foods on a barbecue. Lay two wire coat hangers over a square piece of flexible, lightweight chicken wire. Trim the wire to shape.

2 Push the curved hanger handles firmly inward to form round handles. Fold the edges of the wire over the outer edges of the hangers, tucking in any sharp points.

3 Fold the hangers together at the join. Use the rack for cooking both sides of delicate foods, such as fish and hamburgers, which tend to collapse if turned with tongs.

USING BAMBOO SKEWERS
● **Preventing burning** To grill or barbecue foods on bamboo skewers, first soak the skewers in water for about 20 minutes. This will prevent them from burning during cooking.

ADDING WOOD CHIPS
● **Soaking** To extend the lives of hickory or oak wood chips, soak them in water for a few minutes. Then scatter the wood chips onto the coals to add aroma to the barbecue.

PREVENTING STICKING
● **Oiling a grill** Brush a barbecue grill with oil to prevent foods from sticking to it. Heat the grill to a high temperature before you place any food on it for cooking.

GRILLING SUCCESSFULLY
● **Using foil** Line the grill pan with a layer of foil, shiny side up, to reflect heat back onto food while it cooks. This will also make it easy to clean the pan after cooking.
● **Preheating a grill** Always preheat a grill for at least five minutes before cooking.
● **Absorbing fat** When grilling fatty meat, place a few pieces of stale bread in the bottom of the grill pan to absorb fat spills.
● **Turning meat** Use tongs, instead of a fork, for turning meat to prevent the loss of juices due to piercing.
● **Grilling low-fat foods** Brush low-fat foods, such as chicken, with oil to keep them moist.

TURNING FRANKFURTERS
Thread frankfurters from end to end

Using skewers
Thread frankfurters or sausages onto flat metal skewers to make it easy to turn them on a barbecue or grill. The skewers also conduct heat, which helps reduce the cooking time.

FRYING AND SAUTÉEING

Frying and sautéeing are quick methods of cooking that seal in food juices effectively. Control the heat carefully to cook foods evenly and prevent overheating. Delicate foods, such as fish fillets, may need to be coated before frying to give them a little extra protection from the heat.

CHECKING TEMPERATURE

Testing with bread
If you do not have a thermometer to check oil temperature, drop a piece of bread into the oil. When the bread browns, usually in about a minute, the oil is hot enough to add food for frying.

REUSING OIL

Paper towel retains food debris

Straining impurities
Before reusing oil left over from frying, filter out any food debris left in it. Line a sieve with an absorbent paper towel, hold the sieve over a bowl, and then pour the oil through it.

HEALTHY TIP

Brush pan with oil to prevent sticking

Using a ridged frying pan
To "dry" fry fatty foods such as bacon or sausages, use a heavy frying pan with a ridged base. The ridges hold the food above its own fatty juices, which can be poured off when cooking is finished.

COATING & BROWNING FRIED FOODS

● **Drying food** Dry food thoroughly by patting it with a paper towel before dipping it into batter for frying. This will help the batter cling to the food, coating it evenly.

● **Mixing butter and oil** To obtain a golden color when shallow-frying, use a mixture of half butter and half oil. The butter browns easily, and the oil prevents it from burning.

PREVENTING PROBLEMS

● **Controlling odors** Wear a shower cap when frying if you want to prevent smells from getting into your hair. After you have finished frying, remove the pan from the heat and cover. Let cool.
● **Avoiding spattering** Always dry food thoroughly to remove surface moisture before adding it to hot oil. If the oil starts to spatter, cover the pan with an upside-down metal colander or a wire-mesh pan guard.

USING A WOK EFFECTIVELY

Clip-on draining rack

Deep-frying in a wok
Use a wok for deep-frying foods, since the shape will allow you to use less oil than with conventional frying methods. If the wok has a curved base, use a wok stand to steady it.

● **Testing heat** To test whether a wok is hot enough before adding oil, hold the palm of your hand a few inches above the surface of the bottom of the pan until you feel the heat rising from it. Alternatively, wait until a wisp of smoke rises from the bottom of the empty wok.
● **Shaking the wok** When stir-frying food in a wok, keep shaking the pan and stirring the food constantly over a high heat. This will ensure that the food cooks evenly and quickly using minimal fat.
● **Using chopsticks** Use long wooden chopsticks to turn food cooked in a wok; they will stay cool to the touch.

SAFETY

● **Paying attention** Always stay near a pan of fried food while it is cooking.
● **Controlling temperature** Check the temperature of oil with a thermometer, and keep it just below smoking point.
● **Preventing fire** If fat catches fire, turn off the heat, and cover the pan. Do not use water to put out the fire.

ROASTING POULTRY

Poultry needs to be cooked thoroughly to kill all harmful bacteria. Chicken is ready when the juices run clear, not pink, when the flesh is pierced through the thickest part. Duck and squab are suitable for serving slightly less well cooked, with just a touch of pink in the flesh.

ROASTING SUCCESSFULLY
● **Using the cavity** Tuck a bunch of herbs, a lemon, or a whole onion inside the cavity of a chicken or turkey before roasting. The flavor will penetrate the meat, and will make tasty juices for gravy.
● **Resting poultry** Allow poultry to rest for about 20 minutes after roasting. This will make it easy to carve. Turn off the oven and leave the bird inside, or remove and cover with foil.
● **Using roasting bags** Cook poultry in a roasting bag to eliminate the need for basting. If you want to crisp up the skin, open the bag for the final 20 minutes of cooking.
● **Using a microwave** If you "roast" poultry in a microwave that does not have a browning option, sprinkle the bird with paprika to add color.

COVERING WITH BACON
● **Using bacon slices** Keep the breast of birds such as turkey, pheasant, or squab moist and tender by laying strips of bacon over the breast area.

Use flat of knife blade to stretch bacon

Maintaining shape
To retain the shape of small birds such as squab, wrap bacon slices around them. Stretch each slice first by pressing firmly along its length with a round-bladed knife to elongate it. Then wrap slices around the bird.

ROASTING TURKEY
● **Maintaining moisture** Roast a turkey breast-down for the first hour of cooking to keep it moist. Then turn the turkey over to finish cooking.

Place turkey on celery

Laying on a bed of celery
Before placing turkey in a roasting pan, cover the base of the pan with celery sticks, which act like a roasting rack. The vegetables will add flavor to the meat juices for a delicious gravy.

ROASTING DUCK
● **Crisping skin** For crisp duck skin, prick the skin all over with a fork, sprinkle with salt, and roast on a rack to lift the bird above the fatty juices.

Protecting wings
To prevent the wing ends of a duck from overcooking before the rest of the bird has finished cooking, wrap them in foil before roasting. Remove the foil for the final 30 minutes of cooking to allow the wings to brown.

ROASTING CHICKEN
● **Browning skin** To boost the golden-brown color of a roast chicken, add a pinch of ground turmeric to the oil or butter that you use for basting.

Flavoring with wine
Pour about ⅔ cup (150 ml) red or dry white wine into a large, clean, empty food can. Sit a chicken on the can, then stand in a roasting pan. The wine will flavor meat juices that collect in the can.

TRADITIONAL TIP

Wrapping in cheesecloth
Instead of covering a large chicken or turkey with foil for roasting, dip a double layer of cheesecloth into melted butter or oil, and lay it over the bird's skin. The cheesecloth will allow the skin to brown and become crisp during cooking without trapping steam.

ROASTING MEAT

For a successful meat roast, it is important to place it in a hot oven at the start of cooking to seal in the tasty juices. Reduce the heat once the meat starts to brown. Remove chilled meat from the refrigerator 20 minutes before roasting, so that it comes to room temperature.

ROASTING FATTY MEAT

Rub powder into surface

Using dry mustard
When roasting a cut of beef or pork with a high fat content, cover the surface with dry mustard powder. This will counteract the fattiness and add flavor to the gravy.

CHECKING TEMPERATURE

Insert thermometer away from bone

Using a thermometer
Insert a meat thermometer into the thickest part of the meat, avoiding the bone. Bone conducts heat more quickly than flesh, so it may give a false reading. Leave the thermometer in during cooking.

PREPARATION BASICS

● **Choosing meat** The best cuts of beef, veal, or lamb will be labeled "Prime;" the best pork is "US No. 1." Prime meat may be difficult to find in grocery stores; fortunately the next grade of meat, "Choice," is also good.
● **Noting weights** Always take note of the weight and the cut of meat before discarding the label.
● **Trimming meat** Cut away excess fat from meat before roasting. Prime and Choice meat should still have sufficient marbling to keep the roast moist.

PREPARING ACCOMPANIMENTS

Roast meat and poultry are often associated with standard accompaniments – roast pork is usually accompanied by apple sauce, for example. There are no set rules, however, and trimmings can be varied to suit your taste, and to add extra color and texture to dishes.

SAVING TIME
● **Thickening gravy** To thicken the consistency of gravy quickly, whip in 1–2 tbsp (15–30 ml) instant potato buds.
● **Lowering fat content** A fat separator is a timesaving tool if you make roasts regularly. After roasting meat or poultry, pour pan juices into the separator, and pour off the rich, lower-fat juices. Discard the remaining fat, and use only the juices when making gravy.
● **Microwaving cranberries** Cook 2 cups (250 g) cranberries in 1 cup (225 ml) water on High until the water and juices are boiling. Continue to cook on High for a further five minutes, until the berries begin to burst. Sweeten with sugar to your liking.

IMPROVING GRAVY

Skim surface with paper towel

Skimming off fat
To remove a layer of fat from meat or poultry gravy, drag an absorbent paper towel lightly across the surface of the liquid. Repeat, if necessary, to remove any traces of fat that are left before serving the gravy.

ADDING EXTRAS
● **Flavoring gravy** Stir a generous dash of brandy or port into plain gravy to pep up the flavor for serving with a special roast. Boil for two minutes before serving.
● **Making stuffing balls** When stuffing a roast of meat or poultry, make more stuffing than you need. Roll the extra into balls, and place in the juices around the roast for the last 20 minutes of cooking. Alternatively, put extra stuffing in a separate pan, add pan juices, then bake with the roast for the last 20 minutes.
● **Glazing a roast** Just before serving, brush the surface of a roast with warmed apricot or cranberry jelly to give it an attractive, sweet-tasting glaze.

FISH AND SHELLFISH

F ISH COOKS SIMPLY AND QUICKLY, and in its many forms it can be cooked by most methods. Whole fish cooked on the bone has the best flavor. Filleted fish is versatile enough to be fried, poached, grilled, or even barbecued.

ADDING FLAVOR

M ost types of fresh fish need little flavor enhancement, but it is a good idea to use different accents to stimulate appetite and add variety. With a squeeze of lemon and a sprinkling of herbs, or with unusual marinades or glazes, fish can take on new dimensions.

FLAVORING OIL

Sliced ginger

Ginger

Adding fresh ginger
Before shallow-frying or stir-frying fish, add a few thin slices of fresh ginger to the oil for extra flavor. Stir over medium heat for 3–4 minutes, then remove, and cook the fish.

MARINATING RAW FISH
● **Choosing a marinade** Use an oil-based marinade for white fish to moisten and add flavor. Use an acidic marinade, based on citrus juice or vinegar, for oily fish to offset its richness.
● **Using yogurt** Spread a yogurt-based marinade, such as a tandoori mixture, over fish that is to be grilled. This will seal in the juices and produce a spicy low-fat crust.
● **"Cooking" in a marinade** Cut about 1 lb 2 oz (500 g) fresh, white fish into thin strips, and add the juice of four limes or lemons. Chop and stir in an onion, a chili, and a clove of garlic. Chill for 3–4 hours. The marinade will "cook" the fish, and it will be ready to eat cold.

FLAVORING FISH

Dribble marinade over warm fish

Seasoning with marinade
Slash the flesh of small, whole fish at intervals before you grill or fry them. Flavor with a marinade of white wine and herbs or spices after cooking. Let stand until cold before serving.

FLAVORING OILY FISH
● **Using mustard** Spread herring or mackerel fillets with a thin layer of mustard. Then roll the fish in raw oatmeal or rolled oats before frying.

Citrus slices layered on fish

Sandwiching fillets
Add flavor to fillets of mackerel or herring by sandwiching the fillets together with lemon, lime, or orange slices and thyme sprigs. Bake in the oven, or tie firmly with string and grill.

USING COATINGS
● **Mixing with herbs** Instead of coating white fish fillets in plain bread crumbs, stir in a few crumbled dried herbs, curry spices, or crushed, dried chilies.
● **Using coconut** Dip pieces of monkfish or other white, firm fish in lightly beaten egg. Then toss the pieces in grated fresh coconut before frying. This will give the fish an unusual, nut-flavored covering.
● **Adding sesame** For extra flavor, add 1 tsp (5 ml) sesame oil to the egg you use for coating fish. Stir sesame seeds into bread crumbs to add flavor and texture to a coating.

FLAVORING WITH HERBS
● **Adding herbs** Tuck sprigs of fresh herbs into the cavity of a whole fish before cooking, so that the flavor of the herbs penetrates the flesh of the fish.

Baking with fennel
Bake whole fish such as sea bass on a bed of sliced fennel stalks, which will add a subtle flavor. Arrange the fennel in an even layer in a buttered ovenproof dish, then lay the fish over it.

GRILLING AND BARBECUING

Most whole fish, particularly oily fish, cook well on a barbecue or grill and need little more than an occasional brushing with oil to prevent them from drying out or sticking. Delicate fish fillets and steaks need careful basting and turning, or wrap them in foil.

GRILLING SUCCESSFULLY
● **Making kebabs** When making fish kebabs, add other quick-cooking ingredients, such as mushrooms or cherry tomatoes, which will cook in the same amount of time as the fish.
● **Slashing flesh** When cooking a whole fish or thick fillets, slash the thickest parts of the flesh to help the heat penetrate evenly, and speed up grilling.
● **Turning fish** Place a layer of oiled foil over the grill rack so that the fish will turn easily without sticking. Alternatively, grill fish steaks on a preheated cookie sheet, so that there is no need to turn them.
● **Preventing sticking** Preheat the grill rack to a high heat before cooking to seal in juices and prevent sticking.

GRILLING FISH FILLETS
● **Positioning fish** To prevent damage to the flesh, brush fish skin and grill rack with oil, and place fish skin side down.

Using skewers
Thread small fish fillets onto wooden skewers for easy turning on a barbecue, and to prevent the fish from breaking up. Soak the skewers in water before use to keep them from burning.

GRILLING SHELLFISH
● **Keeping moist** Wrap shelled mussels or scallops in slices of bacon to keep them moist. Grill after threading onto skewers.

Butter prevents oysters from drying out

Grilling fresh oysters
Place fresh oysters in the deep halves of their shells on a grill pan. Top each with a spoonful of herb butter, and scatter with bread crumbs. Cook on a hot grill pan or under a broiler until bubbling.

ROASTING AND BAKING

Roasting fish at a high temperature seals in flavors and produces tender, moist flesh. Baking in foil or baking parchment bundles prevents the fish from drying out and allows it to cook in its own juices, which can be added to a sauce or poured over the fish before serving.

COOKING FISH IN BUNDLES

Buttered parchment

1 Bake small, whole fish or fish fillets in bundles. Cut a heart-shaped piece of waxed baking parchment to enclose the fish. Butter the center, and place the fish on one side. Add any flavorings.

Follow shape, tucking in ends with fingertips

2 Fold the other side of the paper over the fish, and tuck and fold along the edge, starting from the rounded end. Finish at the pointed end with a double fold to secure the bundle. Bake on a cookie sheet.

PRESERVING FLAVOR
● **Wrapping in foil** When baking a whole fish such as salmon, wrap it loosely in foil so that the fish stews in its own juices, keeping it moist.
● **Making crispy skin** Baste the skin of sea bass or trout with butter, and season. Roast the fish at a high temperature – about 450°F (230°C).
● **Baking in salt** Place a whole fish on a layer of rock salt. Completely cover it with salt to seal in the juices, then sprinkle with water. Bake at 400°F (200°C) until the salt is hard and dry, then break it with a hammer, discard the salt and skin, and serve.

FRYING

Frying is traditionally a popular method of cooking fish, and need not greatly increase the fat content of your diet. If you heat the oil before adding the fish, an outer crust will form instantly and hardly any fat will be absorbed, leaving the flesh tender and moist.

WORKING WITH OIL

● **Choosing oil** Use good-quality, clean oil for frying fish, since delicate fish flavors can be destroyed by strongly flavored or tainted oil. Lightly flavored oils, such as corn or sunflower, are ideal.

● **Heating the oil** For a crisp coating, make sure that the oil is hot enough before frying fish. For deep frying, the temperature of the oil should be 375°F (190°C).

● **Frying from frozen** To deep-fry fish from frozen, heat the oil to approximately 350°F (180°C), which will allow the inside of the fish to cook before the coating browns.

FRYING SHELLFISH

● **Leaving tails** When peeling shrimp for frying, remove the heads, legs, and skins, but leave the tails on. Use the tail to hold a shrimp when dipping it into the coating mixture.

FRYING JUMBO SHRIMP

Roll shrimp in seasoned cornstarch

Coating in cornstarch
Prepare jumbo shrimp for frying by dusting gently with seasoned cornstarch, then dipping in lightly beaten egg white. The cooked shrimp will have a light, crisp coating and remain juicy inside.

MAKING BATTER

Adding beer
To make a light, crisp batter for coating fish, substitute beer for the liquid, or add a tablespoonful of brandy. Alternatively, lighten the batter by folding a beaten egg white into the mixture just before coating and frying the fish.

ADDING EXTRA FLAVOR

● **Combining oils** When shallow-frying fish fillets, add a subtle, Asian flavor by mixing 1 tbsp (15 ml) sesame oil with a lightly flavored oil, such as sunflower, before cooking.

COATING & WRAPPING

● **Mussels** Dip mussels in a light batter and deep-fry in hot oil for about 30 seconds.

● **Fish fillets** When coating delicate fish fillets, dip first in flour, then in beaten egg. Coat evenly with fine bread crumbs to seal in flavor and prevent the fish from breaking up.

● **Whole fish** To coat small, whole fish, such as whitebait or sardines, in seasoned flour, place the flour and fish in a plastic bag, then shake well to coat evenly.

● **Peeled shrimp** For a light, crisp, golden coating, wrap peeled shrimp in thin strips of phyllo dough, enclosing all but the tail, before frying.

PREPARING SQUID

Diamond pattern will look attractive after cooking

Scoring flesh
Before frying the pouch flesh of squid, score its smooth surface lightly with a sharp knife, making a diamond pattern. This method of scoring the flesh will help the heat penetrate the flesh evenly during cooking.

PREVENTING SPITTING

● **Using a colander** If fish begins to spatter during frying, overturn a colander on top of the pan. This will prevent the grease from escaping, but let steam out.

STIR-FRYING

● **Choosing seafood** Choose a firm-textured, meaty piece of seafood, such as monkfish or squid, for stir-frying; softer-textured seafood breaks up.

● **Using delicate fish** To stir-fry delicate fish, such as cod, coat the pieces in cornstarch before cooking. Shake the pan instead of stirring it to keep the fish pieces whole.

● **Cooking small batches** To keep the heat high enough to seal in the juices, stir-fry a small quantity of fish at a time.

● **Keeping pieces separate** Toss pieces of squid in a little sesame oil before stir-frying to help keep them separate.

POACHING FISH

Poaching is a classic method of cooking fish and also one of the most healthy, since the fish is cooked in liquid with no fat added. Poaching is most suitable for cooking whole fish, such as salmon, and delicate white fish fillets, which require gentle, even cooking.

POACHING PERFECTLY

● **Handling fish gently** To poach a delicate fish, place it in warm liquid that just covers it. Slowly bring the liquid up to barely simmering.

● **Serving fish cold** To cook a whole fish or fish fillets to be served cold, bring the liquid up to simmering and steam gently for one minute. Turn off the heat, and allow the residual heat to cook the fish.

● **Using stock** Give your guests slotted spoons to poach fish at the table in a flavorful stock. Mongolian- or Chinese-style steamers or a fondue set can be used to cook the fish. Serve the stock as a soup.

COOKING LARGE WHOLE FISH

Fitting in a large pan
If you do not have a special pot in which to cook a large, whole fish, accommodate the fish in a large saucepan by curling it gently to fit inside the pan, with its backbone facing upward. Serve on a round platter.

Using a dishwasher
Double-wrap a salmon or any other large fish in foil. Seal thoroughly. Place it on the upper rack of an empty dishwasher. Run a wash cycle at 150°F (65°C), without prewash or dry. Remove, and cool in the foil.

STEAMING FISH

Steaming is a healthy method of cooking, suitable for fish fillets or thin steaks. The main rule is that the fish should not touch the water. You do not need a steamer, but if you steam fish often, it is useful to have a steaming compartment that fits over a saucepan.

COMBINING FOODS

Cooking over potatoes
When steaming fish, make economical use of energy by placing the fish in a steamer over a pot of boiling potatoes. Cover and simmer for 10-15 minutes, depending on thickness.

STEAMING SUCCESSFULLY

● **Steaming large fish** To steam a large, whole fish that will not fit into a steamer, pour a shallow depth of water into a deep roasting pan. Place the fish, covered tightly with foil, on a rack in the pan above the water level, and simmer on the stovetop for five minutes per 1 lb (450 g) weight.

● **Using individual baskets** Use Chinese-style steamer baskets, which stack easily, to steam and then to serve individual portions of fish.

● **Topping off liquid** Always keep a kettle of water close to boiling point while you are steaming foods, so that when topping off the liquid in the steamer, the added water will not lower the temperature.

BRIGHT IDEA

Cooking on a plate
Place small fish fillets or steaks between two heatproof plates, and cook over a pan of rapidly boiling water. The fish will cook evenly and quickly in its juices. Pour the juices over the fish to serve.

SOUPS, STOCKS, AND SAUCES

M AKING YOUR OWN SOUPS, STOCKS, AND SAUCES is rewarding, since you can make nutritious and inexpensive dishes that are far superior to anything you could buy, using simple, fresh ingredients and a few basic cooking skills.

MAKING SOUPS AND STOCKS

T he basis of a good homemade soup is a flavorful stock. Bouillon cubes save time, but it is relatively easy and inexpensive to make your own stock using leftover vegetables or the bones from a roast. There is an infinite variety of soups that you can create in your kitchen.

MAKING SOUPS

● **Sweating vegetables** Before adding stock, cook vegetables first by "sweating" in a tightly covered pan with a little butter. Add a few tablespoonfuls of wine or dry sherry for extra flavor. Cook over low heat for one hour, shaking now and then to prevent sticking.
● **Using lettuce leaves** Instead of discarding the large, tough outer leaves of lettuce, shred them like cabbage, and cook in a stock. Purée when soft, and stir in a little cream.
● **Using leftovers** Make a quick vichyssoise with cooked potatoes. Fry an onion or a leek until soft, then purée it with the potato and vegetable stock. Add cream to taste.

PURÉEING VEGETABLES

Press vegetables through sieve

Using a ladle
To purée cooked vegetables by hand for adding to soups, put them into a large sieve over a bowl, and squash them with a ladle. This is quicker than using a wooden spoon for pressing, and requires less effort.

THICKENING SOUPS

Stir in a small amount at a time

Using a beurre manié
To thicken a soup quickly and easily, mix together equal amounts of butter and all-purpose flour to a thick paste. Drop small spoonfuls of the mixture into the hot soup, and stir over the heat until sufficiently thickened.

ADDING VARIETY

● **Using spices** Stir mild curry powder into carrot or parsnip soup to add a warm flavor.
● **Adding texture** Before puréeing vegetables for a soup, set aside a ladleful of the cooked, chopped vegetables to add texture to the soup.
● **Crumbling cheese** Liven up creamed or canned soups by stirring in some crumbled blue cheese before serving.
● **Making pistou** Crush three garlic cloves with 2 tbsp (30 ml) pine nuts, a handful of basil, and 2 tbsp (30 ml) olive oil. Stir the mixture into vegetable soups to taste.

USING STOCKS

Ice cubes   *Fat*

Stock

Removing fat
To remove fat from the surface of stock effectively, add a few ice cubes. When the fat has set around the ice, lift it off.

● **Cooking on low heat** To make a really rich, clear stock, simmer it slowly over very low heat. Boiling a stock tends to give a cloudy appearance.
● **Reducing stock** To store cooked stock, reduce it first by boiling it in an uncovered pan until it is very thick and syrupy. The stock will then set when cooled, and this will keep longer than a liquid.
● **Using leftovers** Add leftover vegetables, trimmings, or peelings to stock for flavor. Do not use potatoes, since they will make the stock cloudy.

MAKING EGG-BASED SAUCES

Sauces incorporating eggs are made either by creating a thick emulsion, as in mayonnaise or hollandaise, or by gentle cooking, as in the case of custard or cream sauce. Egg-based sauces take longer to make than many other sauces, but their rich, creamy textures are unmatched.

CORRECTING FAULTS
● **Adding ice** If you overheat hollandaise sauce, and it is just starting to curdle, stir in an ice cube to cool it quickly.
● **Rewhisking hollandaise** To smooth a curdled hollandaise sauce, add it drop by drop to a spoonful of vinegar in a clean bowl, whipping hard until the sauce rethickens.
● **Using egg yolk** If mayonnaise separates, beat a fresh egg yolk in a clean bowl, and whip in the mayonnaise drop by drop until the mixture thickens.
● **Adding cornstarch** If a custard sauce begins to curdle, plunge the base of the pan into cold water, then push the sauce through a sieve. Whip a teaspoonful of cornstarch into the sauce, and reheat gently without boiling until thickened.

MAKING MAYONNAISE
● **Reducing fat** For a white, low-fat mayonnaise, use whole eggs instead of just the yolks, or mix the mayonnaise with plain yogurt in equal parts.

Add leaves to color mayonnaise

Using a blender
Put all the mayonnaise ingredients except the oil into a blender. Run the machine, and add the oil in a thin stream until the sauce thickens. Then add any extra ingredients, such as watercress.

MAKING HOLLANDAISE
● **Using a microwave** Heat 7 tbsp (100 g) butter in a large cup on High, and whip in two egg yolks and flavorings. Cook on Medium for one minute.

Bowl placed over unheated burner

Avoiding curdling
To make hollandaise sauce without a double boiler, prepare it in a bowl placed in a roasting pan containing simmering water. Make sure that the bowl is not directly above the heat source.

MAKING OTHER SAUCES

There are numerous different types of sauce in addition to custard and the emulsions produced by traditional sauce-making methods. Flour-thickened mixtures are useful, and sauces made from simple purées, salsas, and cream reductions provide interesting alternatives.

MAKING SALSAS
Salsas are an essential part of Mexican cuisine, adding powerful flavors and rich colors to simple meals.

● **Saving time** Place chilies, garlic, onions, tomatoes, and seeded peppers in a food processor. Pulse until finely chopped for a *salsa cruda*.
● **Mixing fruits** Combine finely chopped fresh mango, pawpaw, and chilies to serve with grilled fish or chicken.
● **Creating mild flavors** To reduce the strong flavors of raw garlic and onions, simmer for 5–8 minutes before use.

WORKING WITH SAUCES
● **Adding cornstarch** To thicken a smooth sauce, blend 1 tsp (5 ml) cornstarch into 2 tsp (10 ml) cold water, add to the sauce, and stir over moderate heat until thickened.
● **Correcting lumpy sauces** If a sauce or gravy has become lumpy, pour it into a food processor, and process until smooth. Alternatively, press the sauce through a sieve.
● **Making purées** Use smooth purées of vegetables such as peppers for colorful, simple, low-fat sauces. Grill the peppers to remove the skins, then purée in a processor.

TRADITIONAL TIP

Deglazing a pan
Add wine, stock, or cream to the concentrated juices or sediment left in a roasting pan after cooking meat or poultry. Bring to a boil, and stir well.

GRAINS, PASTA, AND LEGUMES

THE WIDE VARIETY OF GRAINS, PASTA, AND LEGUMES now available from all over the world presents many choices for healthy meals that are easy to prepare. They form the basis of substantial main dishes and delicious side dishes.

GRAINS

Grains are usually boiled or steamed, either on their own or combined with a variety of other ingredients in dishes such as pilafs or risottos. Whole grains take longer to cook than processed white grains, but most varieties of grain will cook within about 30 minutes.

REMOVING STARCH

Rinsing basmati rice
Basmati rice needs to be rinsed thoroughly to keep the grains separate. Place it in a bowl of cold water, and swirl the rice around by hand. Drain, and repeat until the water is clear.

COOLING COOKED RICE

Using a wooden spoon
To cool cooked rice quickly for use in salads, drain through a sieve and place over a bowl. Prod the rice at intervals with a wooden spoon handle to release the steam and heat.

STEAMING COUSCOUS

Lining a colander
If you do not have a couscous steamer, line a metal sieve with a piece of cheesecloth, and place it over a pan of boiling water. Pour the couscous into the sieve and cover. Steam until tender.

TRADITIONAL TIP

Making a stomach settler
As a cure for an upset stomach, boil white rice without having rinsed it first, then strain off the starchy cooking liquid. Allow the liquid to cool, then give it to the patient to drink.

COOKING PERFECT RICE
● **Presoaking rice** Reduce the cooking time of rice and other grains by soaking them first in cold water for 30 minutes.
● **Cooking on a low heat** When cooking glutinous rice, use a large pan, and simmer on the lowest heat possible. Keep the lid on during cooking, and let stand for 10 minutes after draining.
● **Using a microwave** Place 1 cup (250 g) white rice in a large bowl with 2 cups (450 ml) boiling water. Cook on High for nine minutes. Cook brown rice for about 15–20 minutes.
● **Forking rice** Fluff up cooked rice by separating the grains with a fork before serving.

ADDING VARIETY
● **Cooking in stock** Add extra flavor to plain boiled grains by cooking them in a rich meat, chicken, or vegetable stock rather than water.
● **Coloring rice** If you do not have saffron for tinting rice and risottos, stir in a pinch of turmeric after cooking.
● **Using coconut milk** Simmer long-grain rice in coconut milk to accompany Asian dishes. Use about 1½ cups (400 ml) coconut milk to ¾ cup (200 g) rice, and cook until the liquid is absorbed.
● **Using pesto** Replace the butter or olive oil in cooked polenta with a roughly equal quantity of pesto sauce.

PASTA

There are only a few simple rules to follow when cooking fresh or dried pasta. Cook it lightly, in plenty of rapidly boiling water, until it is *al dente* – which translates literally as "to the tooth." This means the pasta is tender to the bite, but still offers a slight resistance in the center.

COOKING LONG PASTA

Feed pasta in as it softens

Feeding into a pan
To fit long spaghetti into a small pan of boiling water, hold it in a bunch, and put one end into the water. As the ends of the pieces soften, bend the pasta slightly, and push in the rest gradually.

COOKING STUFFED PASTA

Skimmer will not split pasta

Using a skimmer
To lift cooked, filled pasta such as ravioli out of water without damaging or bursting it, use a flat, metal skimmer or a flat, slotted, draining spoon. Toss in oil or sauce to prevent sticking.

COLORING PASTA

To add color and flavor when making pasta dough, mix in additional ingredients.

- **Tomato** Add 2 tsp (10 ml) tomato paste per egg to the beaten eggs, and stir well.
- **Spinach** Thaw ¼ cup (50 g) frozen, chopped spinach per egg. Squeeze well before adding to the beaten eggs.
- **Saffron** For rich, golden pasta, add a pinch of ground saffron to the flour.
- **Beets** Stir 1 tbsp (15 ml) cooked, puréed beet per egg to the pasta dough.

LEGUMES

Peas, beans, and lentils are a valuable source of protein and are versatile enough to be used in all kinds of dishes, including casseroles, pâtés, dals, and salads. Dried beans take some time to cook, but the cooking is simple, and they are less expensive than canned varieties.

COOKING TIMES

Most legumes need to be soaked in cold water for at least 4–8 hours. Alternatively, soak in boiling water for about one hour. The following cooking times are a rough guide only; recommended times may vary from one type to another, so check carefully.

- Split lentils: 15–20 minutes.
- Whole lentils, aduki beans, mung beans, split peas: 25–30 minutes.
- Black-eyed peas, Great Northern beans, lima beans, peas: 45 minutes.
- Black beans, white kidney beans, red kidney beans: about one hour.
- Pinto beans, chickpeas: 1¼ hours.
- Butter beans, fava beans: 1½ hours.

COOKING BEANS
- **Seasoning** Season beans toward the end of their cooking time, since salt can prevent them from softening.
- **Cooling** If you are cooking beans to serve cold, cool them in their cooking water rather than drying in a colander. This stops their skins from splitting.
- **Pressure cooking** If you are using a pressure cooker, cook beans on High for a third of their normal cooking time.

DIGESTIVE AID

Boil dried, soaked beans vigorously for 10 minutes, then drain and start again with fresh water. This process reduces the "gassiness" associated with eating beans. Simmer gently until the beans are tender.

PREPARING SNACKS
- **Making a dip** Mash cooked, drained butter beans well with a fork. Add crushed garlic, chili paste, and olive oil to make a rich, spicy dip. Serve with vegetable sticks.

Flour seasoned with ground pepper

Making chickpea nibbles
Mix cooked or drained canned chickpeas with seasoned whole-wheat flour and crushed garlic. Fry in a little butter and oil over high heat until crisp and golden. Serve with cocktails.

DESSERTS

A HOT OR COLD DESSERT rounds off a meal nicely. Whatever level of skill you possess, and however much time you have to prepare, it is always possible to make a delicious dessert that will bring the meal to a satisfying end.

BAKING PIES AND TARTS

There is no more memorable way of enjoying an abundance of ripe fruits in season than by baking them in a golden, homemade pastry case. Alternatively, dairy products or many pantry ingredients can be used to produce a quick, convenient filling for a delicious dessert.

PREPARING FILLINGS
● **Dicing cheese** Add tiny cubes of a tangy, mature cheese to complement a sweet apple filling in a pie.
● **Creating a quick filling** Make a festive dessert by mixing fresh seedless grapes with a few spoonfuls of store-bought mincemeat. Spoon into a pastry shell, and bake until hot. Serve with whipped cream.
● **Glazing fruits** To glaze and sweeten fresh fruits for a colorful tart or pie filling, warm a few spoonfuls of seedless raspberry jelly with a squeeze of lemon or orange juice in a pan. Brush the glaze over the fruits.

MAKING TOPPINGS

Pinch phyllo into ruffles

Using phyllo dough
Instead of laying sheets of pastry or phyllo flat on top of a fruit filling, crumple them slightly for a "chiffon" effect. Brush with butter, bake as usual, and sprinkle with confectioners' sugar.

FRUIT TART TOPPINGS

● **Marshmallows** Arrange marshmallows to cover the fruits. Grill until golden.
● **Marzipan** Cut marzipan into dice, and scatter over the tart. Bake or grill until golden.
● **Almond crumble** Mix equal amounts of ground almonds, brown or raw sugar, and flaked almonds. Sprinkle the mixture over the fruits before baking to form a golden crust.
● **Meringue** Whip one egg white until stiff, then whip in ¼ cup (55 g) superfine sugar. Pipe a meringue lattice over the fruits, and bake for a delicious, decorative topping.

MONEY-SAVING TIP

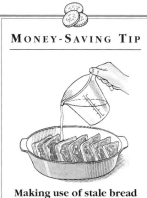

Making use of stale bread
Spread slices of stale bread with butter and marmalade or jam, and layer in an ovenproof dish. Add two eggs beaten in 1¼ cups (300 ml) milk. Bake in a moderate oven.

ADDING EXTRA FLAVOR

Distribute coconut evenly

Sprinkling coconut
To add extra flavor to a fruit tart or pie, sprinkle a layer of dried coconut over the base before adding the filling. This will also help prevent the base from becoming soggy.

ADDING VARIETY
● **Baking upside-down tarts** Use a cake pan to make an upside-down fruit tart. Butter and sugar the base, add the fruits, and top with rolled-out pastry. Bake and invert.
● **Making sweet pizza** Roll out puff pastry or bread dough, and top with slices of fruits such as apples, pears, or plums. Sprinkle with brown sugar and spices, dot with butter, and bake in a hot oven until bubbling and golden.
● **Latticing phyllo strips** Cut phyllo dough into long strips with scissors to make a quick lattice for a pie or tart. Use two sheets together, brushed with butter, for the best effect.

MAKING OTHER HOT DESSERTS

Hot desserts are warming and satisfying, and they can be very versatile. Whip up lemon pancakes for an informal occasion, or try flambéed crêpes suzettes for a dinner party. Add variety to puddings by stirring in dried fruits, spices, an extract such as vanilla, or citrus-fruit zest.

USING BATTER

● **Adding cocoa** To make delicious chocolate-flavored pancakes, replace 2 tsp (10 ml) of the quantity of flour used in the recipe with cocoa powder.

● **Baking easy tarts** To make a quick and easy fruit dessert, pour waffle batter over sugared fruit slices in a heated, greased cake pan. Bake in a hot oven until golden.

● **Making a light batter** For a crisp, light fritter batter, separate the eggs, and mix the yolks with the flour. Whip the egg whites until stiff, and fold into the mixture. Use the batter to coat sliced apple, pineapple, or banana.

● **Deep-frying pancakes** Place a spoonful of fruit in the centers of cooked pancakes. Fold the pancakes into squares, dip in batter and deep-fry until golden. Dust with sugar, and serve with fruit sauce.

FINISHING SOUFFLÉS

Caramelizing the top
Give a hot, sweet soufflé a golden, caramelized finish on top by sprinkling with confectioners' sugar at the end of cooking. Sprinkle quickly, and bake for 4–5 minutes to brown.

USING WAFFLE BATTER

Making beignets
Use waffle batter for making beignets as an alternative to waffles. Carefully drop spoonfuls of the batter into hot oil, and fry until puffy and golden. Serve the beignets topped with maple syrup or vanilla sugar.

UNUSUAL DESSERTS

● **Making Baked Alaska** Lightly brown crumpled phyllo dough under the broiler. Use to top scoops of ice cream, and cover with warm chocolate sauce.

USING A MICROWAVE

● **Baking apples** Peel and core apples, then fill with a pat of butter and brown sugar. Bake, covered, in the microwave until soft. Brown under the broiler if desired.

● **Cooking puddings** Use a very large, deep container to cook milk-based puddings in a microwave, since the milk will rise up the sides.

● **Setting meringue** Cook a meringue topping on a dessert in a microwave to save time. Scatter toasted nuts over the surface if it is too pale.

● **Melting chocolate** To melt chocolate in the microwave, break it up and heat for 1–2 minutes per ounce (25 g). Remove and stir until smooth.

FLAVORING MILK

Citrus zester

Adding lemon zest
To lift the flavor of a plain pudding such as rice or bread, use a citrus zester to grate a few strips of lemon zest over the pudding, and stir to mix in evenly before cooking. Orange zest can also be used.

● **Flaming cherries** When flaming Cherries Jubilee, be sure to use cherry-flavored liqueur as the alcohol. It will intensify the flavor of the fruit.

QUICK DESSERTS

● **Filling croissants** Cut open warmed croissants, and fill with hot stewed plums, then scatter with flaked almonds.

● **Pan-frying bananas** Peel and thickly slice some bananas, and sauté in a little butter and brown sugar for two minutes. Sprinkle with orange juice and a dash of rum.

● **Grilling soft fruits** Sprinkle kirsch over frozen, mixed fruits in an ovenproof dish. Top with mascarpone cheese and brown sugar, and broil until hot and bubbling.

● **Making fruit compotes** Warm a mixture of canned fruits, their juices, grated lemon zest, and cinnamon in a pan. Serve with whipped cream.

COLD DESSERTS

There are several types of cold dessert, from fresh, light fruit salads and mousses to rich, creamy egg custards, cheesecakes, and filled meringues. They all have the advantage that they can be made in advance, leaving you free to prepare and serve other courses.

PREVENTING PROBLEMS

● **Preventing skin** Lay a piece of waxed paper over puddings and custards as they cool, to prevent a skin from forming on the surface.
● **Slicing meringue** Prevent a soft meringue dessert from sticking when being sliced, either by buttering the knife blade first, or by dipping the knife into boiling water.
● **Adding sparkle** Pep up the flavor of an oversweetened or plain fruit salad by adding a splash of sparkling wine just before the dessert is served.
● **Making crème caramel** Rinse the dish being used in hot water before pouring very hot caramel into it. This will help prevent the dish from cracking.

FINISHING CRÈME BRÛLÉE

Spray water evenly over surface of sugar topping

Caramelizing sugar
For a perfect, golden caramel topping on crème brûlée, sprinkle the set custard with a thick layer of superfine sugar, and spray with a fine water mister. Caramelize under a hot broiler.

MAKING PAVLOVAS

Shape meringue on plate

Preventing breakage
Spoon the meringue mixture for a pavlova onto a ceramic, ovenproof pizza plate so that it can be baked and served in the same dish. You will thus avoid cracking it while transferring it.

GELATIN-SET DESSERTS

Gelatin is the most common setting agent used in cooking. It is available in powdered form and should be thoroughly dissolved in hot water before use. Agar-agar, a vegetarian setting agent made from seaweed, is used in much the same way.

USING GELATIN

● **Dissolving gelatin** Always add gelatin to hot liquid to dissolve. Do not add the liquid to the gelatin.
● **Preparing fruits** Cook fresh pineapple or kiwi fruit before using in gelatin-set desserts; this destroys the enzyme that keeps gelatin from setting.
● **Eating outdoors** If serving a dessert outdoors in warm weather, slightly increase the amount of gelatin used. Add an extra 1 tsp (5 ml) gelatin for every envelopeful.
● **Turning out set desserts** Wet a mold for a thin gelatin mixture such as jelly to make turning out easy. Lightly oil a mold for a thick mixture.

DECORATING MOLDS

Gelatin holds fruit in place when set

Layering with fruits
Set fruits in a gelatin mold by swirling a little unset gelatin into the mold. Arrange the fruits around the base or sides. Chill, to set. Continue layering the fruit until the mold is full.

SERVING SET DESSERTS

● **Retaining flavor** Remove a gelatin-set mixture from the refrigerator 15 minutes before serving, since overchilling will reduce the flavor of a dessert.
● **Using water** Before unmolding a gelatin mold onto a serving plate, rinse the plate in cold water. Unmold, and slide into position.
● **Unmolding** To unmold set mixtures, dip the mold briefly in hot water. Put a plate over the mold, flip it over, and shake to dislodge the dessert.
● **Serving frozen** A cold soufflé that has not set can be served frozen. Put it in the freezer until firm, remove the paper collar, and serve.

CHOCOLATE DESSERTS

When using chocolate in either hot or cold desserts, buy the best you can afford. The better the quality, the more chocolatey tasting your dessert will be. Use cocoa to add a chocolate flavor to cooked mixtures, but remember to include some sugar to taste.

SHAPING CURLS

Cool marble board

Using a zester
Make decorative chocolate curls using a citrus zester. Spread melted chocolate evenly over a cool surface, and let stand until just set. Pull the zester across the surface to remove small curls.

MAKING EDIBLE LEAVES

Paint chocolate over leaf with small, soft brush

Imprinting leaves
Select clean, unblemished rose leaves or other nonpoisonous leaves. Brush melted chocolate evenly over each leaf. Let set, then very gently peel off the leaf to reveal its imprint.

USING CHOCOLATE
- **Melting chocolate** To melt chocolate without a double boiler, use a heatproof bowl over hot, not boiling, water.
- **Making curls** Add store-bought chocolate couveture to melted chocolate to make it pliable when shaping curls.
- **Adding gloss** Add a rich gloss to a chocolate sauce or a chocolate topping by stirring in two pats of unsalted butter.
- **Substituting cocoa** If you run out of baking chocolate, use 3 tbsp (45 ml) of cocoa and 1 tbsp (15 ml) of butter for every 1 oz (25 g) needed.
- **Replacing alcohol** Replace the alcohol in a chocolate dessert with the same amount of black coffee, if preferred.

ICE CREAMS AND SORBETS

Ice creams are based on simple mixtures and can be produced easily with or without an ice cream maker. Ice cream mixtures based on heavy cream and egg custards are very successful made by hand, but sorbets and frozen yogurt benefit from machine churning.

MAKING ICES
- **Flavoring ices** Slightly over-flavor or oversweeten sorbet and ice cream mixtures, since freezing masks flavors.
- **Using gelatin** To make a firm, scoopable sorbet, add a little dissolved gelatin to the mixture before freezing.
- **Sweetening with honey** For a soft texture, use honey rather than sugar to sweeten ices.
- **Making ices by hand** Whisk handmade ices at frequent intervals while freezing to break up ice crystals and produce a smooth texture.
- **Maturing ices** Mature the flavor of ices in the freezer for 24 hours. Soften at room temperature before serving.

USING AN IMPROVISED BOMBE MOLD

Fill center with soft-fruit sorbet

Hot towel loosens bombe from basin

1 To make an ice cream bombe without a mold, set a freezer-proof bowl in a basin of ice. Pack the base and sides of the bowl with firm but slightly softened ice cream. Fill the center, and freeze.

2 To turn out the bombe, wrap the bowl briefly in a dish towel that has been wrung out in hot water. Run a knife around the inside edge of the bowl, then invert the bombe onto a serving plate.

BAKING

H OME BAKING IS ONE OF THE MOST REWARDING cooking skills. While you are
learning basic techniques, follow recipes and measure ingredients carefully.
Once you have gained confidence, you can adapt recipes to your own taste.

MAKING CAKES

T here are four basic techniques used in
making cakes: melting, creaming, cutting
in, and beating. Whichever method you use,
preheat the oven and prepare the pans first,
since you are most likely to get a good rise if the
cake is baked as soon as possible after mixing.

LINING TINS
● **Cutting spares** If you
often use a particular pan for
baking, cut several thicknesses
of waxed paper at a time, and
keep the spares for future use.
● **Protecting the edges** Line a
cake pan for a fruit cake with
a double layer of waxed
paper to protect the edge of
the cake from excessive heat.
● **Greasing pans** Use oil to
grease a cake pan; it is easier
to brush on than butter and is
less likely to burn or stick.
● **Adding paper** Place a small
square cut from nonstick paper
in the base of a greased and
floured pan to ease removal.

MAKING RING PANS

Dried beans

Using a food can
Make a ring pan by placing a tall
food can, weighed down with pie
weights, in the center of a round
cake pan. The beans will stop the
can from moving when the batter
is poured around it.

MAKING HEART SHAPES

Combining two cakes
Bake a round and a square cake,
with the diameter of the circle
and the sides of the square the
same length. Cut the circle in
half, and place one half on each of
two adjacent sides of the square.

REMOVING FROM PANS
● **Allowing standing time**
Leave a sponge cake in the pan
for 2–3 minutes to let it contract
and firm up before removing
it from the pan. Let a fruit
cake cool completely.
● **Loosening sides** Run a knife
around the inside of the pan
to loosen the sides of a cake.
● **Using a can** To remove a
cake from a loose-bottomed
pan, rest the base on a tall can,
and push the sides down.
● **Inverting pans** Prevent a
cake from drying out by
inverting it onto a cooling rack
and placing the pan over it.
● **Using an oven rack** Use an
oven shelf as a cooling rack.
Raise it above the counter by
placing it on a springform ring.

HEALTHY TIP

Dusting with bran
Grease a cake pan as usual,
then, instead of flour,
sprinkle a little wheat or oat
bran inside it to add fiber as
well as flavor to the cake.
Turn the pan to coat the base
and sides evenly.

TESTING DONENESS

● **Pressing the top** Apply
light pressure to the top
of a sponge cake with your
fingertips. The top should
feel firm and should spring
back into shape without
leaving an indentation.
● **Checking the edges** Look
closely at the edges of a
cake. They will have shrunk
away slightly from the sides
of the pan if the cake has
cooked thoroughly.
● **Listening closely** Listen to a
cake. A sizzling noise means
that it is still cooking.
● **Using a skewer** Test a cake
by inserting a metal or
bamboo skewer into its
middle. The skewer will be
clean if the cake is cooked.

ADDING FLAVORINGS AND FILLINGS

A simple sponge or a plain fruit cake can be transformed through the imaginative use of fillings and flavorings. Try enhancing a basic sponge cake with scented leaves or extracts, or create a lavish showpiece in minutes by adding a dash of liqueur and a rich frosting.

ADDING FLAVOR

Place lemon-scented geranium leaf in center of pan

Using a geranium leaf
Before adding sponge cake batter to a pan for baking, place a lemon-scented geranium leaf in the bottom of the pan. As the cake cooks, the leaf's delicate scent will permeate it.

SANDWICHING CAKES

Filling will hold layers together

Spreading a filling
Before sandwiching two halves of a sponge cake together, spread a filling, such as frosting, onto both halves. Press them gently together so that they will remain in position when the cake is cut.

HEALTHY TIP

Making a low-fat filling
For a low-fat filling, mix together 7 oz (200 g) reduced-fat cream cheese made from skim milk with 2 tbsp (30 ml) honey, then flavor with finely grated citrus zest. Use as a filling or topping for a sponge or carrot cake as an alternative to a rich cream-cheese frosting.

DISGUISING MISTAKES

Even the most experienced cook can make a mistake when baking. However, most problems can be rectified. If a cake appears burned, for example, it is often only the outer crust that is affected. Remove the crust with a knife, and disguise the top with frosting.

RESCUING SPONGE

● **Correcting curdling** If a sponge cake mixture begins to separate during mixing, add 1 tbsp (15 ml) flour, then beat the mixture thoroughly.

● **Mending cracks** To repair a cake that has cracked while being removed from the pan, brush the pieces with warmed apricot jam. Reassemble the cake in the pan to cool.

● **Concealing cracks** To hide cracks in a roulade or jelly roll, pipe cream over them. Sprinkle with confectioners' sugar, cocoa, or grated chocolate.

● **Moistening sponge** Sprinkle a dry sponge cake with fresh orange or other fruit juice.

USING SUNKEN CAKES

Cut out center from cooled cake

Cutting out the center
If a round fruit or sponge cake has an undercooked, sunken center, make it into a ring cake by cutting the center out neatly with a sharp knife. Cover the ring with frosting.

MOISTENING DRY CAKES

Dribble liqueur slowly to soak in evenly

Adding liqueur
To moisten overcooked or dried-out fruit cake, turn the cake upside down, and pierce it with a skewer several times. Spoon brandy, whisky, or rum over the surface and let stand for 24 hours.

DECORATING CAKES

You do not need special skills to decorate cakes impressively. The simplest, most basic techniques are often the most effective, so there is no need to spend hours in the kitchen. Cool, dry conditions are best for sugar and icings, so avoid working in steamy kitchens.

APPLYING TOPPINGS
● **Pouring icing** To ice a sponge cake quickly, place it on a wire rack over a cookie sheet and pour glaze or melted chocolate over the surface in one movement, smoothing around the sides with a knife. Let set.
● **Softening almond paste** If almond paste dries out and is hard to roll, warm it in a microwave on Medium for 30 seconds. Knead the paste until it is soft enough to roll.
● **Using fondant** Roll out ready-made fondant icing on a surface lightly dusted with sifted cornstarch instead of confectioners' sugar. Cornstarch will be easier to brush off the cake than confectioners' sugar.
● **Smoothing fondant** To smooth the sides of a cake iced with fondant, roll a straight-sided jar around them. Dust the jar first with cornstarch to prevent it from sticking.

DECORATING WITH SUGAR
● **Using a doily** To decorate a plain cake, place a paper doily on top and sprinkle the cake with confectioners' sugar. Lift the doily off to reveal a lace pattern.

Shake confectioners' sugar through sieve

Using stencils
Cut out paper shapes, and arrange these stencils on top of the cake you wish to decorate. Sprinkle the cake with confectioners' sugar, then remove the shapes to reveal the stenciled design.

USING FLOWERS
● **Washing flowers** Wash delicate edible flowers with a fine water mist before using. Shake off excess water, and dry on an absorbent paper towel.

Brush gently with egg white

Coating edible flowers
Decorate edible flowers with a thin coating of sugar. First, brush egg white onto the petals with a soft paintbrush. Sprinkle the petals lightly with superfine sugar, and let dry for 24 hours.

COLORING ICING

Drip coloring into icing

Using a skewer
Control the addition of small amounts of liquid food coloring to icing by using a skewer or a toothpick. Dip it into the bottle, and use it like a dropper to drip the coloring into the icing.

FILLING PIPING BAGS

Working with a cup
To fill a piping bag without mess, fit the bag with a nozzle, place in a measuring cup, and turn the top of the bag over the top of the cup. The bag is held open while icing is spooned in.

MAKING A PIPING BAG

If you do not have a piping bag to ice a cake, improvise with one of the following:

● **Using a plastic bag** For plain icing, snip a corner off a strong plastic bag without a seam, and insert a nozzle.
● **Making a paper cone** Cut an 8-in (20-cm) square of waxed paper, and fold it diagonally to make a triangle. Lift a bottom corner, and curl it around to meet the tip of the triangle at the front. Then curl the other corner around the back to meet the tip. Snip the point off the cone, and pipe through the hole.

BAKING SMALL CAKES AND COOKIES

Baking small cakes and cookies is enjoyable as well as practical: techniques are simple, and cooking times are short. Make them to eat yourself or to give away to friends. Cupcakes and muffins should be eaten as fresh as possible, but cookies can often be stored for several days.

COOKING MUFFINS

Baking in a microwave
Use straight-sided cups to bake muffins in a microwave, rather than a microwave muffin tin. Brush the cups with oil before adding the mixture. Bake the muffins in small batches.

USING A MICROWAVE
● **Using a flan dish** Use a round porcelain flan dish to cook bar cookies in the microwave. Allow to cool, then cut into wedges.
● **Adding color** To add color to microwaved cookies and cakes, brush them with honey and scatter with toasted nuts.

MAKING SMALL CAKES
● **Using a piping bag** When making a large batch of cupcakes, spoon the cake batter into a piping bag fitted with a large, plain nozzle. Pipe the mixture into cupcake liners, and bake.
● **Topping with sugar** Create a crunchy topping for plain sponge cakes by sprinkling them lightly with brown sugar before baking.
● **Creating a surprise** Include a surprise in plain cakes by pressing a small square of chocolate into the center of the uncooked mixture.

MAKING COOKIES

Press rim firmly into dough

Cutting out circles
Use the rim of an upside-down wine glass to cut rounds from rolled-out cookie dough if you do not have a cookie cutter. Dip the rim into flour before using it to cut out sticky mixtures.

PREPARING AHEAD
● **Storing cookie dough** Roll up firm cookie dough and wrap it in foil. Store in the refrigerator for several weeks, baking batches as you need to.
● **Improving flavor** Store gingersnaps in a tin for several days to improve their flavor. Refresh in a hot oven to serve.

SHAPING DELICATE COOKIES AFTER BAKING
● **Using a jar** Use a fish server to lift almond tuiles onto the sides of clean jelly jars as they come out of the oven. This will allow them to cool quickly and will result in them setting in a curved shape.
● **Rolling on a wooden spoon** Shape cooked brandy-snap mixture into rolls around the handle of a wooden spoon while the mixture is still warm. Gently slide the roll off the handle, and cool on a rack. If the mixture sets before it has been shaped, return it to the oven for 30 seconds.

MAKING BISCUITS
● **Helping biscuits to rise** To help biscuits rise and soften the gluten in the flour, use buttermilk or sour cream instead of milk, and equal quantities of baking soda and cream of tartar instead of baking powder.
● **Rolling biscuit wedges** Instead of cutting out round biscuits, roll the dough into one smooth circle, and cut into wedges with a sharp knife. Bake, then pull apart to serve.
● **Adding savory flavor** To give plain biscuit dough a savory flavor, sift 1 tsp (5 ml) of celery salt with the flour, or stir in some herbs.

SHAPING STICKY DOUGH
● **Wetting hands** To prevent cookie dough from sticking to your hands, wet them in cold water before handling it.
● **Chilling dough** If cookie dough is too sticky to handle, wrap it in plastic wrap, and chill for 30 minutes. If it is still sticky, work in some flour.

Mold mixture over top of orange

Shaping over an orange
To shape delicate cookies or mold brandy-snap mixture into baskets, arrange each portion of cookie mixture gently over an orange as soon as it comes out of the oven. Let them set.

MAKING BASIC BREADS

Baking your own bread is easy, satisfying, and takes surprisingly little time. Use a food processor to take the hard work out of kneading, and reduce rising times by using fast-action yeast. Alternatively, let dough rise overnight in the refrigerator so that it is ready to bake the next day.

USING YEAST

● **Substituting dried yeast**
When substituting dried yeast for fresh in a recipe, use 2 tsp (10 ml) dried yeast for ½ oz (15 g) fresh yeast.
● **Using fast-action yeast** Add fast-action yeast directly to a dry flour mix, not to liquid, or its action will be delayed.
● **Freezing dough** If you are making dough that is to be frozen before baking, increase the quantity of yeast by about one third, since freezing will kill some of the yeast.
● **Adding potato water** Save the water from boiled potatoes to add to bread mixes. It will feed the yeast, giving a good rise, and add to the flavor.

HELPING DOUGH RISE

Make bowl airtight with plastic wrap

Covering with plastic wrap
To encourage dough to rise, place it in a bowl, and cover with plastic wrap that has been brushed with oil. The dampness and warmth created inside the bowl will speed up the rising.

BAKING LARGE LOAVES

● **Testing for doneness** To make sure that a large loaf is cooked properly, turn it out of the pan, and tap the bottom with your knuckles. If it sounds hollow, the bread is thoroughly cooked. If not, return it to the oven for a few minutes to finish cooking.

Place both doughs in same pan

Combining doughs
If some members of your family like whole-wheat bread and others prefer white bread, bake the two kinds of dough end to end in a large loaf pan. Then you can slice the loaf from either end.

CREATING CRUSTS

● **Baking crusty loaves** For a really crisp crust all over a loaf, take it out of the pan when it is cooked. Then return it to the oven, placing it directly on the shelf, for five minutes more to make sure the crust is crisp all over. Cool the loaf on a wire rack before storing.

Making soft crusts
For soft crusts on bread rolls or loaves, dust the tops with flour before baking, and cover with a clean dish towel when cooling. Also, add milk to the dough mix instead of using just water.

RISING DOUGHS

● **Adding ascorbic acid** When using fresh yeast, speed up rising times by adding a 25-mg tablet of ascorbic acid for every 8 cups (1 kg) flour.
● **Warming flour** To help dough rise on a cold day, warm the flour first in an ovenproof bowl in the oven at 225°F (110°C). Alternatively, put the flour in a microwave on High for 10 seconds.
● **Using a microwave** Place dough in an oiled bowl, brush with oil, and cover with waxed paper. Stand the bowl in a shallow dish of hot water, and microwave on Low for four minutes. Let stand for about 20 minutes. Repeat the process until the dough is doubled.
● **Testing the rise** To test whether dough has risen enough, press it lightly with a floured finger. The dough should spring back without leaving an indentation.

ENHANCING FLAVOR

Even the most basic breads are transformed by adding extra flavors to the dough. Stir herbs or spices into the dry flour mix to ensure even distribution, or knead in chunky additions, such as olives, just before shaping. Brush tops of loaves or rolls with glaze for last-minute flavor.

ADDING EXTRAS

● **Chopping ingredients** Knead a few chopped olives, herbs, walnuts, or sun-dried tomatoes into plain bread dough for a Mediterranean flavor.

● **Mixing flours** Reduce the strong flavor of buckwheat flour by mixing it half and half with rice flour.

● **Adding spicy glaze** Brush the tops of loaves with a mixture of oil and curry paste or pesto sauce before baking for a spicy, golden crust.

● **Glazing with herbs** For a crisp, savory crust on bread, dissolve 2 tsp (10 ml) salt in 2 tbsp (30 ml) warm water, and brush over the tops of rolls. Sprinkle with herbs and bake.

MAKING SAVORY BREADS

Adding celery salt
Give plain bread a subtle, savory flavor by substituting celery salt or garlic salt for table salt. If the salt crystals are large, dissolve them first in the liquid that will be used to mix the dough.

MAKING SWEET GLAZES

Using honey
Brush bread loaves or rolls with warmed honey as soon as they are removed from the oven for a glossy, sweet glaze. Alternatively, brush with corn or maple syrup for the same effect.

SHAPING AND DECORATING DOUGH

Bread dough can be shaped before baking, whether in a loaf pan or on a cookie sheet. Traditional shapes such as braids or twists can be adapted for large loaves or small rolls. If you are short on time, decorate dough by scoring a lattice pattern on the surface with a sharp blade.

DECORATING LOAVES

Snip dough with scissors

Snipping with scissors
To decorate a plain loaf quickly, use scissors to cut slashes across the top of the dough before rising or baking. The cuts will open out when the dough rises, making a patterned top.

MAKING ROUND LOAVES

● **Shaping a cottage loaf** Top a ball of dough with a smaller ball. Poke a hole through the center with your finger to secure them.

Cutting a cross
Cut a deep cross in a plain, round loaf before proving, using a floured, sharp knife. The cuts will open out to form an attractive crown shape when the loaf of bread is baked.

CREATING VARIETY

● **Using seeds** Scatter sesame or poppy seeds over soft rolls after glazing to make an attractive and tasty topping.

● **Marbling dough** Make two batches of dough; one whole-wheat, one plain. Pull off small pieces, then knead together before shaping to give the dough a marbled effect.

● **Sprinkling pans** After greasing loaf pans, sprinkle lightly with cracked wheat or rolled oats before adding bread dough to give the crust a nutty texture.

● **Baking rolls in clusters** Instead of baking rolls separately, pack them closely together in a pan or place on a cookie sheet. Serve them to be pulled apart as required.

WORKING WITH PASTRY

Pastry forms the basis of many kinds of dish, whether they are hot or cold, savory or sweet. Whatever type of pastry you are making, the same rules will apply. Always keep your tools, work surface, and hands cool. Try to handle the pastry lightly and as little as possible.

MAKING SHORTCRUST
● **Cooling hands** If your hands are warm, hold your wrists under cold water for a few minutes before handling pastry.
● **Enriching pastry** To make a rich, light-textured pastry, add an egg yolk with the water.
● **Letting pastry rest** Cover shortcrust pastry with plastic wrap, and place it in the refrigerator for 30 minutes before rolling out to prevent it from shrinking when baked.
● **Making quick pastry** To mix a quick dough, sift 1 cup (100 g) flour and a pinch of salt into a bowl. Stir in 2½ tbsp (40 ml) oil, 1 tbsp (15 ml) iced water, and a squeeze of lemon juice. Mix to a dough with a fork.

HELPING PASTRY RISE
● **Using water** Before using a cookie sheet for baking choux, flaky, or puff pastry dough, sprinkle it lightly with water instead of greasing it. The water will evaporate in the heat of the oven, and the steam will help the pastry rise.

AVOIDING SOGGY PASTRY

● **Using a cookie sheet** Bake a pie on a cookie sheet, the heat of which will help cook the pastry base. Preheat the cookie sheet in the oven while the oven heats up.
● **Using metal tins** Use a metal pie tin for baking a pie or tart. Metal will conduct heat to the pastry quickly.
● **Sealing with egg white** Brush the base of a pie shell with egg white to seal it and prevent leakage before adding a liquid filling.

USING TRIMMINGS

Grate pastry straight from freezer

Making a pastry topping
Coarsely grate frozen pastry over fruits as a topping, then bake until golden. Wrap leftover pastry trimmings in a freezer bag, and freeze so that they can be used in the future for this purpose.

USING FROZEN PASTRY
● **Preparing** Make and shape puff pastry ready for use. Freeze it until needed, then thaw before baking.
● **Thawing** Thaw frozen pastry by placing it in a microwave on Defrost; 7 oz (200 g) of pastry will need 2½–3 minutes.

PREVENTING PROBLEMS
● **Ensuring an even rise** Brush only the top surface of puff or flaky pastry when glazing with beaten egg or milk, avoiding any cut or fluted edges. The pastry will then rise evenly.
● **Avoiding leakage** When adding a filling with beaten eggs to a ready-made pie shell, heat the case in the oven first, so that the filling starts to set as soon as it touches the pastry.
● **Preventing overbrowning** When baking a fruit pie, allow the pastry to brown and rise first, then reduce the oven temperature to finish cooking.

HEALTHY TIP

Adding fiber
Instead of using all-purpose flour to roll out pastry dough, sprinkle the countertop with rolled oats, wheat germ, or bran. Roll out as usual for a finished pastry that has added texture and contains beneficial dietary fiber.

MAKING SWEET PASTRY
● **Adding sugar and egg** Mix a sweet shortcrust pastry for fruit pies by adding ¼ cup (50 g) of sugar and one egg yolk to every 1 cup (100 g) of flour. Bake at a lower temperature (about 375°F/190°C) than ordinary shortcrust pastry.

Adding ingredients
To add flavor and texture to shortcrust or puff pastry, stir finely chopped nuts such as walnuts or ground almonds into the flour. Alternatively, add spices or finely chopped herbs.

SHAPING PASTRY DECORATIVELY

There is a variety of ways in which you can use pastry as a decorative trim. Shortcrust pastry is the most versatile, since it holds its shape during cooking. Cut leftover pastry into decorative shapes, and bake them separately to keep on hand for use as a quick garnish.

MAKING LATTICE TOPS
● **Using trimmings** Cut rolled-out pastry trimmings into long, thin strips. Arrange them over a pie filling to form a lattice.

Space slits evenly

Cutting slits
To make an easy lattice top for a pie, roll out a circle of pastry to fit the top of the pie, then cut short slits parallel to each other. Stretch the pastry gently to open the slits and create a lattice top.

DECORATING EDGES
● **Cutting shapes** Roll out pastry trimmings, and cut into small leaves, hearts, or flowers. Overlap around the edges of a pie or tart before baking.
● **Making a braid** Roll spare pastry into long, thin strips, and braid these together. Arrange them around dampened pastry edges, and tuck in the seams.
● **Marking with a fork** To seal the edges of a double-crust pie quickly and easily, flatten the edges together with the floured prongs of a fork.
● **Pinching edges** Seal the edges of a double-crust pie by pressing them between your finger and thumb at an angle. This will create a rope effect.

BRIGHT IDEA

Using a pastry label
Use pastry trimmings to cut out a shaped, edible label to decorate a pie and indicate its contents. Alternatively, cut out letters from the pastry to spell out the name of the pie's contents. Brush with beaten egg before sticking on.

USING PHYLLO DOUGH

Phyllo is a delicate pastry that needs gentle handling. Nevertheless, it is easy to use for pies, tartlets, and filled pastries. Work quickly, and cover sheets you are not using to prevent them from drying out, since phyllo dough will become difficult to handle if it dries out.

WORKING WITH PHYLLO
● **Brushing with oil** Use olive or nut oil to brush phyllo before baking savory pastries. Use butter or a light-flavored oil for baking sweet pastries.
● **Brushing with egg** For those on a low-fat diet, brush phyllo lightly with egg white instead of oil. This will give the pastry a crisp texture when baked.
● **Baking in a microwave** Brush filled phyllo bundles with butter, and cook in a browning dish in a microwave on High until the pastry is crisp. Turn the bundles over halfway through the cooking period.
● **Making spring rolls** Use phyllo to make spring rolls. Seal with egg white, and deep-fry in hot oil for 2–3 minutes.

STORING PHYLLO
● **Storing for later** Wrap unused phyllo dough from a package in plastic wrap and refrigerate. Use the pastry within 3–4 days.

Keep pastry moist with damp towel

Preventing drying
Work with one sheet of phyllo at a time, and keep the rest moist by covering with a lightly dampened dish towel. To keep phyllo dough for long periods, cover it with plastic wrap first.

USING LEFTOVER PHYLLO
● **Using damaged sheets** Use up dried out or broken sheets of phyllo by inserting them between whole sheets.

Cup pastry in hand to shape

Making "moneybags"
To use up small pieces of phyllo dough, brush with oil, stack together, and place a spoonful of fruit in the center. Gather up the sides, pinch together firmly, leaving a ruffled edge, and bake.

PRESERVING

I N THE PAST, PRESERVING WAS AN ESSENTIAL PART of a cook's calendar to ensure that pantries were well stocked all year round. This is no longer necessary, but preserving is a skill worth having and has rewarding end results.

PREPARING TO PRESERVE

The basic principle of preserving is to take food at the peak of freshness and maintain its nutritive value at that stage. Little special equipment is necessary, but it is worthwhile to spend some time preparing equipment for use to ensure that your preserves are a success.

USING EQUIPMENT

● **Choosing pan material** For making acidic preserves such as chutneys and pickles, use a stainless steel pot, since aluminum or copper may react with the acid.
● **Choosing the right-sized pot** Use a large pot for making jam to allow room for expansion. The pan should be half full when all the sugar is added.
● **Warming a thermometer** To prevent a thermometer from cracking, warm it in hot water before placing in hot preserves.
● **Hooking a spoon** To prevent a wooden spoon from sliding into a pan, attach a wooden clothespin to the handle at right angles to it. Hook the pin over the side of the pan.

WEIGHING INGREDIENTS

Using bathroom scales
To weigh a large amount of ingredients easily, use bathroom scales. First, note the weight of the pot. Then weigh the ingredients in the pot, and deduct the weight of the pot.

PREVENTING SCUM

Applying glycerin
Brush the inner sides of a pot with glycerin before making jams and jellies. This will prevent scum from forming on the surface of the preserves during cooking.

PREPARING JARS

Jars placed upright

Preventing cracking
To prevent jars from cracking when filled with hot preserves, first wash them thoroughly. Stand them on a cookie sheet covered with newsprint, and place in a warm oven for 10 minutes.

STERILIZING LIDS

Plunging into boiling water
Sterilize the metal lids of the canning jars by placing them in boiling water for six minutes. Remove the lids with food tongs to protect your hands, and drain on absorbent paper towels.

CONSIDERING OPTIONS

● **Using a microwave** If you want to cook jams, jellies, or chutneys in a microwave, plan to make only a small amount at a time. To allow for expansion of the ingredients during cooking, use a heatproof bowl that is three times larger in volume than the quantity of preserve you are making in each batch.
● **Pressure cooking** Reduce the cooking times recommended in recipes for jams and jellies by making them in a pressure cooker. You will also need to use only about half the liquid specified in the recipe.

MAKING JAMS AND JELLIES

A successful jam or jelly is characterized by a firm, clear set, a bright color, and a good fruit flavor. Use fresh, undamaged produce, ideally mixing ripe with unripe fruits. Pectin is the setting agent found naturally in fruits, and unripe fruits contain the highest pectin levels.

STRAINING JELLIES

Ladle fruit pulp into jelly bag

Using a stool

To use a jelly bag to strain jelly, turn a small stool upside down, place a bowl on its base in the center, and tie the jelly bag to the legs of the stool. Fill with fruit pulp, and let drain.

PREVENTING PROBLEMS

● **Preventing mildew** Pick fruits for preserves when conditions are dry, since moisture on the fruits may cause mildew.

● **Using sugar** Cook fruits for jam until tender before adding sugar, which may toughen the skins. Always warm sugar first so that it will dissolve quickly and help give a clear set.

● **Removing scum** Skim jams and jellies to remove scum for a clear set. The last traces can be removed with a paper towel.

● **Distributing fruits** If jam or marmalade contains pieces of fruits or peel, let cool slightly before pouring into jars. This will prevent the pieces from rising to the surface.

● **Covering jam** Place jam jar covers on immediately after canning to discourage bacteria.

SELECTING FRUITS

Some fruits have a tendency to set much better than others.

● **Good** Apples, blackberries, cranberries, concord grapes, crabapples.
● **Average** Raspberries, plums, apricots, grapefruit, oranges, sour cherries.
● **Poor** Pears, sweet cherries, strawberries, rhubarb, peaches.
● **Good combination** Apples and raspberries, cranberries and peaches.

CANNING FRUITS

Successful canning is dependent on efficient sterilization. Modern canning jars extend the lives of preserves, and are available with screwband closures for a good seal. Preserves make delightful presents, particularly if they are decorated with ribbons and pretty gift tags.

PACKING JARS

Arranging slices

Make jars of canned fruits look attractive by arranging slices of fruits such as orange, star fruit, or kiwi fruit against the sides before filling. Pack firmly, avoiding gaps, since fruits rise when cooked.

PREVENTING SPLITTING

Prick skin with toothpick

Pricking fruits

To prevent fruit skins from bursting, prick whole fruits such as cherries, apricots, and plums before packing them into bottles. This will also aid the absorption of syrup by the fruits.

DEALING WITH LIDS

● **Testing the seal** To make sure that the seal on a canning jar is good after bottling, remove the screw cover, and lift the jar by its lid. If the lid stays in place, the seal is good.

● **Loosening bands** Once canning fruits have completely cooled, and the jar is properly sealed, slightly loosen the bands on screw-on closures so that they do not become stuck.

● **Releasing a lid** To loosen a lid that is firmly stuck on a jar with a screwband closure, stand the jar in hot water for a few minutes, then lever off the lid carefully with a knife.

MAKING CHUTNEYS AND PICKLES

Preserving fruits and vegetables in sugar and vinegar is a traditional cooking method that improves their flavors during storage. A good chutney is smooth in texture and mellow in flavor. This result is achieved through lengthy, slow cooking and maturation in the jar.

USING SPICES
● **Substituting whole spices**
If you wish to substitute whole spices for ground when following a chutney recipe, you should double the quantity.

Strike spices with rolling pin

Bruising spices
If you are using whole spices such as cloves or cinnamon to flavor chutneys or pickles, bruise them lightly to release their flavors. Wrap them in cheesecloth, then add to the other ingredients.

USING SALT
● **Choosing the right salt** Buy rock salt for pickling or dry salting, since table salt contains additives that change the flavor and color of ingredients.

Sprinkle salt over vegetables

Retaining crispness
Make sure vegetables stay crisp by using dry salt instead of brine for salting before pickling. Sprinkle vegetables with salt, and let stand overnight to draw out the juices. Rinse and dry before use.

TRADITIONAL TIP

Testing a brine solution
To check whether a brine solution is concentrated enough for salting foods before pickling, lower a fresh egg into the solution. If the egg floats, the concentration of salt is about right. Make sure that you add about ¼ cup (50 g) salt for every 2 cups (500 ml) water.

PRESERVING LEMONS

Salting lemon quarters
Cut six lemons into quarters, not quite cutting them through at one end. Rub salt into the cut surfaces, and pack the lemons into a canning jar. Add the juice of one lemon and 1 tbsp (15 ml) salt. Top off the jar with boiling water, and seal. Refrigerate 2-3 weeks before using the lemons and the liquid in casseroles, soups, and salad dressings.

COOKING CHUTNEYS
● **Reducing liquid** To make sure that a chutney thickens to a good consistency, always cook it uncovered so that the excess liquid evaporates.

Testing before canning
To check whether a chutney is cooked and ready for canning, pull a wooden spoon through it, across the base of the pan. If it parts easily and there is no running liquid, it is cooked.

ADJUSTING RECIPES
● **Enriching color** Use brown sugar to give a rich color to chutneys with a short cooking time. Use white sugar to darken chutneys only if the recipe has a prolonged cooking time.
● **Lightening color** For a pale color and mild flavor, use white vinegar in chutneys, pickles, and relishes. Also, add the sugar only after the basic ingredients have reduced.
● **Reducing sugar** If you want to reduce the amount of sugar used in a chutney recipe, then add dried fruits such as dates or golden raisins instead.
● **Keeping onions soft** Soften onions before pickling by cooking them in a little water for a few minutes before adding vinegar, which has a slightly hardening effect on them.

DRYING FOODS

Drying is a traditional preserving method originating from the observed effects of the sun and wind on fish, fruits, and vegetables. These natural preserving processes can be imitated in the kitchen to dry particular foods by controlling temperature and ventilation.

DRYING HERBS

Leaves arranged in single layer

Using a microwave
Arrange fresh herb leaves on absorbent paper towels, and place in a microwave with a glass of water. Cook on High for about 30 seconds, and repeat until the leaves have dried thoroughly.

VARYING METHODS
● **Hanging bundles** Tie bundles of mixed fresh summer herbs such as parsley, mint, sage, and thyme. Before hanging them up to dry for the winter, cover with cheesecloth to keep them free from dust.
● **Stringing spices** Thread cotton string through fresh chilies so that they can be hung up for drying.
● **Drying in an oven** To dry mushrooms, first remove the stalks, since these tend to toughen. Thread the mushrooms onto bamboo skewers, and arrange on the shelf racks of an oven on the coolest setting until the mushrooms are crisp and dry. Store in a dry place.

PREVENTING PROBLEMS
● **Avoiding browning** To stop apples from browning during drying, soak in salted water for a few minutes. Use 1 tsp (5 ml) salt to 2 cups (500 ml) water.

Place slices on paper towels

Lining racks
When drying fruits or slices of fruit for decorative purposes, lay sheets of cheesecloth or paper towels between the fruits and the drying rack to prevent the ridges from leaving marks on the fruits.

CURING AND SMOKING FOODS

Curing is a method of preserving food by immersing it in dry salt or a salt solution. Curing is now done mainly to add flavor. Many meats are cured before smoking, both to ensure good preservation and to add flavor. Most fish can be preserved simply by smoking.

PREPARING FOODS
● **Cheese** Remove any rind or wax from hard cheeses such as Cheddar or Emmental before home smoking. Cut the cheese into 1-in (2.5-cm) thick chunks, and smoke at 60°F (16°C) for 2–4 hours.
● **Nuts** Blanch whole nuts such as almonds or hazelnuts, then spread them in a single layer across a fine wire mesh screen before smoking.
● **Poultry** When smoking a whole bird such as a chicken or turkey, cover the breast with bacon strips or pork fat to prevent overdrying.
● **Meat and fish** Instead of salt-curing meat and fish, soak in a marinade for several hours to add a salty flavor.

STORING IN WOOD ASH
● **Keeping cured meat** Wrap salt-cured meat in cheesecloth, and roll in wood ash to deter insects. Hang in a cool place.

MAKING YOUR OWN GRAVLAX

Lay fresh dill on fish

1 Lay a fillet of salmon skin side down in a wide dish, and rub with oil. Cover with a layer of salt and sugar, then top with chopped dill and crushed peppercorns.

REMOVING SALT
● **Soaking** Remove excess salt from food that has been cured for longer than one week by soaking in cold, fresh water.

2 Cover with another fillet of salmon, skin side up. Wrap with plastic wrap, and place in the refrigerator for 12 hours, turning the fish over halfway through. Serve thinly sliced.

FREEZING

Successful freezing maintains foods at peak freshness, with the minimum loss of vitamins, color, or texture. Freezing converts water within the cells that make up food to ice, a process that must be done quickly to prevent damage to the cells.

PREPARING TO FREEZE

Most foods require only simple preparation before freezing. It is essential to blanch vegetables, since this will destroy the enzymes that cause deterioration and preserve color, flavor, texture, and nutrients. Secure packing is vital for all foods to keep them airtight.

PREFORMING LIQUIDS

Top of freezer bag turned over open carton

Using a cardboard pack
Preform liquid in a freezer bag for easy storage in the freezer. Put the bag upright in an empty, straight-sided cardboard container. Pour the liquid in and freeze. Lift out the bag, and seal the top.

PREFORMING CASSEROLES

Use enough foil to cover casserole completely

Making a foil lining
Line a casserole dish with foil, and freeze a casserole in it. Lift out of the dish, and overwrap for storing in the freezer. To cook the casserole, unwrap, and return to the dish to defrost and cook.

BLANCHING TIMES

The following blanching times are for medium pieces of common vegetables.

- Asparagus: 2–4 minutes.
- Brussels sprouts, broccoli: 3–4 minutes.
- Cabbage (shredded), red or green: 1½ minutes.
- Carrots: 3–5 minutes.
- Cauliflower, celery, peppers: 3 minutes.
- Corn: 4–8 minutes.
- Eggplants: 4 minutes.
- Green beans: 2–3 minutes.
- Onions, parsnips, spinach: 2 minutes.
- Peas: 1–2 minutes.
- Snow peas: 2–3 minutes.
- Turnips: 2½ minutes.
- Zucchini: 1 minute.

USING FRESH PRODUCE

- **Cooling quickly** Plunge foods into iced water after blanching. Drain well before freezing.
- **Retaining color** Dip cut fruits such as apples into lemon juice or ascorbic acid before freezing to retain color and supplement vitamin content.
- **Using excess fruits** If you have a glut of fresh fruits, stew with sugar, and freeze in pie tins lined with aluminum foil. When the fruits are firm, remove from the dishes, and overwrap before storing. Use frozen packs as ready-made pie fillings in the future.

OPEN-FREEZING FOODS

Keeping pieces separate
To keep delicate fruits or vegetable pieces separate while frozen, open-freeze them on cookie sheets until firm, then pack them into containers or freezer bags for storing.

PREVENTING PROBLEMS

- **Open-freezing cakes** Freeze frosted or decorated cakes until solid before wrapping so that the tops are not squashed.
- **Preventing damage** Protect the top of a pie or delicate dessert by putting an upturned foil pie tin over it. Secure the pie tin to the dish with tape.
- **Avoiding drying** If food does not fill a container, pack the space with crumpled paper to stop the food from drying out.
- **Omitting garlic** Leave garlic out of food to be frozen – it can taste musty when frozen. Add garlic to food after thawing.

STORING AND LABELING

Keep your freezer well organized, and rotate foods as you would in a pantry so that you use foods within their recommended storage times. Reuse suitable food containers for freezing, but always make sure that they are thoroughly clean before filling them.

PACKAGING FOOD
● **Repacking meats** When freezing prepacked meats, always remove the packaging, and rewrap. Cut off the label, then tape it onto the new packaging to save relabeling.
● **Using lids** To pack home-made burgers easily so that they do not stick together, and for easy removal, save plastic coffee can lids, and place each burger on a lid for stacking.
● **Recycling containers** Collect plastic containers with snap-on lids for use in the freezer. Some plastics become brittle at low temperatures, so if you are not sure, line containers with freezer bags.

STORING COOKED FRUITS

Mold paper so it presses down on fruits

Using crumpled paper
When freezing food with liquids such as fruits in syrup, prevent the pieces of food from rising above the surface of the liquid by pressing a sheet of crumpled waxed paper over the food.

LABELING CONTAINERS

Marking a container
For easy labeling of foods in plastic containers, write the details on the container with a wax-based pencil. This will write easily on plastic and the writing will not rub off in the freezer.

PREPARING FREEZER STANDBYS

A freezer offers a wonderful opportunity for keeping timesaving supplies handy. Freeze containers of garnishes and decorations for use when time is short before a dinner party. Freeze leftovers for those days when you need a meal with the minimum amount of preparation.

SAVING TIME
● **Making extra meals** Freeze ready-cooked meals on foil plates. Arrange the food on the plates, ensuring that meats are covered with gravy or sauce, then cover with plastic wrap or foil, seal, and freeze.
● **Making butter balls** Prepare butter balls or curls in advance for entertaining, drop into iced water, then drain and pack into boxes to freeze. Remove and thaw at room temperature about an hour before use.
● **Slicing citrus fruits** Freeze slices of lemon or lime in plastic bags. Add the frozen slices to cocktails.
● **Scooping in advance** Before a dinner party, scoop ice cream or sorbet onto paper-lined trays. Refreeze, ready to serve.

FREEZING CHOCOLATE
● **Protecting with paper** When freezing delicate chocolate shapes, protect the shapes by placing sheets of absorbent paper towels between the layers that are to be stacked.

Using a cookie cutter
Spread melted chocolate onto a cold surface, let set, and use a small cookie cutter to cut into shapes. Layer in a box with waxed paper. Use from frozen to decorate cakes and desserts.

STORING USEFUL BASICS
● **Keeping milk** Freeze spare cartons of milk. Thaw in the refrigerator for two days or at room temperature for six hours.
● **Freezing leftovers** Store leftovers in portion sizes, so that you can take out exactly the number you need.
● **Freezing tomatoes** Freeze whole tomatoes in plastic bags. They can be added directly to casseroles or soups.
● **Keeping spare pastry** Roll out pastry trimmings, and cut into shapes such as leaves or hearts. Freeze in containers, and use straight from the freezer to decorate pies before baking.
● **Using ice trays** Make extra sauce or gravy, and freeze in ice-cube trays, then thaw just the amount you need.

DRINKS

T HE MAIN ADVANTAGE OF CREATING both hot and cold drinks at home is that you can concoct special flavors and blends. The possibilities are endless, from nonalcoholic, flavored fruit drinks to highly spiced, mulled party punches.

FRUIT AND VEGETABLE JUICES

F ruit and vegetable juices are hard to beat for nutrients and fresh flavor. If you enjoy fresh juices, an electric juicer is a worthwhile investment. Otherwise, keep a variety of ready-made juices on hand to mix and match flavors and create refreshing drinks at any time of day.

ENHANCING FLAVORS

Add flower water to plain juice

Adding flower water
Make the flavor of a plain fruit juice more interesting by adding a few drops of orange flower water or rosewater. Stir the juice thoroughly before serving.

PRESSING JUICES
● **Pressing apples** If you are making apple juice in an electric juicer, add a handful of red fruits such as strawberries or raspberries to give the juice a rosy glow and add flavor.
● **Using pulp** Instead of discarding the high-fiber pulp that is left behind after pressing juice, use it in your cooking to add flavor. Add carrot or celery pulp to soups or bread, and include apple or peach pulp in fruit cake recipes.
● **Maintaining color** Add a squeeze of fresh lemon juice when pressing apples or pears to keep their color and prevent them from turning brown.

MAKING SWIZZLE STICKS

Stir juice with spring onion to impart flavor

Using scallions
Use scallions as edible swizzle sticks. Trim root ends and the tops of the leaves – leaving some green for color – just before serving to release flavor.

ADDING INTEREST
● **Using garlic** To pep up the flavor of vegetable juice, rub a cut clove of garlic around the inside of a glass or pitcher before adding the juice, or add a pinch of garlic or celery salt.
● **Chopping herbs** Improve the flavor and color of plain vegetable juices by adding chopped fresh herbs. Try basil, parsley, or lovage in tomato juice, and use tarragon or coriander in carrot juice.
● **Adding fruit and fizz** To make a refreshing summer drink, add chunks of fresh fruits to fresh fruit juice, half-fill tall tumblers, and top off the juice with soda or sparkling mineral water.

CHILLING DRINKS

Add frozen grapes

Adding frozen fruits
Instead of using ice to chill juices, freeze fresh fruits such as grapes or lemon slices. Add these to drinks just before serving to chill and decorate.

HEALTHY TIP

Making nut-milk shakes
For a nutritious, milk-free shake, place a handful of blanched almonds or cashews in a blender with a few strawberries or a banana. Add water to cover, and purée.

SPICED DRINKS

Mulled wines and spice-infused drinks are suitable for many occasions, whether as festive party punches or soothing bedtime drinks. Spices such as ginger, cinnamon, and cloves give a depth of flavor to even the simplest hot punch, with or without the addition of alcohol.

VARYING FLAVORS
● **Using star anise** Add pieces of whole star anise to mulled wine for a rich, spicy flavor.
● **Flavoring coffee** Make an invigorating winter coffee blend by adding ground spices to ground coffee, or grinding whole spices such as allspice, ginger, nutmeg, or cinnamon with fresh coffee beans.
● **Mixing juices** Combine equal quantities of cranberry juice and ginger ale, and mull the mixture gently with cloves or cinnamon to make a delicious nonalcoholic punch.
● **Using savory spice** Sprinkle a few toasted cumin seeds on top of the yogurt-based drinks that often accompany curries.

USING FRUITS

Studding with cloves
To add a spicy flavor and decorate a hot party punch, press whole cloves into the skins of several apples, then float the fruits in the punch while heating and serving the beverage.

SPICING HOT CHOCOLATE

Stir with cinnamon stick

Using a cinnamon stick
Add a mild hint of spice to hot chocolate or cocoa by adding a cinnamon stick. Alternatively, add a pinch of ground cinnamon to the chocolate or cocoa powder during preparation.

TEAS AND TISANES

Tea is an ancient drink that, depending on the particular choice of ingredients added, can be served as a soothing healer or as a refreshing, stimulating reviver. Most teas are usually served hot, but iced tea can be a very welcome cooler on a hot summer's day.

USING HERBS
● **Adding mint** To use fresh mint in iced tea, place a few sprigs in a large pitcher, bruise them with a wooden spoon, then add tea. Pour into glasses, and garnish with mint sprigs.
● **Soothing headaches** Try sipping rosemary tisane to relieve a tension headache. Put a few fresh rosemary sprigs in a pot, pour over boiling water, and infuse for 4–5 minutes.
● **Using alternatives** If herbal teas are not to your taste, try infusing herbs with ordinary black tea, adding sugar to taste.
● **Flavoring green tea** Plunge mint sprigs into freshly made, boiling hot Chinese green tea for a refreshing green tea in the Moroccan style.

ENHANCING FLAVOR
Spoon herbs into pot with tea

Using everyday teas
Bring an interesting flavor to a pot of ordinary leaf tea by adding a few dried herbs, such as dried camomile flowers, while the tea is brewing. Serve plain, or with lemon and sugar if preferred.

USING FRUITS & FLOWERS
● **Adding zest** To make a delicate, fruit-scented tea, add a thinly pared strip of citrus zest to a pot of Indian tea.
● **Making flower teas** Mix a few dried, scented rose petals or jasmine flowers with dry tea leaves, so that the delicate scent mingles with the tea.
● **Creating an exotic flavor** Make a fruit-scented tea by pressing a little juice from a freshly cut mango into tea.
● **Making tea punch** Combine iced tea with chilled fruit juice for a thirst-quenching summer drink. Pineapple or apple juice complements black tea.
● **Adding vanilla** Add a vanilla bean to the tea caddy to infuse a rich flavor during storage.

ENTERTAINING

THROWING A SUCCESSFUL PARTY can be satisfying as well as enjoyable. There are no guaranteed methods to ensure success, but whether the occasion is formal or informal, large or small, good organization and careful advance planning will certainly help. You need to select an appropriate menu, invite a good mixture of guests, and create a pleasant atmosphere in which they feel comfortable. At the end of the party, you will be able to wave good-bye to happy guests with a great feeling of satisfaction and the knowledge that they – and you – thoroughly enjoyed the occasion.

PLANNING A TIMETABLE

When you are cooking for a large number of guests, it is worth planning the occasion well in advance to save yourself time and effort closer to the day. Prepare detailed checklists and timetables, taking all tasks into consideration. This will make the occasion easier to tackle.

PLANNING IN ADVANCE		
COUNTDOWN	PLANNING	ACTION NEEDED
4 WEEKS OR MORE BEFORE	Choose site, theme of occasion, and menu; draw up guest list.	Reserve party room; send invitations; arrange rental or loan of equipment.
2–3 WEEKS BEFORE	Make shopping lists; plan cooking schedule; list other jobs.	Order flowers, alcohol, and soft drinks; cook dishes that will freeze.
1 WEEK BEFORE	Monitor guest acceptances and regrets; decide on seating plans.	Order food; write name and menu cards; wash table linen; clean silver.
3 DAYS BEFORE	Check china and cutlery; finalize numbers of guests and equipment.	Cook food to be reheated or served cold; wash china/glasses.
1 DAY BEFORE	Update cooking schedule; check list of other tasks to be done.	Buy food for last-minute preparation; prepare vegetables/salads; set tables.
PARTY MORNING	Make list of jobs to be done by helpers and hired staff.	Buy fresh bread; arrange flowers and bar; set tables; prepare hot food.
1 HOUR BEFORE	Check tasks as they are completed; allow time for relaxation.	Finish off hot food in oven; put out canapés and cocktail snacks.

PLANNING MENUS

The dishes you choose in a party menu must depend not just on personal taste, but on the season, the occasion, and on limitations such as time and budget. Try to appeal to the eye as well as the appetite, keeping the menu simple, and choose tried-and-true recipes.

SELECTING RECIPES
● **Choosing a main course** Unless you wish to use a particular appetizer or dessert, plan the main course first, then choose an appetizer and dessert to complement it.
● **Keeping courses simple** Help yourself by choosing a simple, cold appetizer that can be prepared in advance.

BALANCING MENUS
● **Varying courses** Create an overall balance of color, texture, and flavor in the menu. Avoid choosing courses that are similar, for example, all egg- or cheese-based.
● **Offsetting rich dishes** Balance a rich or spicy main course with a plain appetizer and a light, refreshing dessert.

PREVENTING PROBLEMS
● **Planning alternatives** In case you are unable to get hold of a particular ingredient, have an alternative dish in mind.
● **Checking diets** Check in advance whether guests have special dietary requirements.
● **Limiting courses** Unless you have extra help, keep to three courses to minimize work.

ESTIMATING QUANTITIES

It is a strange fact that the more people you cater for, the less food you need to allow per head, especially for buffets. If you are catering for 100 people, allow full quantities for about 85. Appetites vary from person to person, but allow half portions for children or elderly guests.

ASSESSING FOOD QUANTITIES			
BUFFET FOODS	**10 PORTIONS**	**20 PORTIONS**	**40 PORTIONS**
Soups, hot or cold	½ gallon (1.75 liters)	1 gallon (4 liters)	2 gallons (8 liters)
Cold, sliced meats off the bone	2 lb (900 g)	3 lb 14 oz (1.75 kg)	7 lb 11 oz (3.5 kg)
Boneless meat for casseroles, etc.	2 lb 3 oz (1 kg)	5 lb (2.25 kg)	10 lb (4.5 kg)
Roast meat on the bone, hot or cold	3 lb 14 oz (1.75 kg)	6 lb 10 oz (3 kg)	14 lb 5 oz (6.5 kg)
Cheese for a cheeseboard	12 oz (350 g)	2 lb (900 g)	2 lb 12 oz (1.25 kg)
Crackers for cheese	1 lb 1 oz (500 g)	1 lb 10 oz (750 g)	2 lb 3 oz (1 kg)
Fish, filleted (in cooked dishes)	2 lb 12 oz (1.25 kg)	5 lb (2.25 kg)	10 lb (4.5 kg)
Poultry on the bone (oven-ready weight)	7 lb 11 oz (3.5 kg)	15 lb 7 oz (7 kg)	2 x 7 lb 11 oz (2 x 3.5 kg)
Rice or pasta (uncooked weight)	1 lb 1 oz (500 g)	1 lb 9 oz (700 g)	2 lb 12 oz (1.25 kg)
Vegetables (uncooked weight)	3 lb 5 oz (1.5 kg)	6 lb 10 oz (3 kg)	12 lb 2 oz (5.5 kg)
Fresh fruits or fruit salad	3 lb 5 oz (1.5 kg)	6 lb 1 oz (2.75 kg)	12 lb 2 oz (5.5 kg)
Ice cream	½ gallon (1.75 liters)	¾ gallon (2.5 liters)	1¼ gallons (5 liters)

TABLE SETTINGS AND DECORATIONS

AN ATTRACTIVE TABLE SETTING ENHANCES A MEAL, whether it is a formal dinner or an informal party. Use your imagination or look in books and magazines for inspiration to create an attractive table setting suitable for the occasion.

PREPARING TABLECLOTHS

In addition to serving a decorative purpose, a tablecloth protects the surface of the table. White linen or cotton damask tablecloths are conventionally used for formal occasions, but you may prefer to choose a cloth to match the setting or to follow the theme of the occasion.

PROTECTING TABLES

Plastic protects table

Covering with plastic
Prevent spills from damaging a polished table top by placing a layer of plastic wrap or oilcloth over it before laying the main tablecloth. Alternatively, use a plastic tablecloth.

WEIGHTING CLOTHS

Slip coin inside hem

Using coins as weights
Weight a tablecloth to be used outdoors by removing a few stitches around the hem and slipping coins or curtain weights inside. Alternatively, you can tack weights onto the cloth.

PREVENTING FLAPPING

Knot loosely to prevent corner from lifting

Tying knots
Knot the corners of a cloth when eating outdoors to prevent them from flapping. Place the cloth over one of a contrasting shade or slip bouquets of dried flowers into each knot for decoration.

FINDING ALTERNATIVES
● **Using sheets** If you need extra tablecloths for a large party, improvise with sheets or lengths of cheesecloth.
● **Using several cloths** If you have only small tablecloths, use a plain sheet as an undercloth, and lay several small, pretty tablecloths diagonally on top to cover a large table.
● **Using a blanket** If you do not have an undercloth, use a thick blanket underneath a tablecloth to prevent the top of the table from being marked.
● **Substituting rugs** For a party with an Arabian or Oriental theme, lay brightly colored kilims or rugs over large tables.

DECORATING PLAIN TABLECLOTHS

Making herb bouquets
Make small bouquets of fresh herbs, such as rosemary or thyme, to attach to a plain tablecloth. Tie the bouquets with ribbon, and pin them to the cloth in each corner.

● **Decorating with stencils** Use stencils and fabric paints to decorate a plain cloth. Stencil a border around each place setting.
● **Spray painting** Brighten up plain fabric or paper cloths with spray paints in colorful, abstract designs for children's parties.
● **Scattering petals** Scatter rose petals or other edible flowers over a cloth for a romantic touch.
● **Adding sparkle** At a festive event, sprinkle gold or silver stars over the tablecloth.
● **Using wallpaper borders** Decorate the edges of a plain cloth with a pretty wallpaper border, securing it around the edges with double-sided tape.

SETTING TABLES

The same basic principles apply to setting any table, whether for an informal or a formal meal, although the menu dictates which cutlery is used. To avoid overcrowding the table at the start of a meal, additional cutlery can be brought to the table with the appropriate courses.

LAYING A TABLE FOR DINNER

Large goblet for red wine

Dessert spoon laid above fork

Water glass

Small wine glass for white wine

Butter knife

Plate set for first course

Napkin placed on side plate

Forks to left of plate in order of use

Knives and spoon to right of plate, knife blades toward plate

Laying a setting
However many courses there are, lay the cutlery in the order it will be used, working from the outside inward. To save space, you can place both the dessert spoon and fork at the top of the setting. Arrange glasses at the top right-hand corner, with the main wine glass placed above the tip of the main knife.

CHOOSING GLASSWARE

If you have taken care with your choice of drinks, you will want to choose glassware equally carefully to complement the drinks and the table setting. When calculating how many glasses you need for entertaining on a large scale, allow an additional 10 percent for breakage.

CHOOSING WINE GLASSES

Choosing the right shape
To enjoy the bouquet of either white or red wine, serve it in glasses that are narrower at the rim than in the body. This shape enhances a wine's bouquet.

USING GLASSWARE
● **Removing labels** To remove sticky labels from new glasses, rub with lighter fluid.
● **Removing water marks** If glasses are dulled by water marks, restore their sparkle by soaking in water with a little vinegar. Rinse thoroughly in cold water, drain, and dry.
● **Washing crystal** Wash fine lead crystal glasses by hand in warm water and detergent. Rinse in clear water, and dry while warm. Washing lead crystal in a dishwasher will dull the surface of the glasses.
● **Serving champagne** Serve champagne in slender flutes, which show off the bubbles and color of the wine.

CHOOSING PITCHERS
Sturdy handle allows good grip when pouring

Fruit and ice remain in pitcher to flavor and cool

Pouring fruit punch
Serve fruit punches and iced drinks from a glass pitcher that has a pinched pouring lip or a filter to prevent fruit slices or ice cubes from falling into the glass.

CHOOSING TABLEWARE

The careful selection of tableware is essential to the visual success of a dinner party and to show off the food at its best. Choose simple yet striking colors and shapes when deciding which china, cutlery, and linen to use. Arrange them so that they do not detract from the food.

MIXING & MATCHING TABLEWARE

Contrasting side plate

Underplate contrasts with dinner plate

Patterned napkin

Mixing colors
If you do not have enough matching tableware for all your guests, then mix and match what you have, combining colors and styles to dramatic effect. Layer contrasting colors on top of one another.

FINDING SERVING ALTERNATIVES

● **Using disposable platters** Buy large, disposable foil platters for buffet foods. To make them look decorative, line with lettuce leaves before arranging the food on top.

● **Using wicker containers** For an unusual presentation, serve bread and canapés in wicker containers. Line baskets with napkins for bread, and trays with lettuce leaves for canapés.

USING LARGE PLATTERS

Arranging ingredients
If you do not have a plate that fits the size of a quiche or tart exactly, choose a large platter. Place the quiche in the center, and fill the space around it with a mixed salad or pretty garnish.

MAKING CENTERPIECES

Even on an informal occasion, a colorful centerpiece of flowers or fruits will bring an extra-special touch to the table. Make sure that the size and shape of a centerpiece allows your guests to see one another across the dining table. Stabilize vases with stones or marbles.

USING FRUITS

Carve pattern with sharp knife

ARRANGING FRUITY, FLORAL DISPLAYS

Apple wedge

Fruit holds stem in place

Citrus slice adds color and prevents other fruits from browning

Making a melon basket
Make a dessert centerpiece for serving fruit salad by making a melon basket. Cut a slice from the melon, and scoop out the flesh. Carve the melon skin to decorate, then fill with fruit salad.

Using fruits
Arrange flowers for a buffet-table centerpiece in a glass dish packed with pieces of fresh fruit. The fruits feed the flowers, keeping them fresh.

DECORATING PLACE SETTINGS

Whatever the occasion – whether formal or informal – imaginative place settings will help make guests feel welcome and break the ice as they sit down to eat. Always keep decorations simple and fresh, and use edible flowers if they will be in contact with the food.

CREATING AN INDIVIDUAL DISPLAY

Decorate underplate with flowers before serving food

Using flowers
To give a place setting a fresh, seasonal touch, arrange edible flowers or fresh herbs around a dinner plate on a wide underplate. Spray the flowers gently with water to keep them fresh for as long as possible.

GIVING EDIBLE FAVORS

Gathered edges of net form pretty frill

Tying net bundles
Make edible favors for guests to take home as mementos. Place Jordan almonds and chocolates on small circles of fine nylon net. Then gather up the net, and tie each bundle with ribbon.

DECORATING PLATES & PLACEMATS
● **Stenciling underplates** Decorate large underplates by stenciling around their rims. Using nontoxic paints, spray holly leaves, hearts, stars, or a band of gold or silver color.

● **Decorating placemats** For a themed adults' or children's party, cut out paper shapes of hearts or cartoon characters to decorate plain placemats. Secure in place with glue.

SETTING THE SCENE
● **Making a pastry garland** For a romantic occasion, shape shortcrust pastry or cookie dough into small hearts. Pierce a hole in each with a skewer, and bake. Thread the hearts together with ribbon to make a garland around each plate.

● **Decorating chairs** To trim chairs for a wedding, use wired florist's ribbon to fashion extravagant bows, and attach one to the back of each guest's chair. Alternatively, tie on small bouquets of fresh flowers to match the bride's bouquet.

● **Adding roses** Place a single red rose across each place setting as a romantic gift for each guest at a wedding or anniversary celebration.

● **Lighting candles** Just before the guests are seated, place a red apple with a long taper candle stuck in it at each setting. Lower the lights when all the candles are lit.

USING FRUITS & SPICES
● **Making spice bundles** Gather together small bundles of warm, winter spices such as cinnamon sticks and ginger with a few bay leaves. Tie together with ribbons as festive gifts for your guests.

Use toothpick to make holes in skin

Decorating citrus fruits
Make spice-scented pomanders as gifts to decorate each table setting. Stud small oranges or limes with cloves, then tie a patterned ribbon around each, and finish with a decorative bow.

USING FINGER FOODS
● **Making edible treats** For a summer party, thread two or three fresh strawberries onto wooden skewers with a mint leaf between the fruits. Place a skewer on each plate for a predinner appetizer.

Tuck herb sprigs between bread sticks

Decorating with herbs
Decorate a country-style table setting by tying each napkin loosely around two or three bread sticks. Add a few sprigs of fresh rosemary or bay leaves for a delicate scent.

MAKING MENU CARDS

Menu cards are most commonly used for formal dinners, but there is no reason why they cannot be used for any occasion. Follow the same theme that was used on the invitations. Guests may like to keep the menu cards as a fun memento of a special occasion.

COVERING MENUS

Tying with cord
To make a handwritten menu look more formal, place it on top of a large piece of colored cardboard. Put the cardboard and menu together with decorative cord, and finish with a bow.

DECORATING CARDS

Using a stencil
Stencil a border onto a menu card using a food motif that reflects the menu. Cut a stencil from thin cardboard in the shape of your choice, then use a stiff brush to apply paint evenly.

DESIGNING INFORMALLY
● **Using marker pens** For festive occasions or special anniversaries, use silver or gold marker pens to write out menus and decorate the edges of simple menu cards.
● **Writing on plates** For an informal party, buy plain paper plates, and write menus on them with colored felt-tip pens. If you have children, they can decorate the menus. (Do not eat off the plates.)
● **Making a collage** Make plain menu cards look festive by cutting up old greetings cards and gluing on images.

DESIGNING PLACE CARDS

Name cards and seating plans can serve a useful purpose even on small, informal occasions. A successful seating plan will place guests so that they enjoy one another's company, avoid confusion as guests sit down at the start of a meal, and help shy guests break the ice.

CREATING MARKERS
● **Using fruits** Spray fruits such as apples, pears, or lemons with gold paint, let dry, then attach gold name tags for festive settings.
● **Baking gingerbread men** Make and bake gingerbread men, and tuck them into small envelopes, each labeled with a guest's name.
● **Piping icing** Cut cookie dough into decorative shapes, bake and cool them, then pipe a guest's name and a decorative motif onto each cookie with colored icing.
● **Painting eggs** For a spring party, paint eggs with guests' names incorporated into the design. Place in pretty egg cups, one at each setting.
● **Saving time** Buy gift tags to use as festive name cards if you are short of time.

USING THEMES
● **Making masks** For a themed costume party, buy plain party masks, and decorate them yourself in a way that reflects the theme. Individualize the masks by incorporating a guest's name into each design.

MODELING FIGURES
● **Using dough** Mix water and flour to make a paste, shape into figures, and bake in a low oven for two hours until dry. Inscribe a guest's name on each figure, decorate it with acrylic paint, and then varnish.

MAKING A POP-UP PLACE CARD

Cut with craft knife

1 Draw a shape in the center of a sheet of thin cardboard, and color if desired. Mark a fine line to indicate where the fold will be. Cut carefully around the shape above the fold line.

2 Fold the card along the marked line. The upper part of the shape will extend above the fold. Inscribe the guest's name on it, and then position the card on the table.

FOLDING NAPKINS

Folded table napkins can enhance a table setting on a special occasion, and knowledge of a few simple folds is all that you require. The best fabrics to use for folding are starched linen and cotton, which hold their shape well. Even paper napkins can be folded successfully.

FOLDING SIMPLE NAPKIN FANS

Pleat evenly

Tie pleats together with ribbon

Hold center pleats of napkin

1 To make a simple napkin fan, first starch and iron a fabric napkin, or use a good-quality paper napkin. Starting from one side, fold the napkin into evenly spaced accordion pleats all the way across.

2 Continue until the whole napkin is pleated, and press the pleats firmly in place. Fold the pleated napkin in half. Tie a small, decorative ribbon bow around the base of the pleats, above the folded end.

3 Place the napkin on a dinner plate, hold the two center pleats together, and open out the pleats to either side to form a fan shape. A napkin fan can also be placed upright in a wine glass.

CREATING NAPKIN RINGS

Napkin rings add a finishing touch to rolled or folded napkins, and there are many ways of creating decorative devices to hold napkins prettily as part of a table setting. Keep them simple, so that they enhance rather than detract from the food and the other table decorations.

FOLLOWING THEMES

● **Creating lavish effects** Buy opulent curtain braids and tassels to wrap around napkins for a sophisticated celebration.
● **Weaving raffia** For a rustic, harvest, or country theme, weave strips of raffia or straw into napkin rings. Tuck dried flowers into the ring.
● **Using ribbons** Tie simple colored ribbons around napkins to follow a color scheme, or buy special, festive ribbons to suit the occasion.
● **Celebrating anniversaries** Wind strings of imitation pearls or other costume jewelry around table napkins for an anniversary celebration.
● **Threading shells** Make a marine-themed napkin ring by threading small shells onto fine wire, then twisting the ends together to make a ring.

USING FRESH HERBS

● **Attaching herb sprigs** To bring a pleasant scent to the dinner table and decorate simple, rolled napkins, tuck sprigs of herbs or herb flowers into plain napkin rings.

Tying with chives
Tie freshly cut chive fronds around a plain, rolled napkin. Cut the chives so that they are as long as possible. The longer the fronds, the easier it will be to tie them. Trim the ends to neaten.

USING FOOD AND FLOWERS

● **Making garlands** Make garland napkin rings to match bridal flowers. Bend a piece of florist's wire into a ring, and bind it with ribbon. Cut sprays of flowers such as mimosa or freesia, and bind them around each ring with fine wire.
● **Using leaves** Select flat-shaped leaves from plants such as iris, and tie around a simply folded napkin in a loose knot.
● **Threading candies** Thread colorful licorice candies onto heavy thread, and tie to make edible napkin rings.
● **Baking bread rings** Instead of bread rolls, shape dough into rings, glaze with egg, and sprinkle with poppy or sesame seeds. Bake until golden, and slip one onto each napkin before serving.

COCKTAIL PARTIES

COCKTAIL PARTIES CAN BE FORMAL OR INFORMAL, offering a simple glass of sherry or a choice of cocktails, depending on the particular occasion. If you are inviting more than 20 guests, consider hiring a bartender to serve drinks.

MAKING AND SERVING CANAPÉS

Food is essential at any cocktail party, but there is no need to spend hours preparing elaborate dishes. Simple canapés or dips are all that is needed. Offer your guests a choice of finger foods and other tidbits that can be eaten with one hand, in one or two bites.

SKEWERING CANAPÉS

Thread small pieces onto toothpick

SERVING CANAPÉS WITH STYLE

Use pastry brush to glaze

Making tricolor sticks
Thread cubes of feta cheese onto toothpicks or wooden skewers between squares of raw green and red peppers to make tricolor sticks. If you prefer, cook the peppers under the broiler.

Using a mirror
Arrange bite-sized finger foods on a mirror tile instead of a plate for an unusual presentation at a formal cocktail party. Leave space between the canapés to achieve the best effect.

Making a dough platter
Roll out shortcrust pastry or bread dough in a round shape. Edge with shaped leftover dough, place on a cookie sheet, glaze with lightly beaten egg, and bake until golden. Use to serve canapés.

QUICK AND EASY CANAPÉS

- **Piped celery** Pipe soft, herb-flavored cream cheese into the hollows of celery sticks.
- **Paté-filled mushrooms** Remove the stalks from small cup mushrooms, and pipe paté into the hollows left by the stalks.
- **Blue-cheese grapes** Mix equal amounts of blue cheese and butter. Cut large black or green grapes in half, and sandwich back together with the mix.
- **Mini-biscuits** Make mini-sized savory biscuits, and bake until golden. Cool, and top with cream cheese and an olive.
- **Chicken-liver toasts** Sauté chicken livers quickly in a little butter and sherry. Cut into bite-sized pieces, and spoon onto small, French-bread toasts.

- **Nachos bites** Spoon a little spicy guacamole or hummus onto tortilla chips, and sprinkle with paprika to garnish.
- **Bacon twists** Twist thin slices of smoked bacon with strips of puff pastry. Bake at 400°F (200°C) for about 15 minutes, or until the pastry is firm and golden brown.
- **Salami cones** Wrap thin slices of salami carefully around melon sticks, and secure each one by piercing with a toothpick.
- **Almond olives** Stuff pitted olives with whole, salted, or smoked almonds.
- **Ham with kiwis** Wrap thinly sliced smoked ham around wedges of peeled kiwi fruit, and secure each with a toothpick.

PREVENTING PROBLEMS
- **Preventing soggy pastry** To serve vol-au-vents and other pastries with moist fillings, bake the pastry cases in advance, but add the fillings only one hour before serving.
- **Making bite-sized foods** Make canapés small enough to be easily held in the hand and to be eaten in one mouthful to prevent mess.
- **Serving in stages** Serve hot and cold canapés in small batches over a period of about an hour, instead of serving them all at the same time.
- **Clearing space** Make space so that guests can put down their drinks and not juggle food and drinks. Clear away empty glasses and food debris.

MAKING CRUDITÉS AND DIPS

Crudités and dips make excellent food for serving at informal cocktail parties, since they are simple to make and can be prepared in advance. Serve plenty of crudités and savory chips for dipping, and make the dippers small enough to be eaten in one mouthful.

PREPARING & PRESENTING CRUDITÉS

Deep serving dish allows ice to melt without spilling

Colorful mixture of vegetables for dipping

Making an ice ring
Keep vegetables fresh by serving them in an ice ring. Fill a large ring mold with water and freeze. Unmold onto a deep serving dish, and arrange vegetables in the center. Garnish around the ice ring to finish.

SIMPLE DIPS

- **Tuna** Drain a can of tuna, and mash with plain yogurt. Add chopped dill to taste.
- **Deviled sauce** Mix tomato ketchup with a small amount of Worcestershire sauce.
- **Pesto** Stir pesto sauce into light sour cream.
- **Blue cheese** Mash equal amounts of blue cheese and soft cream cheese, softening with a little milk if necessary.
- **Avocado** Mash avocado with a little mayonnaise, and add lemon juice to taste.

MAKING AND SERVING DRINKS

Offer drinks to guests as they arrive. Make sure that there is a good selection of soft drinks as well as alcoholic drinks. If you are serving only one or two different drinks, pour them out in advance, and place them on trays to serve. Mix cocktails in pitchers for easy serving.

CHILLING & SERVING

- **Chilling bottles** If you are short of refrigerator space for chilling bottles, fill the tub with ice, and store the bottles in it until you need them.
- **Freezing fruit juice** To prevent drinks from being watered down by plain ice cubes, freeze fruit juice into cubes as an alternative.
- **Rinsing glasses** Rinse all traces of detergent from glasses before pouring champagne, since detergent destroys the bubbles.
- **Serving soft drinks** Always include fresh fruit juices and mineral waters among soft drinks for nondrinkers.
- **Making punch** Serve a mixed punch at a large party. This is particularly suitable for large numbers, and can be less expensive than serving a wide selection of wines and spirits.

PREPARING & PRESENTING DRINKS

Strawberry stirrer adds flavor

Fizz created by dissolved, brandy-soaked sugar cube

Cucumber garnish

Rim frosted with food coloring and superfine sugar

Twist of peel adds flavor

Napkin placed under iced drink absorbs moisture

Adding finishing touches
It is worth taking care to serve drinks well, and some of the most effective ideas are quick and simple to achieve. If you want to add a garnish to a cocktail, make sure that you choose a large enough glass so that the drink will not overflow.

BUFFETS

PREPARING A SELF-SERVICE, BUFFET-STYLE MEAL is the easiest way to cater for a large number of people, since it allows you to provide for a range of different tastes, ages, and appetites, as long as you organize the food well in advance.

ARRANGING A BUFFET TABLE

For an appealing buffet, try to add variety to the appearance of dishes by varying their shapes and heights. Select food, tableware, utensils, and accessories such as napkins so that colors, textures, and shapes complement or contrast with one another in an imaginative way.

PLANNING THE LAYOUT OF A BUFFET TABLE

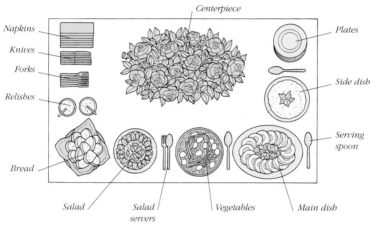

Centerpiece

Napkins

Knives

Forks

Relishes

Bread

Plates

Side dish

Serving spoon

Salad

Salad servers

Vegetables

Main dish

Arranging dishes
When arranging the dishes on a buffet table, start with the plates, then side dishes, followed by the main dish, and finally vegetables and salads, with serving utensils alongside. Breads, any relishes, cutlery, and napkins are usually positioned at the end of the selection. Place decorations in the middle of the table.

ORGANIZING BUFFETS
● Positioning a buffet table
Leave room behind a buffet table so that you have easy access for replacing dishes.
● **Taping wires** If you place the buffet table in the center of a room, make sure that all electrical wires are taped down safely to the floor.
● **Grouping chairs** Make sure that there are enough chairs, and position them together in groups of three or more so that guests can sit and chat.
● **Setting drinks aside** Place drinks, glasses, and cups on a separate table to avoid congestion at the buffet table.
● **Leaving space on the table** Leave space between dishes on the buffet table so that guests can put down glasses or plates when serving themselves.

KEEPING FOODS COLD
● **Making a cold plate** Fill a dish with water, and freeze. Put it in a plastic bag, then place a plate on top to keep food cold.

Rest food platter on ice

Using crushed ice
Remove chilled foods from the refrigerator just before serving. To keep food cold on the table, fill a wide dish with crushed ice, and nestle a serving dish into it.

CALCULATING QUANTITIES

Use this checklist to figure quantities for buffet foods. Use the guide on p. 118 to calculate main- and side-dish quantities.

● **Bread** A large, thinly sliced loaf has 18–20 slices. One baguette serves 10 people.
● **Butter** 2 tbsp (25 g) butter will cover seven slices of bread.
● **Green salad** A large iceberg lettuce will serve 10 people, a romaine will serve eight, and a Boston, four.
● **Celebration cake** A 5-lb (2.25-kg) sheet cake can be cut into about 50 slices.
● **Wine** A small (70-cl) bottle fills six glasses; a large (1-liter) bottle, nine.
● **Ice** 20 lb (10 kg) ice cools two cases (24 bottles) of wine.

PRESENTING FOOD

Take care with the presentation of food for a buffet table in order to show off the food at its very best. If you are feeding a large number of guests, replenish serving dishes and clear away empty plates frequently so that the table always looks attractive for your guests.

USING LARGE PLATTERS
● **Stacking sandwiches** Cut sandwiches into quarters, and place them with the points upward to show the fillings.

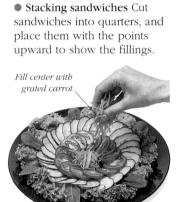

Fill center with grated carrot

Arranging a salad
Instead of tossing salad in a bowl, arrange ingredients in a colorful pattern on a large, wide platter. Spoon dressing, if desired, over the salad before serving.

DISPLAYING FRUITS

Making a fruit pyramid
Cut the flesh from a large pineapple, leaving the central core and leaves. Attach to a cake stand. Build up seasonal fruits around the core into a pyramid.

BRIGHT IDEA

Making a cake stand
If you do not have a cake stand for a buffet table, use a large plate or platter. Stand it on an upside-down sugar bowl or soufflé dish. Make sure that the plate is centered. Secure the two firmly with removable putty.

SERVING DRINKS

If guests are to help themselves to drinks at a buffet party, punch is ideal, since it is easy to serve. Offering a punch is also a good way to make alcohol go further. Warm hot punches over low heat if you wish to prevent the alcohol from boiling off, and serve in heatproof cups.

SERVING COLD DRINKS
● **Making a punch bowl** You can use any large, glass bowl as a punch bowl. Decorate the edges with frosted sugar or fruit slices, and drape edible flowers around the sides. Tie ribbon to the ladle handle to serve.
● **Keeping punch chilled** To keep a fruit punch cold, and to serve it in an unusual way, cut the top off a large, round watermelon. Scoop out the flesh, and freeze the shell for 2–3 hours. Add the punch, and serve from the shell.
● **Flavoring ice cubes** To chill and flavor fruit cups, freeze strawberries, maraschino cherries, or mint into ice cubes.

SERVING COCKTAILS

Replace lid when straw is in place

Using melon shells
For an unusual way of serving a fruit cocktail, cut a slice from the top of a small melon and scoop out the flesh. Before filling, cut a hole in one side of the lid for a straw to fit through.

SERVING HOT PUNCHES
● **Mulling wine** To keep mulled wine or a hot punch warm, make the drink in an electric slow-cooking crockpot placed on the buffet table.
● **Floating apples** For a festive winter punch, float a few sweet apples and spices in a hot wine or ale punch. The apples will poach gently, and after an hour or so will make a delicious dessert.
● **Doubling up cups** If you are serving hot punch in disposable paper or plastic cups, test the cups first to check that they are heatproof. Double up cups to make them comfortable to hold.

DINNER PARTIES

Aᴅɪɴɴᴇʀ ᴘᴀʀᴛʏ ɪs ᴀɴ ᴇxᴄᴜsᴇ to show off cooking skills that you may not necessarily use in everyday cooking. Plan carefully, and prepare as much as possible in advance so that you are able to enjoy time with your guests.

PRESENTING FOOD

Good presentation of food needs only basic decorating skills and simple but effective garnishes. Elaborate presentation of food can be reserved for formal occasions, but always make sure that the way in which the food appears enhances rather than overshadows your cooking.

MOLDING VEGETABLES

Using a pastry cutter
To serve cut vegetables, place a round pastry cutter on each plate, and spoon in the cooked vegetables, packing them firmly. Lift off the cutter, leaving the vegetables molded to shape.

ARRANGING FOOD
● **Adding height** Pile stir-fried dishes high in the center of a plate so that the helping looks attractive and generous.
● **Fanning slices** To arrange sliced food decoratively, such as an avocado or a chicken breast, slice the food, and lift it whole onto a plate with a spatula. Then fan out the slices evenly.
● **Tieing bundles** Use a chive "ribbon," or thin strips of green leek blanched for 30 seconds, to tie vegetable sticks or baby vegetables together in small bundles.

SHAPING CHOCOLATE

Making chocolate baskets
Spread melted chocolate evenly over 7-in (18-cm) circles of waxed paper to within 1 in (2.5cm) of the edges. Mold over upside-down cups, let set, and peel off the paper. Use for serving desserts.

SERVING CREAMS AND SAUCES

Connect drops of cream with toothpick

Spoon sauce carefully to create pattern

Feathering cream
Flood a plate with chocolate sauce or fruit purée, then carefully spoon drops of heavy cream onto it at regular intervals. Draw the tip of a toothpick through each drop to make a chain of feathered heart shapes.

Designing a pattern
Serve two sauces of similar consistency but contrasting colors together to create an impact. Create a simple but effective pattern by swirling one around the other, for example, on each side of a plate.

● **Making shapes** Spoon a little sauce into a small piping bag, and pipe the outline of the shape you want on a plate. Carefully spoon the rest of the sauce to fill in the shape.
● **Setting purées** Dissolve 1 tsp (5 ml) gelatin in every 1 cup (250 ml) hot fruit purée, then pour the purée while still hot onto a serving plate. Chill the purée until set, then arrange the dessert however you wish.
● **Creating a marbled effect** Marble dark and white chocolate sauces by stirring them together very lightly immediately before serving.
● **Enhancing gravy** Sprinkle fine strips of citrus zest, such as lemon or lime, into plain gravy to accompany grilled meat.

ADDING FINISHING TOUCHES

Garnishes add an attractive finishing touch to a dish, particularly if you are cooking for a special occasion. Remember, however, that it is the dish that is important: garnishes should complement, not compete with, the ingredients. Prepare elaborate garnishes in advance.

ENHANCING GARNISHES

● **Shaping with a canelle knife** Before slicing a cucumber as a garnish, run a canelle knife or the prongs of a fork down its sides at intervals. The slices will then have a fluted edge.

● **Dipping in parsley** Add color to lemon or tomato wedges by dipping their edges into finely chopped parsley after cutting. Alternatively, dip the edges of tomatoes into finely grated Parmesan cheese.

● **Deep-frying parsley** To prevent parsley sprigs from becoming limp, deep-fry them first in hot oil until they are bright green and crisp. Drain on a piece of paper towel.

GARNISHING WITH FRUITS

● **Preparing strawberry fans** To decorate summer desserts, leave the leafy tops on fresh strawberries, and use a sharp knife to cut thin slices through the fruits, leaving the slices attached at the stem end. Hold each stem, and lightly press the slices into a fan shape.

Use sharp knife for accurate cutting

Cutting apple leaves
Cut a series of long, V-shaped notches in the side of an apple, each notch slightly bigger than the one before. Remove the pieces from the apple, and push each piece along on top of the one below to form a leaf shape.

PREPARING VEGETABLE GARNISHES

Slice horizontally to produce hearts

Making carrot hearts
For a romantic dinner garnish, shape a peeled carrot by cutting a groove down one side. Cut the opposite side to a point, so that cross-sections form heart shapes. Slice for individual hearts.

GARNISHING QUICKLY

● **Using trimmed leaves** Keep the central leaves from a head of celery, and scatter them over savory dishes to add color.

● **Scattering nuts** Keep toasted, flaked almonds in a jar for scattering over hot and cold savory or sweet dishes as an instant garnish.

● **Sprinkling sugar** As a quick, effective topping for hot or cold desserts, shake sifted confectioners' sugar lightly over the surface of the dish.

● **Using zest** Make a last-minute garnish for savory and sweet dishes by using a zester to grate fine strips of zest from citrus fruits. Scatter the zest over the food before serving.

● **Grating coconut** Use a vegetable peeler to grate curls of fresh coconut over main courses or desserts. Remove the flesh from the shell, but retain the brown skin. Grate across the skin and the flesh to keep the skin on the curls.

Cut leaves into thin ribbons

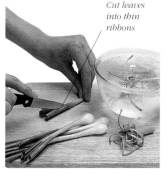

Making scallion tassels
Trim scallions, and cut short lengths from the leaf ends. Cut slits lengthwise, extending halfway along each piece from the leaf end. Place in iced water until the sliced leaf ends curl.

SAVING TIME

● **Preparing ahead** When entertaining, make garnishes such as lemon twists, scallion tassels, and tomato wedges in advance. Place on a plate, and add to the food at a later stage. Cover them with plastic wrap, and they will stay fresh for up to four hours.

EDIBLE FLOWERS

The following flowers are edible, and are therefore good for decorative purposes. The large flowers of some vegetables, such as zucchini, and the flowers of some herbs are also edible. If you cannot identify a flower, do not eat it.

Apple blossom	Lavender
Borage	Marigold
Calendula	Nasturtium
Clover	Orange
Dandelion	Pansy
Daylily	Primrose
Elderflower	Rose
Geranium	Violet

SERVING WINE

Alcoholic drinks stimulate the appetite and enhance the flavor of food, so they can add to the enjoyment of any meal, however simple the food or the setting. If you are unsure about choosing wines, consult a good wine merchant, who will let you taste a selection before you buy.

MATCHING WINE WITH FOOD

There are no strict rules about which wine to serve with which dish, but the following guidelines are useful.

● **Order of drinking** White wine is generally preferred before red, young before mature, and dry before sweet.
● **Appetizers or canapés** Serve crisp white wines, sparkling wines, or dry sherry.
● **Fish dishes** Serve dry white wines such as Muscadet, or young, light reds.
● **Pasta and cheese dishes** Serve robust wines such as Bardolino (red).
● **Creamy dishes** Choose slightly acidic wines such as Sauvignon Blanc (white).

PREPARING WINE
● **Chilling wines** To chill white wines, refrigerate for a maximum of two hours, or bury the bottles in crushed ice for 30 minutes before serving.
● **Accelerating chilling** Put wine in the freezer to cool quickly, leaving only for about five minutes. Set a timer so that you remember to remove it.
● **Loosening wires** To save time, loosen the wires of champagne corks while the bottles are chilling so that the corks are ready to pop.
● **Warming red wines** Pour red wine into a slightly warm decanter to warm quickly, instead of heating the wine directly. Uncork young red wine about an hour before serving to develop the flavor.

TRADITIONAL TIP

Decanting wine
Decant bottle-aged wine or port to remove sediment. To do this easily, insert an unbleached coffee filter into the neck of a glass pitcher, and pour the wine gently into it.

SERVING NONALCOHOLIC DRINKS

Whatever the occasion, offer your guests a selection of nonalcoholic drinks. Always have mineral water available for both drinkers and nondrinkers, as well as fruit juices and cordials. Some people may prefer wine "lookalikes" such as grape juice or alcohol-free wines.

ADDING FLAVOR
● **Stimulating the appetite** Add a thin slice of fresh lemon or lime to each glass of mineral water to sharpen the appetite.
● **Accompanying spicy food** Serve a refreshing, lassi-style yogurt drink with spicy food, such as an Indian curry, instead of wine or beer. Place 1 cup (250 ml) plain yogurt in a blender with 2 cups (500 ml) water, ½ tsp (2.5 ml) salt, and a sprig of fresh mint. Blend until smooth, then serve in tall, chilled glasses.
● **Adding celery sticks** Use a small, trimmed piece of celery as a swizzle stick for stirring tomato or vegetable juice.

MAKING MILK SHAKES

Shake until frothy before pouring

Using a screw-top jar
If you do not have a blender with which to make a milk shake, mix fruit purée and ice cream with milk in a large screw-top jar and shake. Alternatively, beat the mixture with a balloon whisk.

ALCOHOL-FREE COCKTAILS

● **Cranberry spritzer** Stir equal parts cranberry juice, white grape juice, and sparkling mineral water.
● **Raspberry mint fizz** Pour ¼ cup (50 ml) raspberry syrup into a tall glass. Add a handful of crushed mint leaves and ice. Top off with soda water.
● **Shirley Temple** Shake several dashes of grenadine into a glass. Top off with lemon-lime soda for a bubbly froth. Finish with a maraschino cherry.
● **Peppermint cream** Shake peppermint cordial with cream and a little crushed ice.

CATERING FOR SPECIAL OCCASIONS

A wedding, birthday, or other celebration is an excuse to prepare elaborate food, but clever presentation and original use of color can also contribute to a memorable meal. Use your imagination to carry the theme of an event through to the table decorations and the food.

MAKING UNUSUAL CAKES

EXTENDING COLOR THEMES TO FOOD

Duck with orange

Tomato and pepper salad

Selecting golden food
For a golden-themed celebration, serve yellow and orange foods such as carrots, yellow peppers, saffron rice, and fruits such as oranges and peaches.

Peach served with brandy snaps

Creating different shapes
For a celebration cake, fill small cream puffs with whipped cream or pastry cream, then pile into a pyramid shape. Tuck roses or mint leaves in the gaps, and sprinkle with confectioners' sugar.

USING FLOWERS
● **Making a cake stand** Instead of using a formal silver cake stand for a wedding or a christening cake, choose a firm wooden box that is slightly larger than the base of the cake, and cover it with a lace cloth. Pin on silk or fresh flowers and ribbons to decorate.
● **Flavoring with flowers** Add a few drops of orange flower water or rosewater to whipped fresh cream, and stir gently. Spoon into pretty bowls, and scatter with fresh orange blossom or rose petals. Serve with desserts instead of plain whipped cream.
● **Floating candles** To make an unusual evening table decoration, half fill a large, wide glass bowl with water. Float small candles and lavish fresh blooms, such as camellias, on the water.

● **Creating a tricolor dinner** Mix red, green, and white foods to carry an Italian theme through the meal. For example, use red and green peppers, or tomatoes and basil, with white cheeses.

● **Using dark foods** For an elegant dinner, create a stunning, almost black theme by using black plates and dark foods such as beets, purple basil, wild rice, black grapes, and blackberries.

CREATING MOLDED ICE DECORATIONS
● **Making ice sculptures** Use an elaborate gelatin mold to freeze an ice sculpture for a celebration buffet table. Unmold and use as a centerpiece for crudités or fresh fruits.

● **Using boiled water** When making ice sculptures and bowls, first boil the water. This will result in clearer ice than if unboiled water is used. Cool completely before freezing.

MOLDING A DECORATIVE ICE BOWL

Tape bowls to ensure evenly shaped ice

Use knife point to push flowers into position

1 Make an ice bowl in which to serve ices. Place a small, freezer-proof bowl inside a larger bowl, and tape the bowls in position. Fill the space in between with water.

2 Push some edible flowers into the water, and freeze. Fill the small bowl with warm water, and lift out. Dip the outer bowl in warm water, and unmold.

PARTY MANAGEMENT

THERE IS NO MYSTERY TO THROWING the perfect party, but careful planning in advance is the best insurance you can have against disasters. Once a party is organized, allow yourself some time to relax before your guests arrive.

OFFERING HOSPITALITY

Whatever the occasion, the most important thing to remember is that the guests come first. Give some thought to creating a warm atmosphere that will make guests comfortable as soon as they arrive, and spend time with them instead of disappearing into the kitchen.

PROVIDING FINGER BOWLS

Add lemon slices to refresh hands

Napkins for wiping hands

Placing finger bowls
If you are serving foods that are to be eaten with the fingers, such as crudités or shellfish, provide each guest with a finger bowl if they are sitting down to eat, or spread finger bowls liberally around the room for a buffet.

● **Scenting water** Add a few drops of orange flower water, rosewater, or lemon juice to the water, or scatter rose petals or jasmine flowers to leave a pleasant scent on the fingers.

● **Warming water** If you are serving sticky or fatty foods, such as spare ribs, warm the water to hand-hot for finger bowls, and put them out just before you serve the food.

> ### PLAN OF ACTION
>
> Remember these points before and during a party.
>
> ● **Checking insurance** Check with an insurance broker in case you need special insurance for a large event.
> ● **Preparing ahead** Do as much as possible in advance to make sure that you are free to welcome guests.
> ● **Circulating among guests** Introduce guests to each other, and "rescue" anyone who is left on their own.
> ● **Drinking alcohol** Do not encourage guests to drink large quantities of alcohol.

WELCOMING GUESTS

● **Creating atmosphere**
Depending on the occasion, tie a garland of fresh flowers, a lantern, or a bunch of balloons on a mailbox or a door to set the scene as guests approach the house.
● **Adjusting lighting** Before your guests arrive for a party, dim the house lights or light some candles around the rooms. Make sure that the light is soft but not too low, so that guests can see their food as well as one another.
● **Checking bathrooms** Check bathrooms to make sure that they are clean, with soaps and towels put out for guests to use. Leave lights on if the switches are difficult to locate.

CREATING A FRAGRANT ATMOSPHERE

Place ingredients in small bowls

Making potpourri
Instead of making a heavily flower-scented potpourri, make a food-based mixture. Combine bay leaves, thinly pared or dried citrus zest, cinnamon sticks, rosemary sprigs, juniper or allspice berries, and star anise. Sprinkle with vanilla or almond extract.

● **Reviving potpourri** Freshen up potpourri that has lost its scent by spreading it onto a cookie sheet and sprinkling it with water or scented oil. Place in a hot oven for five minutes to draw out the fragrances.

● **Positioning bowls** Place bowls of potpourri in the warmest areas of the room, such as on a mantelpiece, on a shelf above a table lamp, or around candles. The warmth will enhance the fragrances.

COPING WITH EMERGENCIES

However carefully you plan and prepare for entertaining, it is a good idea to be well prepared for emergencies. Whether someone experiences a medical problem or there is simply a spill, remain calm so that you can deal with the situation quickly and effectively.

CLEANING SPILLS

● **Preventing permanent stains** If red wine is spilled onto a carpet, splash it with soda water. Pat with paper towels to soak up the excess liquid, and treat with carpet shampoo.

Removing candle wax
If candle wax drips onto a tablecloth, rub it with an ice cube, and chip off the wax. Cover with paper towels, and press with a warm iron. Dab with rubbing alcohol to remove any residue before washing.

PREVENTING PROBLEMS

● **Informing neighbors** If you are throwing a party, let the neighbors know, or invite them over, so that noise will not be a source of irritation.
● **Spot-cleaning** Have on hand a bottle of spot-cleaner or dry-cleaning fluid, ready for dealing with minor spills.
● **Noting useful numbers** At a children's party, make sure that you have each parent's telephone number, and keep the number of the nearest hospital by the telephone.
● **Avoiding spoiled food** If cooking food such as a soufflé, the timing of which is critical, ensure that it will not be ready before it is due to be eaten.
● **Checking allergies** Be aware of any special dietary needs of guests, and ask parents if their children have food allergies.

COPING WITH DRINKERS

● **Preventing drunk driving** If a guest has drunk too much to drive, insist that a sober guest drive them home, or call for a taxi. Alternatively, suggest they stay overnight.

SAFETY

If someone is choking, follow this first-aid technique:

1 Remove food or false teeth from the mouth. Encourage the victim to cough.

2 If coughing fails and the person is making a high-pitched, wheezing sound, stand behind them, and put your clenched fist – thumb inward – underneath the breastbone. Hold the fist with the other hand, and pull firmly upward and inward up to four times.

CLEANING UP

Cleaning up after a party need not spoil the fun. If you work in a sensible, organized manner, the task will be simple and quick. A dishwasher will help, but if you do not have one enlist as many people as possible to help with the washing, drying, and putting away.

WORKING ORDER

Work in a logical order so that cleanup runs smoothly.

● **Clearing** Load glasses, cutlery, plates, ashtrays, and other items onto trays and carry them to the kitchen.
● **Removing food waste** Remove food debris from plates and serving dishes.
● **Soaking utensils** Soak plates, glasses, and cutlery in a sink full of soapy water.
● **Washing dishes** Wash in the sink, or load the dishwasher.
● **Putting away** Rinse, drain, dry, and put items away.

DRYING GLASSWARE

Avoiding damage
Cup the bowl of a stemmed glass in a dish towel when drying it, rotating the glass gently without twisting. Alternatively, rinse in clear water, and drain on a towel.

SAVING TIME & EFFORT

● **Heating water** Make sure that there is plenty of hot water for dishwashing.
● **Clearing the sink** Check that the sink or dishwasher is empty before starting to clean up.
● **Soaking cutlery** Prepare buckets of hot, soapy water, and drop cutlery into them to soak as you clean up.
● **Stocking up** Check that you have plenty of garbage bags, clean rags, detergent, and paper towels on hand.
● **Emptying ash** Empty the contents of ashtrays into an old cookie tin for safe disposal.

CHILDREN'S PARTIES

Good planning is the secret of success for children's parties and will make them fun for you as well as for the young guests. Organize food, space, and activities well in advance, and enlist help from other parents on party day.

PREPARING FUN FOOD

Children's party food should be colorful, fun, and good to eat. Keep it simple and healthy, easy to hold in the hand and to eat in small mouthfuls. Encourage the children to eat more than just sweet foods by making savories in fun shapes and colors to tempt picky eaters.

MAKING NOVELTY CAKES
● **Using a jelly roll** Cover a ready-made jelly roll with colored, ready-to-use fondant icing that is longer than the roll. Pinch the icing at each end so that it resembles a giant piece of candy. Decorate.
● **Cutting blocks** For a young child's party, make individual cakes by cutting a sponge cake into large cubes and covering with fondant. Pipe a child's initial on each piece, and pile up the cakes like toy blocks.
● **Making a clock** Pipe a clock on a birthday cake, with the "time" showing the child's age.

DECORATING BISCUITS

Baking window cookies
Roll out firm cookie dough, and cut into shapes, then remove centers with a small cutter. Fill the holes with crushed, clear, hard candies. Bake as usual.

USING FRUIT NOVELTIES

Fill with ice cream

Carving orange lanterns
Sculpt oranges to look like Halloween lanterns. Slice off the tops, scoop out the flesh, and carve faces into the skins. Fill, and replace the tops to serve.

FEEDING TODDLERS
● **Making traffic lights** Set green, yellow, and red gelatin in clear tumblers. Let each layer set before adding the next.

Pipe melted chocolate for face and tail

Creating meringue mice
Make oval meringues, and bake in a cool oven for 1½ hours. Stick halved chocolate buttons gently into the meringue for ears, and pipe other details such as eyes.

SERVING HOT FOODS
● **Saving time** To make quick, individual pizzas, top English muffins or plain rolls with savory toppings. Grill.

Frankfurters resting against mashed-potato pyramid

Making a tepee
Mold mashed potatoes into a pointed heap on a plate. Pile frankfurters or sausages around the outside of the potatoes to form a decorative tepee shape.

FEEDING TEENAGERS
● **Choosing a theme** Try a Tex-Mex theme for a teenage party. Serve food such as tacos with fillings, salsas, chili con carne, and guacamole.
● **Making mini-kebabs** Thread chunks of salami, cheese, cherry tomatoes, and button mushrooms onto bamboo skewers to serve with dips.
● **Filling pita breads** Serve burgers in sandwich-sized pita breads. They will be easier and less messy to hold than in burger buns.
● **Making iced bananas** Push ice-pop sticks into peeled bananas, and freeze for 30 minutes. Dip in melted chocolate, and roll quickly in dried coconut. Serve while still slightly frozen.

MAKING PARTY DRINKS

Inventing children's drinks for parties can be fun, and you can be especially creative with the trimmings. Wherever possible, try to use healthy, nutritious ingredients, such as fresh fruit juices instead of highly sweetened soda, and use fresh fruits for decoration or in ice cubes.

DECORATING DRINKS

● **Adding ice cream** Put scoops of ice cream into fruit juice just before serving. Half-fill glasses with the drink, add ice cream, and serve.
● **Making lollipops** Freeze fruit juice on lollipop sticks to make drinks on sticks.
● **Decorating milk shakes** Sprinkle fruity milk shakes with grated chocolate or rainbow sprinkles.
● **Freezing juices** Fill separate ice cube trays with apple, cranberry, and orange juices, and freeze overnight. Put mixed cubes into tall glasses, top off with lemonade, and decorate with fresh fruits.

DECORATING GLASSES

Use brightly colored stickers

Using stick-on shapes
Instead of buying decorated party glasses, attach stick-on shapes to the outside of plain tumblers or plastic cups. Remove all the stickers before washing.

ADDING EXTRAS

Making "magic" drinks
Delight children with this special effect. Freeze chocolate chips for 30 minutes, then add a handful to glasses of lemon-lime soda. The chips will bounce up and down.

USING FOOD FOR PARTY GAMES

Incorporate fun foods into party games. Plan energetic games, preferably outdoors, before the children eat. Hunting for edible treasure is popular. Use novelty foods for this or for quiet activities after the meal. If the weather is bad, try egg decorating with food markers.

MAKING EDIBLE GAMES

● **Icing domino cookies** Pipe dots of white icing or cream cheese onto rectangular chocolate cookies or graham crackers to make dominoes. Let the children play with the dominoes and then eat them when the game is over.

Baking a cookie jigsaw
Roll out plain, firm cookie dough. Cut jigsaw shapes in it. Bake and cool, then decorate with colored icing or food colors. Let the children fit the shapes together before they eat the cookies.

ENTERTAINING TODDLERS

Making fruit trees
Encourage small children to eat fruit by making a "tree" for the table. Fill a plant pot with stones, and insert a small branch into it. Hang cherries, or tie other fruits to the branches, for children to pick.

PLAYING OUTDOORS

● **Apple bobbing** Float some apples in a large bowl or bucket of water. Ask each to try to bite an apple without using hands. The first child to do so wins the game.
● **Egg-and-spoon racing** Hold a race with each child carrying a hard-cooked egg in a spoon. The winner is the first to finish without dropping the egg.
● **Passing the orange** Form two teams. Put an orange under the chin of each team leader. The winning team is the first to pass the orange along the team line without using hands.
● **Playing tic tac toe** Bake bread dough into large Os and Xs. Mark a grid on an old sheet, and lay it down. Let the children place the shapes.

BARBECUES

NO MATTER HOW BASIC THE EQUIPMENT AND HOW SIMPLE THE FOOD, barbecues are often more fun and the food better-tasting than meals cooked indoors. They can even free you from the kitchen, and fresh air will sharpen appetites.

SETTING UP BARBECUES

There are many well-designed, sophisticated barbecues on the market today that are very easy to light, control, and clean. It is not essential, however, to spend a lot of money on barbecue equipment. You can improvise very successfully using only basic equipment.

BUILDING A SIMPLE BARBECUE

Sturdy metal rack for grilling

Ordinary household bricks, arranged to your specification

Space under fuel pan for ashes, and to allow air to circulate

Shallow pan or old roasting pan with airholes

Using household bricks
Erect a small, simple barbecue using bricks. Equip it with a metal grill rack and a pan in which to place the fuel. If the barbecue is to be permanent, then line the inside with fireproof bricks.

MONEY-SAVING TIP

Using a cookie tin
To make a small, impromptu picnic barbecue, punch holes around the sides of an old cookie tin. Fill the tin with briquettes, and place a metal grill rack or a piece of chicken wire on top to hold the food for grilling.

PREPARING TO COOK
● **Adding flavor** Instead of buying expensive bags of hickory or oak chips for a flavored, smoky taste, scatter sprigs or twigs of rosemary, thyme, or fennel over the fire just before cooking. Soak the sprigs in water first to make them last longer.
● **Greasing racks** Keep trimmed meat fat for rubbing over a barbecue rack before placing food on it to prevent food from sticking. Alternatively, brush the rack with oil.
● **Heating up** Wait for the flames to die down before starting to cook. Charcoal takes at least 25–30 minutes to heat up, and gas barbecues take 10 minutes. Coals should be ash gray in color.

PREPARING FIRES
● **Using foil** Line the base of a barbecue with foil before adding fuel to reflect heat and to make cleaning easy.
● **Lighting fuel** If you find charcoal briquettes difficult to light, buy a bag of easy-light charcoal. It is clean and safe to use, since you need not handle the charcoal. Just place the specially designed bag of fuel in position, and light it.
● **Burning wood** Choose hardwoods from a sustainable source. Woods such as apple, oak, or cherry will burn slowly without crackling or smoking.

PREVENTING PROBLEMS
● **Avoiding flare-ups** To prevent a fire from flaring up, do not add too much oil to marinades, and trim excess fat from meat.
● **Controlling a fire** Keep a bucket of sand and a garden hose nearby in case a fire flares up out of control.

SAFETY

● **Site** Choose a firm, level surface away from buildings and out of the wind.
● **Children and pets** Keep them away from the fire.
● **Protection** Use long-handled tools and insulated gloves.
● **Fire control** Let the fire heat naturally. Never use lighter fluid.
● **First aid** Keep a first-aid kit handy in case of accidents.

CHAR-GRILLING FOODS

Cooking foods on an open grill directly over charcoal will give them a unique, smoky flavor, and using robust marinades, herbs, and spices will give additional impact. Plan the order of char-grilling carefully so that foods receive the precise amount of cooking that they need.

COOKING EVENLY
● **Precooking foods** Make sure that meat and poultry are well cooked by precooking in the microwave. Transfer them immediately to the barbecue.
● **Parboiling potatoes** Parboil new potatoes for five minutes, then thread them onto metal skewers. Brush with oil, and grill for 8–10 minutes.
● **Using heat zones** Use the cooler, outer edges around the grill to avoid overcooking food that needs gentle heat, such as vegetables or fruits.
● **Controlling heat** If your barbecue has no heat control, raise and lower the grill rack to control the heat. Sear meats such as steaks about 1½–2 in (4–5 cm) above the coals, then raise the rack to finish cooking on a lower heat.

ADDING FLAVOR
● **Spicing vegetables** Toss vegetables such as corn on the cob in butter or oil, and sprinkle with Cajun or curry spice.

Spread pesto with pastry brush

Glazing food with pesto
Brush low-fat food such as turkey or chicken breasts with pesto to add flavor and to keep the flesh moist during cooking. Pesto will also impart a rich Mediterranean flavor to the dish.

QUICK VEGETARIAN DISHES

● **Char-grilled vegetables** Brush halved eggplants, peppers, zucchinis, and onions with oil, and grill until golden and tender.
● **Eggplant rolls** Slice an eggplant lengthwise, brush with oil, and grill until tender. Wrap around sticks of feta cheese and basil leaves, then grill lightly.
● **Garlic bruscetta** Grill whole bulbs of garlic until tender. Brush slices of bread with olive oil, and grill. Squeeze the garlic onto the bread, and sprinkle with basil.
● **Tofu kebabs** Thread cubes of tofu onto kebab skewers with cherry tomatoes, mushrooms, and zucchinis. Brush with oil, and grill.

WRAPPING FOODS

Some foods benefit from a little protection to prevent them from drying out or breaking up in the fierce heat of a barbecue. To seal in juices and keep foods moist, use natural wrappings such as grape leaves, corn husks, or banana leaves, or wrap foods in foil, and cook gently.

USING GRAPE LEAVES

Overlap grape leaves, enclosing food completely

Wrapping fish
Use grape leaves to wrap delicate foods such as fish to prevent them from drying out or breaking up during cooking. If you are using fresh grape leaves, blanch first for one minute to soften.

USING CORN HUSKS

Wrapping chicken
Retain unwanted husks from corn on the cob, and use them to wrap chicken breasts stuffed with dried apricots. Use several layers of husk to keep the chicken moist during cooking.

TRYING NEW IDEAS
● **Using bacon** Slice large sausages lengthwise, and spread with mustard. Wrap in bacon slices, secure with toothpicks, and cook.
● **Making calzone** Use pizza dough to enclose pizza-style toppings. Fold the dough in half, then pinch the edges together to seal them. Brush with oil before grilling.
● **Making fruit bundles** Wrap fruits in foil with a dash of liqueur and a pat of butter.
● **Cooking in skins** Grill whole bananas, turning occasionally, for 6–8 minutes. Slit the skins, and serve with maple syrup.

PICNICS

PICNICKING IS IN MANY RESPECTS THE IDEAL WAY to enjoy good food and company. It enables you to eat in a favorite scenic spot or at an outdoor event. Whatever the occasion, keep picnics simple for maximum fun and minimum fuss.

MAKING PICNIC FOOD

The type of picnic you are planning will determine your selection of food. For a walking trip, food will need to be packed into a small space, and must be eaten without utensils. If you are traveling by car, you can pack more sophisticated foods and equipment.

MAKING SANDWICHES

● **Freezing in advance** Make sandwiches for a picnic in advance, and freeze them. Fillings containing hard-cooked eggs, mayonnaise, or salad are not suitable for freezing.
● **Making crab bites** For bite-sized sandwiches, stamp out shapes from bread using a cookie cutter. Pipe with cream cheese from a tube, and wrap around crab sticks. Secure the bites with toothpicks, and pack into boxes.
● **Mixing breads** Add interest to sandwiches by using whole-wheat and white bread together with a filling between.

ADDING VARIETY

Damp towel prevents bread from cracking

Rolling pinwheels
Cut the crusts from thinly sliced bread, and spread with butter. Place on a dampened dish towel, spread with filling, and roll up inside the towel. Then slice to create pinwheel shapes.

USING WHOLE LOAVES

Wrap tightly in foil

Filling a baguette
Instead of packing individual, filled rolls for a picnic, split a long baguette lengthwise. Brush the surface with olive oil, add a savory filling, and wrap. Slice into portions at the picnic site.

TRANSPORTING DESSERTS

Dip sliced fruit into purée

Serving a fruit dip
Purée fresh fruits, such as strawberries or mangoes, with honey to taste. Pour into a small plastic container, and transport to the picnic site inside a larger container together with sliced fruits for dipping into the purée.

CHOOSING EASY FOODS

● **Serving crudités** Pack a basket of simple, fresh crudités with a tub of a favorite dip and an ice pack for easy eating without plates. Choose vegetables that require little preparation, such as whole baby carrots, baby corn, radishes, mushrooms, and cooked new potatoes.
● **Packing individual portions** Take individual quiches or pies instead of a large one, so that they can be eaten easily without utensils, and there will be no need to slice into portions.
● **Wrapping potatoes** For cold-weather picnics, wrap baked potatoes in foil. Pack in several layers of newsprint or in an insulated bag.

BRIGHT IDEA

Stacking desserts
Make individual mousses or crème brûlées in small ramekins, then stack them together with a piece of cardboard between each one. Wrap the stack in plastic wrap for transporting.

CHOOSING EQUIPMENT

There is no need to buy lots of special equipment for picnics, but an insulated cooler bag with ice packs is essential for keeping food cold and fresh, especially in summer. Disposable plates and glasses are lighter and safer to carry than china and glass.

SELECTING CONTAINERS

● **Packing foods** Use square food containers where possible, since they are easier to stack than round ones and therefore take up less space. Round plastic containers often have good seals, so use these for transporting liquids.

● **Choosing a thermos** Use a wide-necked food thermos to keep foods such as fruit salad cold. They can also be used to keep casseroles or soups hot.

● **Using boxes** If you do not have a picnic basket, use a large cardboard box instead. It will hold more and will be easier to pack than a traditional picnic basket.

USING CAMPING STOVES

Tray provides level base

Making a firm base

If you take a small portable camping stove on a picnic, make sure that you use it safely. Before lighting, place it on a metal tray on a level piece of ground, well away from plants and trees.

PICNIC CHECKLIST

Check that you have packed the following useful items:

● Salt and pepper.
● Paper napkins or towels.
● Corkscrew.
● Sharp knife for cutting bread and other foods.
● Plastic or paper plates, glasses, and cutlery.
● Serving spoons.
● Drinking water.
● Blanket or tablecloth.
● Large umbrella.
● Dampened disposable cloth in a plastic bag.
● Insect repellent.
● First-aid kit.
● Garbage bag.

PACKING FOOD

Packing food for a picnic is largely a matter of common sense. With a little careful planning, your food will arrive at the intended picnic site cool, undamaged, and ready to eat. A general rule is to pack heavy or unsquashable items first, and to put more delicate items on top of them.

TRANSPORTING SALADS

● **Leaving space** Pack salads loosely into rigid containers to prevent crushing and to allow the ingredients to breathe.

Packing a dressing

To keep the crispness of a green salad, toss it with the dressing at the picnic site. Transport the dressing in a screw-top jar packed in the same container as the salad.

PACKING SMALL ITEMS

Tape corkscrew to bottle

Packing a corkscrew

To ensure that you remember to take a corkscrew, and to make it easy to find at the picnic site, tape a corkscrew to a bottle of wine using masking tape.

PREVENTING PROBLEMS

● **Using tissue paper** Place tarts with delicate edges in rigid boxes, and surround them with crumpled tissue paper for protection during transportation.

● **Wrapping glasses and china** Carefully wrap drinking glasses or china plates that you are taking on a picnic in bubble wrap to prevent damage.

● **Packing bottled drinks** Lie bottles on their side in ice in a covered cooler to keep them cool and avoid breakage.

● **Packing foods in order** As much as possible, pack foods in the order they will be needed, with desserts at the bottom.

● **Avoiding spills** Allow carbonated drinks to stand after the journey so that they do not squirt when opened.

IMPROMPTU ENTERTAINING

T HE MOST ENJOYABLE MEALS are often the ones that have not been planned – for example, when guests arrive unexpectedly. You will be able to cope with these occasions easily if you keep certain items on hand and use them creatively.

PREPARING STANDBY FOODS

A lways keep your kitchen pantry well stocked, so that if you have to entertain on short notice you will be prepared. Everyday foods can quickly be transformed into impressive dishes with a little imagination. Keep a stock of luxury foods to add last-minute special touches.

STORING IN THE FREEZER
● **Making individual portions** When freezing main dishes or desserts to keep as standbys, freeze in one-portion packs so that you can remove only as many servings as you need.
● **Freezing stuffings** Make rich fruit or herb stuffings for meat and poultry, and store them in the freezer to use on special occasions in the future.
● **Making bruscetta** Slice ciabatta bread, and reassemble for freezing. When guests arrive, spread the frozen slices with pesto sauce, sprinkle with grated cheese, and bake until golden. Serve with salad.

FREEZING CREAM

Pipe rosettes in well-spaced rows

Piping rosettes
Store whipped-cream rosettes in the freezer, ready for last-minute decorations. Pipe onto a cookie sheet lined with waxed paper. Freeze until solid, then pack in rigid boxes to store.

FREEZING PANCAKES

Interleaving with paper
When you cook pancakes, make more than you need, and freeze those you do not use. Interleave with waxed paper, overwrap, and freeze. You will be able to remove as many as you need.

USING BASIC STORES
● **Serving snacks** Keep jars of olives, nuts, and savory nibbles on hand to serve with drinks while you are preparing a meal for unexpected guests.
● **Making antipasto** Combine canned or bottled ingredients such as artichoke hearts, sun-dried tomatoes, cannellini beans, sardines, and pimentos to make a quick antipasto. Serve with crusty bread.
● **Creating rice dishes** Mix leftover long-grain rice with a variety of foods such as flaked salmon, tuna, or shreds of chicken and vegetables such as peas or corn. Heat all the ingredients gently before serving as a main course, or serve cold as a speedy salad.

PANTRY DESSERTS

Stuffing pancakes
Thaw frozen pancakes in the microwave, fold into quarters, and fill with canned fruits. Heat until bubbling, and serve with whipped cream or ice cream.

● **Baked peach snowballs** Fill the hollows of canned peach halves with crumbled macaroons or graham crackers, cover the peaches completely with meringue, and bake until the "snowballs" are golden.

● **Apple surprise** Mix together applesauce and vanilla pudding or yogurt. Spoon the mixture into serving dishes, and top with toasted nuts.
● **Raspberry rice** Stir frozen raspberries into store-bought rice pudding, and spoon into dessert glasses to serve.
● **Pears in port** Drain canned pear halves, and arrange the fruits in a shallow dish. Pour over enough port to cover, and chill before serving.
● **Fried pineapple rings** Drain canned pineapple rings, and sauté them gently in butter until they are golden in color. Sprinkle with brown sugar and a little brandy. Serve hot with whipped cream or ice cream.

COOKING FOR EXTRA GUESTS

If you find yourself with an extra mouth to feed, and it is too late to go shopping, think quickly and add extras to what you are already cooking. Bulk out casseroles with canned or frozen vegetables, offer bread with each course, and serve fresh fruits as well as a dessert.

ADDING TOPPINGS

● **Topping with cheese** To extend a vegetable dish, cover with a cheese sauce and flaked almonds, then grill.

Shaping a dough topping
Roll out biscuit dough, and cut into shapes with a cookie cutter. Arrange the dough shapes over a casserole filling, and bake in a hot oven for 12–15 minutes.

INCREASING QUANTITIES

● **Adding stock** Increase the volume of a soup by adding a flavorful stock or a glass of dry white wine. Heat until boiling, and then stir in cream or milk to taste before serving.
● **Adding beans** To bulk out cooked rice, stir in a can of drained kidney beans or chick peas and a few chopped herbs.
● **Stirring in oats** Add a handful of oatmeal and a can of chopped tomatoes to extend a bolognese sauce.
● **Serving an appetizer** To make a quick and easy appetizer to accompany a main meal, serve a tomato and onion salad with crusty bread.
● **Serving accompaniments** Serve stuffing or complementary sauces to extend roast meats.

DOUBLING UP DESSERTS

Alternate pudding and whipped cream

Layering with cream
If you have made a pudding or mousse that is not sufficient, increase the number of portions by layering the fruit with whipped cream in tall glasses.

ENHANCING BASIC DISHES

If you are faced with making an everyday family meal into something more exciting for visitors, create a sense of occasion by combining ingredients in unusual ways. Pep up casseroles with crispy, herbed croutons, or spoon desserts into pretty glasses instead of plain bowls.

SERVING SOUPS

Combining colors
Make canned soups special by lightly swirling two contrasting colors together. Cream soups work best, and good partners are tomato with asparagus or celery with green pea.

EMBELLISHING DESSERTS

Finish with cookies for crunchy topping

Layering ingredients
Sprinkle canned fruit with sherry or brandy, and serve with a store-bought dessert such as lemon mousse. Alternate layers of each with crumbled cookies, and spoon into attractive glasses.

BRIGHT IDEA

Flavoring UHT cream
Mask the distinctive flavor of UHT milk or cream by whipping in a few drops of vanilla extract or rosewater before adding it to a dessert.

COOKING MEASUREMENTS

SUCCESSFUL COOKING OFTEN DEPENDS UPON ACCURATE MEASUREMENT. If you lack the experience to guess amounts accurately, make sure that you have sets of measuring cups and standard measuring spoons, and a good oven.

══ EASY MEASURING ══

Many recipes give measurements in both metric and imperial units. Use whichever system you prefer, but do not mix the two, since they are not interchangeable. Teaspoons and tablespoons are always treated as level measurements and should not be heaped.

PROPORTIONAL MEASURES
● **Relative sizes** You can make many recipes (but not those for baking) without using measuring cups. Use a small coffee cup and assume it holds 1 cup (225 ml). Use the same cup for all the measurements in a recipe; correct proportions usually produce good results.

CONTAINER USES
● **Using food containers** Items such as yogurt containers and tomato cans can help you get precise measurements without using measuring cups. A yogurt container, for example, will range from 5 oz (150 ml) to 1 cup (225 ml). Mark the size on the container.

MEASURING FATS
● **Measuring with cups** Hard fats such as butter or lard are easier to measure in cups by using the displacement method. To measure ¼ cup butter, fill a measuring cup with ¾ cup water, then add butter until the water reaches the 1 cup mark.

APPROXIMATE IMPERIAL/METRIC EQUIVALENTS					
WEIGHT		VOLUME		LENGTH	
IMPERIAL	METRIC	IMPERIAL	METRIC	IMPERIAL	METRIC
½ oz	15 g	¼ tsp	1.25 ml	⅛ in	3 mm
1 oz	25 g	½ tsp	2.5 ml	¼ in	5 mm
1¾ oz	50 g	1 tsp	5 ml	½ in	1 cm
2¾ oz	75 g	2 tsp	10 ml	¾ in	2 cm
3½ oz	100 g	1 tbsp/3 tsp	15 ml	1 in	2.5 cm
4½ oz	125 g	2 tbsp/1 fl oz	30 ml	1¼ in	3 cm
5½ oz	150 g	3 tbsp	45 ml	1½ in	4 cm
6 oz	175 g	2 fl oz/¼ cup	50 ml	2 in	5 cm
7 oz	200 g	3½ fl oz	100 ml	2½ in	6 cm
8 oz	225 g	4 fl oz/½ cup	125 ml	2¾ in	7 cm
10½ oz	300 g	7 fl oz	200 ml	3¼ in	8 cm
11½ oz	325 g	8 fl oz/1 cup	225 ml	3½ in	9 cm
12 oz	350 g	9 fl oz	250 ml	4 in	10 cm
14 oz	400 g	10 fl oz	300 ml	4½ in	12 cm
15 oz	425 g	14 fl oz	400 ml	5 in	13 cm
1 lb	450 g	16 fl oz/2 cups	450 ml	5½ in	14 cm
1 lb 2 oz	500 g	18 fl oz	500 ml	6 in	15 cm
1 lb 10 oz	750 g	21 fl oz	600 ml	6¼ in	16 cm
2 lb 4 oz	1 kg	24 fl oz/3 cups	675 ml	6½ in	17 cm
2 lb 12 oz	1.25 kg	25 fl oz	700 ml	7 in	18 cm
3 lb 5 oz	1.5 kg	4 cups	900 ml	7½ in	19 cm
4 lb 8 oz	2 kg	4½ cups	1 liter	8 in	20 cm
5 lb	2.25 kg	6¾ cups	1.5 liters	8½ in	22 cm
5 lb 8 oz	2.5 kg	9 cups	2 liters	9 in	23 cm
6 lb	2.7 kg	11 cups	2.5 liters	10 in	25 cm
6 lb 8 oz	3 kg	13 cups	3 liters	12 in	30 cm

TEMPERATURE CONVERSIONS

Most recipes specify a cooking temperature to ensure the best results. Ovens vary according to type, fuel used, and fluctuations in power, so you may need to make adjustments if a dish is cooking more quickly or slowly than the suggested cooking time in the recipe.

OVEN TEMPERATURE CONVERSIONS			
DESCRIPTION	°F	°C	USES
COOL	225°F 250°F	110°C 120°C	Warming
WARM	275°F 300°F	140°C 150°C	Slow cooking
MODERATE	325°F 350°F	170°C 180°C	Baked goods
FAIRLY HOT	375°F 400°F	190°C 200°C	Baked goods Meats/Poultry
HOT	425°F 450°F	220°C 230°C	Meats/Poultry
VERY HOT	475°F	240°C	Meats/Poultry

MAXIMIZING OVEN USE
● **Baking dishes together** To bake several dishes that each require different temperatures together, adjust cooking times instead. With the oven on a moderate setting, cook dishes requiring a higher temperature for longer, and those needing a lower temperature for less.

CONVECTION OVENS
● **Adjusting times** Reduce cooking times in a fan-assisted oven by 5–10 minutes per hour, or reduce the oven temperature by 20–50°F (10–20°C), since a fan-assisted oven will cook food faster than a conventional oven. Check the manufacturer's handbook for specific timings.

ROASTING TEMPERATURES

Use these roasting times as a rough guide only, since they will vary according to the cut of meat. Meat on the bone will cook more quickly, since bone conducts heat. Beef, lamb, and duck may be served rare, but other meat must be cooked until the juices run clear.

ROASTING TEMPERATURES AND TIMES					
MEAT TYPE		°F	°C	BASE TIME	ADDITIONAL TIME
BEEF	rare	400°F	200°C	20 minutes	20 minutes per 1 lb (500 g)
	medium	400°F	200°C	20 minutes	25 minutes per 1 lb (500 g)
	well done	400°F	200°C	20 minutes	30 minutes per 1 lb (500 g)
LAMB		350°F	180°C	30 minutes	30 minutes per 1 lb (500 g)
PORK		350°F	180°C	35 minutes	35 minutes per 1 lb (500 g)
CHICKEN		350°F	180°C	25 minutes	25 minutes per 1 lb (500 g)
TURKEY		375°F	190°C	20 minutes	20 minutes per 1 lb (500 g)
DUCK		375°F	190°C	30 minutes	30 minutes per 1 lb (500 g)
GOOSE		350°F	190°C	30 minutes	30 minutes per 1 lb (500 g)

NUTRITIONAL INFORMATION

A HEALTHY DIET IS IMPORTANT TO EVERYONE, young or old, and not only helps prevent heart disease, tooth decay, and obesity, but protects against some serious illnesses. Achieving a balanced diet is easy and can be enjoyable.

BALANCING YOUR DIET

The nutritional value of any diet depends upon a good balance of all the essential nutrients. The best way to achieve this is to eat a variety of foods from all the different food groups. Try to eat at least one balanced meal every day, and limit unhealthy snacks.

INCREASING FIBER
● **Serving whole-grain bread** Switch from white to whole-grain bread, and use less filling and more bread in sandwiches.
● **Varying salads** Mix beans, rice, or pasta into green salads.
● **Eating healthy snacks** Serve whole-grain toast with peanut butter instead of sweet cookies.

REDUCING SUGAR
● **Cutting down gradually** If you add sugar to drinks, reduce the amount gradually, and you will not notice the difference.
● **Buying fruits** Keep fruits handy to replace sugary snacks.
● **Adding mineral water** Dilute fruit juices with mineral water to reduce natural sugar intake.

REDUCING FAT
● **Using substitutes** Consider using ground turkey in recipes instead of ground beef or lamb, since it is much lower in fat.
● **Spreading butter thinly** If you like butter on bread, soften it first for a few seconds in the microwave so that it will be easy to spread thinly.

RECOMMENDED DAILY INTAKE OF ESSENTIAL FOODS

Choosing food for a balanced diet
To achieve a balanced diet, you should eat the right amounts of the foods that provide protein, vitamins, carbohydrate, fiber, and minerals every day. This pyramid shows the number of servings of each type of food you should eat, and lists a selection of sample servings.

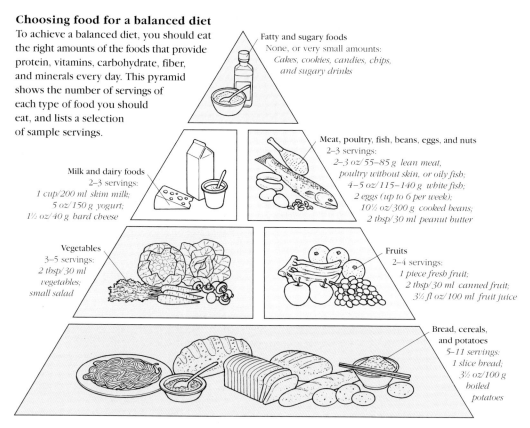

Fatty and sugary foods
None, or very small amounts:
Cakes, cookies, candies, chips, and sugary drinks

Meat, poultry, fish, beans, eggs, and nuts
2–3 servings:
2–3 oz/55–85 g lean meat, poultry without skin, or oily fish; 4–5 oz/115–140 g white fish; 2 eggs (up to 6 per week); 10½ oz/300 g cooked beans; 2 tbsp/30 ml peanut butter

Milk and dairy foods
2–3 servings:
1 cup/200 ml skim milk; 5 oz/150 g yogurt; 1½ oz/40 g hard cheese

Vegetables
3–5 servings:
2 tbsp/30 ml vegetables; small salad

Fruits
2–4 servings:
1 piece fresh fruit; 2 tbsp/30 ml canned fruit; 3½ fl oz/100 ml fruit juice

Bread, cereals, and potatoes
5–11 servings:
1 slice bread; 3½ oz/100 g boiled potatoes

EATING THE RIGHT NUTRIENTS

A well-balanced diet should include all the vitamins and minerals listed below. Many of them cannot be stored in the body, so they need to be included in your diet on a daily basis. Specific dietary requirements vary from person to person, but use this chart as a guide.

IMPORTANT VITAMINS AND MINERALS

NUTRIENT	GOOD SOURCES	FUNCTIONS IN THE BODY
VITAMIN A	Milk and dairy foods, oily fish and fish-liver oils, liver, butter, margarine, spinach, carrots, dried apricots and yellow fruits, nuts and seeds.	Aids vision in dim light; essential for growth of healthy skin and normal development of tissues, especially those that secrete mucus.
B-GROUP VITAMINS	Fortified breakfast cereals, meat, organ meats, fish, cheese, bread, eggs, whole cereals.	Encourage release of energy for growth; repair and maintain nervous system; aid muscle and heart function; encourage healthy skin and hair.
VITAMIN C	Citrus fruits and juice, lightly cooked green vegetables such as Brussels sprouts and cabbage, potatoes, most fresh fruits.	Maintains healthy skin, gums, teeth, and blood vessels; essential for iron absorption. Heavy smoking and drinking increase the need for vitamin C.
VITAMIN D	Fortified milk, oily fish, margarine, eggs, fortified breakfast cereals.	Controls calcium and phosphorus levels in blood; develops strong bones.
VITAMIN E	Vegetable oils, whole-grain cereals, butter, eggs, animal fats, green vegetables, nuts.	Helps body cells function properly; protects essential fats against oxidization.
IRON	Meat, especially liver and kidneys, bread, flour and other cereals, vegetables.	Vital component of red blood cells, which carry oxygen from lungs to cells.
CALCIUM	Milk, cheese, bread and flour, green vegetables, canned sardines and salmon.	Develops strong bones and teeth; aids muscle development and blood clotting.
PHOSPHORUS	Milk and milk products, bread and other cereals, meat and meat products.	Develops healthy bones and teeth; is essential for release of energy.
MAGNESIUM	Milk, bread and other cereal products, potatoes and other vegetables.	Essential constituent of all cells; is necessary for utilization of energy.
SODIUM	Salt, bread, most processed foods.	Essential for maintaining water balance and for muscle and nerve activity.
POTASSIUM	Vegetables, meat and milk, fruits and fruit juices.	Works with sodium in the functioning of muscles and nerve cells.
ZINC	Meat and meat products, milk, bread and other cereal products, oysters, sardines.	Needed for development of reproductive organs, healthy teeth, immune system.
TRACE ELEMENTS	*Copper* meat/vegetables; *iodine* seafood/milk; *fluorine* water/seafood; *selenium* meat/fish/cereals; *chromium* widely distributed.	All known to be essential. Research is ongoing to discover specific roles and consequences of dietary deficiencies.

USEFUL COOKING TERMS

T HIS GLOSSARY EXPLAINS THE MEANING of common cooking terms that are used but not fully explained in the text of this book. The list includes equipment, ingredients, cooking techniques, dishes, and other culinary terms.

- **Al dente** An Italian term describing cooked pasta that is just firm to the bite.
- **Ambrosia** Sweetened fruit purée mixed with yogurt or whipped cream to make a light, refreshing dessert.
- **Antipasti** An Italian term for hot or cold hors d'oeuvres.
- **Au gratin** A French term describing a dish topped with a sauce, sprinkled with bread crumbs or cheese, and grilled or baked until golden.
- **Bain marie** A French term describing a pan or dish half-filled with hot water in which a container of food is cooked. The water is kept heated to just below boiling point.
- **Baking empty** Partly baking a pastry shell for a tart or flan. The pastry is weighed down, with pie weights for example, to prevent it from rising and from remaining uncooked beneath a moist filling.
- **Barding** Tying bacon or pork fat over meat or poultry before roasting to keep it moist and eliminate the need for basting.
- **Basting** Brushing or spooning liquid fat or juices over meat or poultry during roasting to prevent it from drying out.
- **Beignet** A French term describing a sweet fritter lightened with whipped egg whites and often flavored with ground almonds.
- **Beurre manié** A French term for a paste that is made by kneading together equal parts of butter and flour. The paste is then used as a thickener for both sauces and stews.

- **Blanching** Plunging foods into boiling water for a short time to reduce strong flavors, whiten, preserve color, destroy bacteria, or parboil.
- **Bouquet garni** A French term describing a small bunch of herbs, tied together or wrapped in cheesecloth, that is added to stews or casseroles for flavor.
- **Braising** Baking or stewing meat, poultry, or vegetables in a small amount of liquid in a covered pot.
- **Brine** A salt and water solution in which food is immersed for preserving.
- **Brûlée** A French term describing a dish that has been sprinkled with sugar and grilled until a caramelized crust has formed on top.
- **Canapés** A French term describing small, bite-sized appetizers.
- **Caramel** A dark, sweet substance made by heating sugar or sugar syrup.
- **Casserole** A covered baking dish used for cooking stews in the oven; the name of dishes cooked by this method.
- **Char-grilling** Cooking food, unwrapped, on an open grill directly over charcoal to allow the unique, smoky flavor of the fuel to penetrate the food.
- **Clarifying** Removing impurities from butter or stock by heating the liquid, then skimming or straining it.
- **Compote** A mixture of fruits cooked in a syrup. The mixture is usually served warm.
- **Coulis** A French term for a pourable, liquid purée used as a sauce. Usually made of fruit.

- **Creaming** Beating together fat and sugar. Used as the basis of some cake mixtures.
- **Crêpe** A large, thin, French-style pancake with either a sweet or savory filling.
- **Crockpot** An electric pot that simmers food very slowly over a long period.
- **Croutons** A French term describing small pieces of fried or toasted bread used for garnishing soups or salads. A croute is toasted bread on which food is served; en croute describes baked food wrapped in pastry, while a croustade is a fried bread or pastry case in which hot, savory mixtures are served.
- **Crudités** Raw vegetables cut into sticks to be dipped into a sauce as an appetizer or an hors d'oeuvre.
- **Crystallize** To form into crystals. This occurs in sugar- or honey-based syrups. The term also describes the coating of fruits or flowers with sugar.
- **Curdling** The separation of a food, usually as a result of the overheating of or the addition of an acid substance to milk- or egg-based sauces.
- **Decanting** Pouring a liquid such as wine or vinegar from its bottle into a clean container, leaving behind the sediment.
- **Deglazing** Diluting sediment or concentrated juices left in a pan after cooking meat by stirring in a liquid such as water, stock, or wine.
- **Dredging** Sprinkling lightly and evenly with flour or sugar. A dredger has holes pierced in the lid for even sprinkling.

- **Dusting** Sprinkling food lightly with flour, sugar, or spices for a light coating.
- **Emulsion** A mixture of two normally insoluble liquids. Droplets of oil, for instance, are emulsified in vinegar in a vinaigrette dressing.
- **Flambé** A French term describing a dish that is sprinkled with alcohol and set alight. The alcohol burns off, but its flavor remains.
- **Flameproof** Describes equipment resistant to direct heat and oven heat, which can be used on a burner, under a grill, and in an oven.
- **Folding** Incorporating a light mixture into a heavier one – such as whipped egg whites into a cake mixture – by cutting and mixing lightly with a spoon to keep as much air in the mixture as possible.
- **Freezer burn** Dried out and discolored patches on food, caused by a long period of exposure to air in the freezer, resulting in dehydration.
- **Frosting** A fluffy icing used to cover cakes; a coating of sugar around the rim of a glass.
- **Glazing** Brushing the surface of a food with a liquid such as beaten egg, milk, or honey to moisten the food or give the surface a glossy appearance.
- **Hulling** Removing the leafy parts from soft fruits such as strawberries or blackberries.
- **Infusing** Extracting the flavors of spices or herbs by soaking them in liquid heated in a covered pan.
- **Julienne strips** Vegetable pieces that have been cut very finely into matchstick slices.
- **Kneading** Working a dough firmly by pressing, stretching, and folding it with the hands.
- **Liaison** A thickening agent, such as flour, egg yolk, cream, or beurre manié, which is used for thickening or binding sauces and soups.

- **Macerating** Softening food by soaking in a liquid or syrup.
- **Marinating** Soaking food in a seasoned liquid – often a blend of oil, wine, and vinegar – to add flavor or to tenderize the texture.
- **Mocha** A combination of coffee and chocolate.
- **Mousse** A lightly set mixture, which may be sweet or savory, that is usually based on whipped eggs or egg whites.
- **Ovenproof** Describes equipment resistant to oven heat only, not direct heat.
- **Parboiling** Partly cooking food in water or stock.
- **Paring** Peeling or trimming a food, usually vegetables.
- **Peaks** The mounds created in a mixture, such as egg white, that has been whipped to stiffness. Peaks are "soft" if they curl over or "stiff" if they stay upright.
- **Pectin** A substance that is found naturally in fruits and vegetables, and is essential for setting jams and jellies. Artificially produced pectin can be bought from stores.
- **Petits fours** French-style, bite-sized treats and cakes served with coffee.
- **Pilaf/pilau** A spiced, savory rice dish, usually including meat, poultry, or fish.
- **Piquant** A French term meaning pleasantly sharp, pungent, or sour in flavor.
- **Pith** The white, fleshy part of citrus rind that lies just beneath the colored zest.
- **Proving** Letting dough or a yeast mixture rise.
- **Purée** A French term describing food that has been mashed, liquidized, or strained until completely smooth.
- **Ramekin** A small, straight-sided ovenproof dish.
- **Reducing** Thickening a liquid mixture, such as a soup or sauce, by boiling uncovered to evaporate excess liquid.

- **Refreshing** Pouring cold water over freshly cooked vegetables to retain color and prevent further cooking; reviving limp salad ingredients by standing in cold water.
- **Rendering** Melting down solid fat to make drippings.
- **Rising** The expansion of dough or a yeast mixture as a result of the action of the yeast.
- **Roux** A French term describing a mixture of equal amounts of fat and flour, which are cooked together as a basis for thickening sauces.
- **Sautéeing** A French term describing the continual tossing of food in shallow fat so that it browns evenly.
- **Scalding** Plunging fruits or vegetables into boiling water to facilitate the peeling of skins; heating a liquid to just below boiling point.
- **Skimming** Removing the surface layer of impurities, scum, or fat from liquids such as stocks and jams while cooking. This is usually done with a flat, slotted spoon.
- **Sweating** Cooking food, usually vegetables, very gently in melted fat to release juices for flavor, but without allowing the food to brown.
- **Syrup** A concentrated solution of sugar and water.
- **Tang** The prong of a knife blade embedded in the handle.
- **Terrine** An earthenware or china dish used for baking or steaming pâtés and meat loaves; the name given to food that is cooked in this way.
- **Trussing** Tying or skewering meat or poultry into a neat shape before cooking.
- **Tuiles** A French term for thin, sweet cookies shaped to resemble curved tiles.
- **Vintage** Wine from a particular year's harvest.
- **Zest** The outer, colored part of citrus peel, which contains strong flavor in its oils.

149

INDEX

ACKNOWLEDGMENTS

AUTHOR'S ACKNOWLEDGMENTS

I would like to thank Jo Richardson, Judy Garlick, and Sarah Hall for their inspiration, patience, and thoroughness during the making of this book. Many thanks are also due to the rest of the Dorling Kindersley team, especially to Helen Benfield, Colette Connolly, Adèle Hayward, and Samantha Gray for all their hard work. Finally, I would like to thank my husband, Don Last, for giving such enduring support and enthusiasm.

PUBLISHER'S ACKNOWLEDGMENTS

Dorling Kindersley would like to thank the following:

Prop loan Elizabeth David Cookshop, Covent Garden, and MFI Furniture Centres Ltd.

Editorial and design assistance Samantha Gray and Adèle Hayward for editorial assistance, Austin Barlow for design assistance; Chris Bernstein for the index; and Debbi Scholes for proofreading.

ARTWORKS

Illustrators All illustrations by Kuo Kang Chen and John Woodcock, apart from additional illustrations by Geoff Denney on pages 10–11, 12–13, 60–61, 77, 128, and 138.

PHOTOGRAPHY

Photographers Andy Crawford, John Elliot, and Steve Gorton.

Photographic assistants Sarah Ashun and Gary Ombler.

Hand models Penelope Cream, Toby Heran, and Audrey Speitel.